BY MARGUERITE YOURCENAR

Dear Departed

DEAR DEPARTED

Marguerite Yourcenar

Translated from the French

by Maria Louise Ascher

The Noonday Press

Farrar Straus Giroux

New York

Library of Congress Cataloging-in-Publication Data
Yourcenar, Marguerite.
[Souvenirs pieux. English]
Dear departed / Marguerite Yourcenar ; translated from the French
by Maria Louise Ascher. — 1st ed.
Translation of: Souvenirs pieux.
1. Yourcenar, Marguerite—Biography.   2. Novelists, French—20th
century—Biography.   I. Title.
PQ2649.O8Z46913   1991   848'.91209—dc20   [B]   91-11168 CIP

1212-80-024

Contents

Illustrations

La Cruche cassée *reproduced courtesy of the Musée du Louvre,*
© *Photo R.M.N. All other illustrations courtesy of the Petite*
Plaisance Trust, whose assistance is gratefully acknowledged.

Genealogical Chart

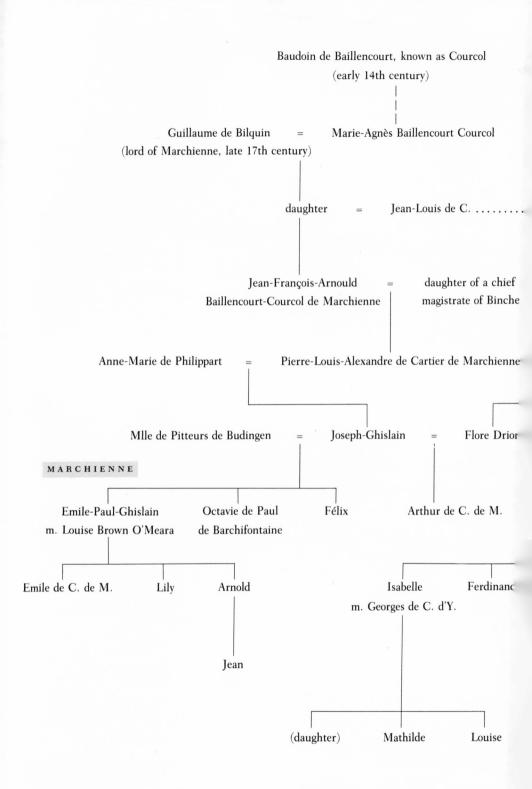

Baudoin de Baillencourt, known as Courcol
(early 14th century)

Guillaume de Bilquin   =   Marie-Agnès Baillencourt Courcol
(lord of Marchienne, late 17th century)

daughter   =   Jean-Louis de C. . . . .

Jean-François-Arnould   =   daughter of a chief
Baillencourt-Courcol de Marchienne   magistrate of Binche

Anne-Marie de Philippart   =   Pierre-Louis-Alexandre de Cartier de Marchienne

Mlle de Pitteurs de Budingen   =   Joseph-Ghislain   =   Flore Drion

MARCHIENNE

Emile-Paul-Ghislain   Octavie de Paul   Félix   Arthur de C. de M.
m. Louise Brown O'Meara   de Barchifontaine

Emile de C. de M.   Lily   Arnold   Isabelle   Ferdinand
m. Georges de C. d'Y.

Jean

(daughter)   Mathilde   Louise

........................Louis-Joseph de C.   =   Marguerite-Pétronille
(cousins)   (early 18th century)

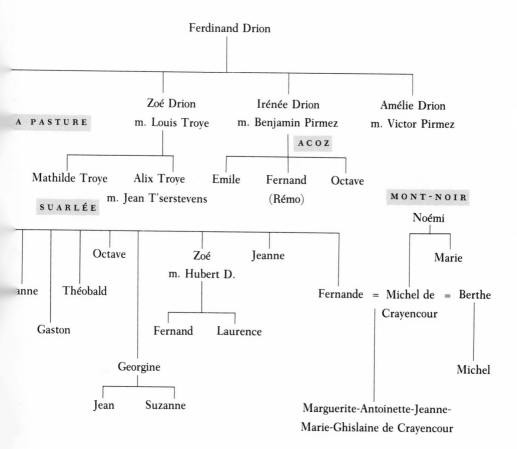

Ferdinand Drion

Zoé Drion   Irénée Drion   Amélie Drion
A PASTURE   m. Louis Troye   m. Benjamin Pirmez   m. Victor Pirmez

ACOZ

Mathilde Troye   Alix Troye   Emile   Fernand   Octave
                m. Jean T'serstevens   (Rémo)
SUARLÉE   MONT-NOIR
                                                          Noémi

        Octave   Zoé   Jeanne   Marie
                    m. Hubert D.
anne   Théobald   Fernande = Michel de = Berthe
                                                    Crayencour
    Gaston   Fernand   Laurence

                Georgine   Michel
            Jean   Suzanne
                                    Marguerite-Antoinette-Jeanne-
                                    Marie-Ghislaine de Crayencour

*What did your face look like
before your father and mother met?*

ZEN KOAN

THE BIRTH

The being I refer to as *me* came into the world on Monday, June 8, 1903, at about eight in the morning, in Brussels. My father belonged to an old family from the north of France, while my mother was a Belgian whose forebears had lived for centuries in Liège and later settled in the province of Hainaut. The house in which the event took place—for the birth of a child is always an event to its father and mother, and to those near and dear to them—was on the avenue Louise, at number 193. It was swallowed up by a high-rise some fifteen years ago.

Having set down these few facts, which mean nothing in themselves and which, nevertheless, for each one of us, lead beyond the confines of our own individual history and even beyond History, I am obliged to pause, dizzied by the hopeless tangle of incidents and circumstances which to a greater or lesser extent shape us all. That girl-child, already fixed by the space-time coordinates of the Christian era and twentieth-century Europe, that speck of pink flesh wailing in a blue cradle, compels me to ask myself a series of questions which are all the more daunting for their apparent banality and which any author worthy of the name will strive to avoid. That the child is in fact myself I can hardly doubt without doubting everything. Still, to overcome in part the feeling of unreality that this identification gives me, I am forced—just as if I were trying to recreate some historical personage—to seize on stray recollections gleaned secondhand or even tenth-hand; to pore over scraps of correspondence and notebook pages which somehow escaped the wastebasket (so eager are we to know the past that we wring from these poor relics more than they contain); and to burrow in registries and archives for original documents whose legal and bureaucratic jargon is devoid of all human content. I am quite aware that such gleanings are deceptive and vague, like everything that has been reinterpreted by the memories of a great many people; flat, like items written on the dotted line of a passport application; inane, like oft-told family anecdotes; and corroded by gradual accretions within us, as a stone is eaten away by lichen or metal by rust. These odds and ends of purported truths are, nevertheless, the only bridge still standing between that infant and me. They are also the only buoy that keeps both of us afloat on the ocean of time. Mildly curious, I set about assembling them here, to see what the completed puzzle will reveal: the image of a certain person and several others, of a milieu, of a place, and here and there a fleeting glimpse of something nameless and formless.

That Brussels was my birthplace was nearly accidental, as many other things were to be throughout my life, and as they doubtless are in every life when one looks closely. Monsieur and Madame de C. had just spent a dreary, overcast summer at the family estate of Mont-Noir, on a hillside in French Flanders, and that lovely spot—even lovelier in those days, before the ravages of the war, than it is now—had seemed to them, as always, the most boring place on earth. The presence of Monsieur de C.'s son by his first marriage, a sullen boy of eighteen, had not enlivened the vacation: he persisted in treating his stepmother with great rudeness, despite her shy attempts to win him over. Their one outing had been in late September—a brief excursion to Spa, the nearest town where Monsieur de C., who enjoyed gambling, could find a casino and try his hand at a martingale or two without Fernande's having to brave the autumn rains on the quais of Ostend. As winter approached, the prospect of spending cold, bleak months in the old house on the rue Marais, in Lille, seemed even less appealing than the summer they had passed at Mont-Noir. Monsieur de C.'s insufferable mother, Noémi, whom he detested more than any other woman he knew, had held sway over these two dwellings for fifty-one years. Daughter of a president of the Lille tribunal, born wealthy, and married by virtue of her fortune alone into a family that still complained of its financial losses during the French Revolution, she never for an instant let them forget that they owed their present affluent existence to her. As widow and mother, she controlled the purse strings and doled out comparatively meager sums for the support of her middle-aged son, who was blithely running up huge debts while waiting for her death. She was inordinately fond of the possessive pronoun. Michel and Fernande grew weary of hearing her say things like "Close the door to my drawing room," "See if my gardener has raked my paths," "Look at my clock and tell me what time it is." Madame de C.'s pregnancy made traveling impossible for the couple, who until then had cured all their troubles by escaping to sunny climes and picturesque retreats. Germany and Switzerland, Italy and southern France being temporarily out of reach, Monsieur and Madame de C. sought a place of their own where they could live in privacy and where the formidable Noémi would be restricted to infrequent visits.

Moreover, Fernande missed her sisters, particularly her older sister, Mademoiselle Jeanne de C. de M., a lifelong invalid, who, as she was suited for neither marriage nor the convent, had settled in Brussels in a modest house of her own choosing. Almost equally, and perhaps more, Fernande missed her old German governess, now living with Mademoiselle Jeanne as her companion and factotum. Severe-looking in her black-embroidered bodice but nevertheless endowed with Germanic simplicity and a mischievous sense of humor, this woman had become a second mother to Fernande, who had lost her own when very young. As a matter of fact, Fernande in her youth had rebelled against these two influences; it was in part to escape from that devout, somewhat drab, woman-centered household that she had married Monsieur de C. Now, after two years of marriage, Fernande saw Mademoiselle Jeanne and Mademoiselle Fräulein as the embodiment of good sense, virtue, serenity, and a gentle, unruffled existence. In addition, raised as she had been to revere all things having to do with Germany, she was determined to have a Belgian doctor, trained at a German university, attend her at the birth—a man who had also taken good care of her married sisters when they had had their own children.

Monsieur de C. gave in. He almost always gave in to his successive wives, just as he would later to his daughter, namely me. He was, without doubt, generous to a degree that I have never seen equaled in anyone else, which caused him to say yes more often than no to those he loved, or even to those whose presence he merely tolerated. Deep down he felt, as well, a basic indifference, the result of a disinclination to take part in ever-irritating disputes and of a feeling that, when you came right down to it, "things don't really matter." Last but not least, he had one of those quicksilver minds that are delighted, even if only momentarily, with every novelty. Brussels, where Fernande wished to settle, would offer the charms of the big city that were lacking in gloomy, sooty Lille. A more prudent man would have thought to rent a house for a few months, but Monsieur de C. always made decisions on the assumption that they were for life. A realtor was hired to find the ideal house. Monsieur de C. went in person to survey the choices offered, of which, not surprisingly, only the most expensive seemed to suit. He bought it on the spot. It was a small mansion, three-quarters furnished, its little garden enclosed by ivy-covered walls. Monsieur de C. was especially taken with the spacious Empire-style library on the ground floor: dominating the room from the mantel was a white marble bust of Minerva with helmet and shield, enthroned on a green marble pedestal. Mademoiselle Jeanne and Fräulein undertook to find a domestic staff, as well as a nurse who would see Fernande through the birth and care for mother and child in the weeks following. Monsieur and Madame de C. arrived in Brussels with countless trunks, many of which contained books destined for the library's shelves, and with Trier the dachshund, whom they had purchased three years earlier while traveling in Germany.

The move provided a welcome distraction. The servants were mustered for inspection: the cook Aldegonde and the chambermaid, her young sister Barbara, or Barb, both born near Hasselt on the Dutch border; and a man hired as gardener and groom, to look after the horse and the smart little carriage that would take the couple on outings to the Bois de la Cambre nearby. Fernande and Michel knew the fleeting pleasure of displaying their new home to any visitor who would admire it. The family came in droves. Monsieur de C. had a high opinion of his sister-in-law Jeanne for her level head and sound judgment and for her courage in the face of her infirmities. He had a somewhat lower opinion of Fräulein and her inane cheerfulness. Moreover, she had done such a thorough job of teaching her charges German that it had become like a mother tongue to them; whenever Jeanne and Fräulein visited Fernande, the three of them spoke nothing but German, which exasperated Monsieur de C.—less because he could not understand their female chatter, which hardly interested him anyway, than because it seemed to him extremely bad manners.

Fernande's brothers came to dinner. Théobald, the eldest, prided himself on his engineering diploma but had never put his training to the slightest use and had no desire to do so. An inveterate club man at the age of thirty-nine, he spent most of his time at his club, thriving on small talk. His fat neck, always chafed by its tight, stiff collar, disgusted his brother-in-law. The younger Octave owed his romantic name in some measure to his "uncle" (really his mother's first cousin) Octave Pirmez, a dreamy, introspective essayist who was one of the fine Belgian prose writers of the nineteenth century. But he owed his name most of all to the fact that he was the eighth of ten children. He was a pleasant-looking man of average height, who cut a rather eccentric figure. Like his "Uncle" Octave of poetic memory, he was fond of traveling, and he amused himself by wandering about Europe, alone, on horseback or in a light gig of his own devising. Once—a rare whim in those days—he even went so far as to take a ship across the Atlantic to visit the United States. Not widely read, though adorned with a thin literary veneer (he had described some of his travels in an unreadable little book printed at his own expense), with a mild interest in antiquities and the fine arts, he seems in his peregrinations to have sought mainly the local color and scenic beauty so beloved of all travelers in those days, from the old Töpffer of *Voyages en zigzag* to the Stevenson of *Travels with a Donkey*. Perhaps, too, he sought a freedom that he could not find in Brussels.

Fernande's three married sisters from the provinces visited less often, hampered as they were by their children, their household duties, and their obligations as patrons of local charities. Their husbands, however, whether for business or for pleasure, managed to make fairly frequent trips to Brussels. Monsieur de C. would join them over cigars and listen to them expound on the burning issues of the day: the Franco-Italian accord of Camille Barrère, the scandalous radicalism of the minister Emile Combes, the Baghdad Railway and Germany's schemes for annexations in the Near East, and, finally, Belgium's commercial and colonial expansion, a topic they never tired of. These gentlemen were comparatively well informed about the vagaries of the financial world; in politics, they parroted conservative commonplaces. All this was of scant interest to Monsieur de C., who, for the moment, had no money to invest in business ventures and who regarded all political news as a type of lie, or at least as a mixture of little truth and much falsehood which he was not inclined to try to sort out. One of the things that had persuaded him to ask for Fernande's hand had been the independence she enjoyed as an orphan; but he had begun to realize that five brothers and four sisters by marriage could be just as bothersome for a husband as a mother-in-law. Until then, the young woman had known scarcely anything of Brussels other than the convent where she had been educated; her social connections had been, so to speak, mere extensions of the family. Her schoolmates were scattered far and wide. The prettiest and most talented, Mademoiselle de T., a Dutch girl whom Fernande had loved with teenage ardor and who had dazzled

Monsieur de C. at the wedding in her rose-colored maid of honor's gown, had married a Russian and now lived thousands of miles away. The two young women wrote each other earnest, affectionate letters. The intolerable Noémi, whom Michel and Fernande had thought they were rid of, still exerted an oppressive influence on the household, for it was she who decided whether or not her son's allowance would be paid out regularly. Last, and especially dispiriting for this Frenchman from the north whose heart lay in the south, it rained there as incessantly as in Lille. "One is always better off somewhere else," Monsieur de C. was fond of repeating. For the time being, they were not much better off in Brussels.

This marriage, already fissured with little cracks, had been decided on by Monsieur de C. shortly after the death of his first wife, to whom he was attached by extremely strong bonds compounded of passion, aversion, mutual resentment, and fifteen years of a restless life spent more or less side by side. The first Madame de C. had died in dramatic circumstances that this man who freely discussed everything spoke of as seldom as possible. He had counted on the renewed zest for life that a fresh and beguiling face would bring him; he had been mistaken. Not that he didn't love Fernande: he was, in fact, almost incapable of living with a woman without becoming attached to her and indulging her every wish. Even apart from her appearance, which I shall try to describe further on, Fernande had charms that were uniquely hers. The most important was her voice. She spoke beautifully, without a trace of a Belgian accent, which would have irritated this Frenchman; she spun stories with delightful imagination and whimsy. He never tired of hearing her recount her childhood memories or of making her recite her favorite poems, which she knew by heart. She

Fernande de C. de M., 1899

Michel de C., about 1909

had, on her own, provided herself with something like a liberal education: she possessed a passing knowledge of classical languages; she had read or was reading everything that was fashionable, as well as some good books that are beyond mere fashion. Like him, she loved history, and, like him, especially or rather exclusively to glean from it romantic or dramatic anecdotes or, here and there, a few shining examples of moral elegance or of pluck amid misfortune. On those empty evenings when one stays at home, they would play a sort of parlor game, taking down from the shelf a large historical dictionary, which Monsieur de C. would open and choose a name from at random. It was rare that Fernande would be uninformed on the subject, whether it concerned a mythological demigod, an English or Scandinavian monarch, or a forgotten painter or composer. Their best moments were still those they spent together in the library, under the gaze of their Minerva, which owed its existence to the chisel of a Prix de Rome recipient of the 1890s. Fernande was capable of spending days at a time peacefully reading or dreaming. She never engaged in female chatter with her husband; perhaps she saved it for her conversations in German with Jeanne and Fräulein.

So many good qualities had their obverse. She had no skill at running a household. On days when guests were expected for dinner, Monsieur de C., acting in her stead, would plunge into long conferences with Aldegonde, seeking to prevent the appearance at table of certain combinations favored by Belgian cooks, such as chicken and rice served with potatoes, or of desserts like prune tart. In restaurants, while he eagerly and discerningly ordered simple fare, he was annoyed to see her choose complicated dishes at random and satisfy herself finally with fruit. The whims of pregnancy had nothing to do with this. From the earliest days of their life together, he had been shocked to hear her say, as he was urging her to try another specialty of the Café Riche: "But why? We still have some vegetables left." Since he himself relished the joy of the moment, whatever it might be, he saw in this a form of spurning a proffered pleasure, or perhaps (something he detested more than anything else in the world) a stinginess instilled by her petit-bourgeois upbringing. He was mistaken in not perceiving that Fernande had ascetic impulses. Yet the fact remains that even for those furthest from being gourmets or gourmands or gluttons, living together means in some measure eating together. Monsieur and Madame de C. were not good partners at table.

Her appearance left something to be desired. She wore outfits from the best dressmakers with a careless grace; yet this casualness annoyed the husband who tripped over a stylish hat or a muff that his wife had dropped on the floor of her room. New dresses, as soon as they were put on, would become creased or torn; buttons would disappear. Fernande had the kind of fingers that lose rings: her engagement ring had fallen off her hand one day when, through the open window of a railway carriage, she was pointing out a splendid landscape to Michel. Her long hair, which he as a man of the Belle Epoque preferred, was the despair of hairdressers, who failed to understand that Madame was incapable of putting hairpins or combs in the right places. There was something fairylike about her, and nothing is more unbearable, to judge from the stories, than living with a fairy. Worse still, she was fearful. The gentle little mare that he had given her languished in the stables at Mont-Noir. Madame would consent to ride it only when her husband or a groom held it on a lead; the innocent caracoles of the animal terrified her. The sea was no more a success with her than the horse. On their last cruise to Corsica and Elba, she had thought twenty times that they would founder in a sea pleasantly ruffled by a light breeze; on the Ligurian coast, she rarely agreed to sleep in the confining cabin of the yacht even when they were anchored in port, and insisted that a table be set up for her on the quai at mealtimes. Monsieur de C. would see once again the suntanned face of his first wife as she trimmed the sails in heavy weather, or recall her as she had looked in the skirt and pink coat of a horsewoman, helping to break in a horse during manège and keeping her seat despite the animal's wild bucking and plunging, glued to the sidesaddle and so shaken that she would end up vomiting.

A thorough understanding of two people thus bound together is possible only if one is privy to their bedtime conferences. The little that I have found out about my parents' love life convinces me that they were fairly typical of the married couple around 1900, with their problems and prejudices which are no longer ours. Michel dearly loved Fernande's slightly pendulous breasts, which were a bit too full for her slender frame, but he suffered, as did so many men of his day, from his ambivalence about feminine pleasure, believing that a chaste woman gives herself only to satisfy the man she loves and troubled sometimes by his mate's coldness, sometimes by her ardor. Doubtless in part because her romantic reading had persuaded her that a second wife ought to be jealous of the memory of the first, Fernande asked questions that to Michel seemed somewhat ridiculous, in any case ill-timed. As the months passed and soon lengthened into years, she discreetly made known her desire to be a mother—a desire that initially had seemed faint within her. The first and only venture that Monsieur de C. had made into fatherhood had not been of a sort to give him confidence, but he held to the principle that a woman who wanted a child was entitled to have one and, barring mistakes, not more than one.

Everything, then, proceeded as he had wished, or at least as he considered natural that things should proceed. Still, he felt he had been trapped. Trapped just as he had been when —to foil the plans of his mother, who envisioned him as the future manager of her estates, destined like his father before him to listen to the complaints of the tenant farmers and to discuss new leases—he had without the slightest warning enlisted in the army. (And he had loved the army, but that decision had nonetheless been the consequence of a family quarrel and a sort of clumsy blackmail aimed at his relations.) Trapped as he had been upon quitting the army, likewise without the slightest warning, for the sake of an Englishwoman's pretty face. Trapped as he had been when, to please his father, who was suffering from an incurable illness, he agreed to break off that already longstanding relationship (how gentle was the green countryside of England; how sweet were those days of sunshine and rain spent roaming together in the fields, and those farmhouse meals!) and marry Mademoiselle de L., someone whom all circumstances made suitable for him—social standing, old ties between the two families, and furthermore a love for horses and for what his mother called living the high life. (And all had not been unpleasant in those years spent with Berthe: there had been the good and the tolerable along with the worst.) At the age of forty-nine, he found himself trapped yet again in the company of a woman for whom he had tender feelings, tinged by a bit of irritation, and with a child of whom nothing was yet known, except that his attachment for it would grow, doubtless to culminate, if it was a boy, in disappointments and disputes, and, if it was a girl, in his giving her, amid great pomp, to a stranger whose bed she would henceforth share. Monsieur de C. from time to time was seized with a desire to pack his bags. But their settling in Brussels had its good points. If the marriage came apart—not by divorce, which was unthinkable in their milieu, but through a discreet separation—nothing would be more natural for Fernande than to stay with the baby in Belgium near her relatives, while he could use business as a pretext to travel in or move back to France. And finally, if the child was a boy, there was the advantage that in those days of armament he could one day opt for a neutral country. It's quite plain: roughly three years in the army had not transformed Monsieur de C. into a patriot ready to give his sons for the sake of recapturing Alsace-Lorraine. He left such grand enthusiasms to his cousin P., a deputy of the Right, who filled the Chamber with his homilies in praise of the French birthrate.

I have fewer details concerning Fernande's state of mind during that winter and can at most infer what she thought about during her sleepless nights, lying in her twin bed of mahogany, separated by a rug from Michel, who was likewise occupied with his thoughts. Mindful of the little I know of her, I proceed from this to ask myself whether that yearning for motherhood, which Fernande expressed from time to time while watching a peasant woman breast-feed her charge or gazing, in a museum, at one of Lawrence's angelic boys, was really as profound as she and Michel believed. The maternal instinct is not as compelling as people like to say it is, for in every age women of the so-called privileged class have blithely entrusted their children, from infancy on, to the care of underlings, in olden times putting them out to be nursed when the convenience or the social situation of the parents required it, more recently leaving them to the often clumsy or negligent care of maids, in our own day to an impersonal day-care center. Consider, too, the ease with which so many women have offered their children to the Moloch of war and gloried in such sacrifice.

But let us return to Fernande. Motherhood was an integral

part of the ideal woman as depicted by the commonplaces she heard around her: a married woman was obligated to yearn for motherhood just as she was obligated to love her husband and to practice the arts of pleasing. Everything that was taught on this subject was, moreover, confused and contradictory: the child was a grace, a gift from God; it was also the justification for acts deemed vulgar and almost reprehensible, even between spouses, when conception did not occur to justify them. Its birth brought joy to the entire family; at the same time, pregnancy was a cross that a devout woman who knew her duty bore with resignation. On another level, the child was a plaything, yet another luxury, a slightly more solid reason for living than shopping trips to the city and strolls in the Bois. Its arrival always meant pink or blue layettes and visits by women friends whom one received dressed in a lace nightgown. It was unthinkable that a woman surfeited with every gift should not have that one as well. In sum, the child would confirm the complete success of her life as a young wife, and this last point was perhaps not without weight for Fernande, who had married relatively late and who on the twenty-third of February had just turned thirty-one.

Nevertheless, though her relations with her sisters were quite affectionate, she had not revealed her pregnancy to them (except to Jeanne, her adviser in all matters) until the last possible moment, behavior hardly suggestive of a young woman rejoicing in her prospects of motherhood. They had not known of her condition until after her arrival in Brussels. The closer her term approached, the more the pious or charming commonplaces left bare a very simple emotion, namely fear. Her own mother, exhausted by ten deliveries, had died one year after Fernande's birth, "of a brief, cruel illness" perhaps caused by yet another, fatal pregnancy; her grandmother had died in labor in her twenty-first year. Some of the folklore imparted in low voices by the women of the family consisted of recipes for use during difficult labors, of tales of infants who were stillborn or who died before they could be baptized, and of young mothers carried off by milk fever. In the kitchen and in the linen room, such stories were not even told in low voices. But the terrors that haunted her remained vague. She was of a time and a milieu in which not only was ignorance an indispensable part of a girl's virginity but women, even wives and mothers, took care not to know too much about conception and parturition and would not have thought they could name the organs involved. Everything that touched on the center of the body was the province of husbands, midwives, and physicians. Fernande's sisters, who overflowed with advice about diet and with tender exhortations, told her in vain that one loves one's child even before it is born; she did not succeed in establishing a connection between her bouts of nausea, her fainting spells, the weight of that thing which grew within her and would come out of her by the most secret route, in a way she only dimly imagined, and the tiny creature, like those enchanting little wax Jesuses, whose lace-trimmed frocks and embroidered bonnets she already possessed. She dreaded the ordeal, whose vicissitudes she could scarcely envisage but during which she would depend solely on her own courage and strength. Prayer was a haven for her; she calmed herself with the thought that she had asked the nuns at the convent where she had been raised to say a novena for her.

The worst moments were doubtless those in the depths of night, when her usual toothache awakened her. One could hear the last carriages roll by, at long intervals, on the cobblestones of the avenue Louise, carrying people home from parties or the theater, the noise agreeably muffled by what was in those days a row of trees four deep. She took refuge in reassuring practical details: the event was not expected until the fifteenth of June, but Azélie the nurse would take up her duties on the fifth; Fernande would have to remember to write to Madame de B., on the rue Philippe le Bon, with whom Azélie was currently engaged, to thank her for freeing Azélie a few days earlier than initially agreed. Everything would be simpler as soon as she had an experienced person with her. Waking without realizing that she had fallen asleep again, she looked at the little clock on her night table: it was time to take the tonic that the doctor had prescribed for her. A beam of sunlight passed through the thick curtains. It would be a fine day; she could go by carriage to make a few purchases or take a walk with Trier in the little garden. The weight of the future ceased to be oppressive, subdivided itself into insignificant worries or futile occupations, some pleasing, others less so, but all distractions, and filling up the hours so as to make one forget them. During this time, the earth revolved.

At the beginning of April, Fernande's toothaches giving her no relief, it was decided that one of her impacted wisdom teeth should be pulled. She lost a great deal of blood. Dr. Quatermann, the dentist, came to the house and gave her the customary prudent advice: ice cubes in the mouth and several hours of rest without solid food or hot drinks, while refraining from all speech. Monsieur de C. settled himself next to her and, in accordance with the dentist's wishes, provided her with a pencil and a sheet of paper on which to write her slightest desires. Afterward he kept the paper, with its almost illegibly scribbled notes. Here they are:

18

Baudouin has already had that.

. . . . .

Quatermann is intelligent, alert, and kind . . . different from Dr. Dubois yesterday.

. . . . .

I am just like Trier—wordless . . .

. . . . .

With this, it hurts to even suck on a bit of biscuit . . .

. . . . .

It's not in the boiling water . . .

. . . . .

Ring . . . Have someone look for a cork . . . Some wine . . .

. . . . .

In the next room, on the fire?

That is all. But it is enough to give me the tone and rhythm of what those two people said in intimate moments, seated near each other in a house that disappeared sixty-nine years ago. I do not hazard any reasons as to what made Monsieur de C. keep that bit of paper, but the fact that he saved it leads one to believe that those evenings in Brussels had not left him with only unpleasant memories.

On the eighth of June, at about six in the morning, Aldegonde was coming and going in the kitchen, pouring coffee into bowls for Barbara and the gardener-valet. The huge coal-burning stove was already glowing, laden with all sorts of containers full of boiling water. Its heat was pleasant; the room, which was below ground level, was cool despite the season. No one had closed an eye all night. Aldegonde had had to prepare meals at odd hours for Monsieur and the doctor, as the doctor had not left Madame's room since the previous evening. She had also had to make cups of broth and eggnog to soothe Madame, who, moreover, had hardly tasted them. Barbara had spent the entire night shuttling between the bedroom on the second floor and the kitchen, carrying trays, water pitchers, linens. In principle, Monsieur de C. would have found it more decent if that delicate girl of twenty were not assisting with the demands of the birth; but one does not have for a chambermaid, daughter of a Limbourg tenant farmer, quite the same consideration as for the young ladies of the city, and in any case Azélie was continually in need of her. Barbara must have gone up and down those two flights of stairs no fewer than twenty times.

I can easily imagine the three servants sitting in the warmth of the stove, long pieces of buttered bread balanced on the edges of their bowls, into which they dipped each mouthful, pitying Madame, for whom the situation looked bad, but enjoying nonetheless this moment of rest and refreshment, which a ring of the bell or renewed screams would surely interrupt before very long. To tell the truth, since midnight everyone had become quite used to the screams. When they stopped and there was a lull, everyone grew afraid. The women would draw close to the half-open door of the servants' stairway; the broken moans would be almost reassuring to them. The milkman passed, his cart drawn by an enormous dog; Aldegonde went to meet him with her copper saucepot, which the man filled, tilting a milk can. If it happened that the can was nearly empty, the last drops would go to the dog, whose drinking bowl hung from his harness. After the milkman came the baker's boy, delivering little loaves of bread still warm from the oven for the morning's breakfast. Then came the charwoman, whom the servants regarded with disdain; it was her job to scour the front steps and the sidewalk in front of the house and to polish the doorbell, the doorknob, and the mailbox lid engraved with the owners' name. Each event gave rise to a bit of conversation. The servants and visitor would exchange sympathetic commonplaces mixed with a few basic truths: The good Lord wants the rich to be the same, in this, as the poor . . . A moment later, Madame Azélie, whose most recent ring of the bell had gone unnoticed, came down for coffee and a slice of buttered bread and announced that the doctor had decided to use forceps. No, they had no need of Barbara's help at the moment. One more person would only be in the way; the doctor needed elbow room.

At the end of twenty minutes, Barbara, summoned by an

imperious ring from Azélie, fearfully entered Madame's chamber. The pretty room looked like the scene of a crime. Barbara, wholly occupied with the orders that the nurse was giving her, had but a timid glance to spare for the ashen face of the woman in the bed, knees bent, feet extending from the sheet and supported by a pillow. The child, already separated from its mother, was wailing in a basket, covered with a blanket. A heated argument had just erupted between Monsieur and the doctor, whose hands and cheeks were trembling. Monsieur was calling him a butcher. Azélie skillfully intervened to silence the barely suppressed outbursts of the two men. Monsieur the doctor was exhausted and would do well to go home and rest. This was not the first time that she, Azélie, had assisted at a difficult birth. Monsieur savagely ordered Barbara to show the doctor out.

He preceded her and went down the stairs almost at a run. He took from a peg in the vestibule a putty-colored overcoat, which he put on over his stained suit, and left.

With the help of Aldegonde, who was called to the rescue, the women restored to chaos a semblance of order. The sheets soiled with the blood and wastes of the birth were rolled in a ball and brought to the washhouse. The viscous and sacred residues of all births, which every adult has some trouble imagining himself to have been furnished with, ended up being burned in the kitchen fire. The newborn was bathed. It was a robust little girl whose head was covered with black down resembling mouse fur. Her eyes were blue. Once again, the gestures made throughout millennia by generations of women were repeated: the gesture of the maidservant who carefully fills a basin, the gesture of the midwife who tests the water with her hand to make sure that it is neither too hot nor too cold. The mother, too exhausted to bear yet another strain, turned her head away when the baby was shown to her. The child was placed in the pretty cradle lined with azure satin that had been installed in the tiny room next door: in a characteristic expression of her piety, which Monsieur de C. according to his mood found either foolish or touching, Fernande had vowed that for the first seven years of its life her child, whatever its sex, would be wedded to blue in honor of the Holy Virgin.

The newborn squalled at the top of her lungs, trying her strength, already displaying that almost terrifying vitality which fills every creature, even the gnat that most people kill with the back of their hand without a thought. Doubtless, as today's psychologists would have it, she cried from the horror of having been forced out of the womb, from the terror of the narrow tunnel she had had to travel through, from the fear of a world where everything—even the act of breathing and of perceiving indistinctly something that is the sunlight of a summer's morning—is strange. Perhaps she has already experienced analogous leave-takings and entrances somewhere else in time. Perhaps vague fragmented memories, obliterated in the adult, neither more nor less than those of gestation and birth, float beneath that little skull still not completely knit. We know nothing of all this: the doors of life and death are opaque, and they are quickly and firmly closed again.

This baby girl hardly an hour old is in any case already caught, as in a net, in the realities of animal suffering and of human pain. She is caught, too, in the futilities of a time, in the major and minor news items of the daily paper (still lying on the bench in the vestibule, since no one has had time to read it this morning), in that which is fashionable and that which is routine. At the head of her cradle hangs an ivory cross adorned with a cherub's head, which by a series of almost absurd coincidences I still have. The object is ordinary—a devotional trinket that was placed there amid the almost equally ritualistic knots of ribbon, but one that Fernande had probably had blessed. The ivory comes from an elephant killed in the forests of the Congo, whose tusks the natives sold for a pittance to some Belgian trader. That great mass of intelligent life, descendant of a dynasty extending back at least to the beginning of the Pleistocene, has been reduced to this. The trinket was once part of an animal that nibbled tender leaves and drank from streams, that bathed in the good warm mud, that used this ivory to battle a rival or parry the attacks of man, that stroked with its trunk the female with which it was mating. The artist who shaped this material could make nothing better from it than a fancy religious bauble: the cherub, thought to represent the Guardian Angel, in which the child will one day believe, looks like those chubby cupids that were mass-produced, likewise, by Greco-Roman artisans.

The openwork and lace of the minuscule bedcover are the product of needleworkers who toil at home, poorly paid by the owner of the elegant lingerie boutique located in the best part of town, or by the intermediary who supplies her. Madame de C., although softhearted, has doubtless never given a thought to the conditions in which these women live; invisible, they weave and embroider, like the Fates, wedding gowns and infants' clothes. Monsieur de C., who has charitable impulses, has taken an interest in the poor of the village of Saint-Jean-Cappelle, below Mont-Noir. He knows of hovels where, early in the morning, the women sit down before their little cushion on the windowsill, to earn a few sous by their lacemaking before they begin the other, exhausting tasks of the day. He regards the profits of the elegant boutique owner as scandalous but pays her bill without a murmur. Perhaps, after all, those women delight in the exquisite designs that take shape beneath their fingers; yet it is also true that they can lose their eyesight to their work. Fernande's husband had not wanted her to hire a wet nurse, finding it repugnant that a mother should abandon her own child to nurse strangers' children for a fee. In this, too, the sordid rural communities of France's Nord have taught him much: he is outraged that a poor girl should choose to take a casual lover, often with the connivance of her own mother, in the hope of donning a wet nurse's beribboned cap in ten or eleven months and of finding a good position with a well-to-do family that she could keep for years perhaps, if later she is promoted from wet nurse to children's nurse. There is in him, as in many men of his time, a Tolstoy in the rough, caught despite himself in customs and conventions from which he has neither the courage nor the desire to free himself completely. But it is out of the question that Fernande should let her breasts become misshapen; the baby will therefore be bottle-fed.

The milk calms the little girl's cries. She has quickly learned to draw almost fiercely on the rubber nipple; the feeling of the good liquid flowing within her is doubtless her first pleasure. The rich nourishment comes from a nursing creature, animal symbol of the fertile earth that gives men not only her milk but later, when her udders are finally exhausted, her lean flesh, and last her hide, tendons, and bones, which are made into glue and bone charcoal. Torn from her familiar pastures, she will die a death that is almost always agonizing, after the long, lurching journey in the cattle car that will convey her to the slaughterhouse, often bruised, deprived of water, frightened in any case by those jolts and noises so new to her. Or else she will be herded the whole way under the hot sun, by men who will goad her with their long prods and mistreat her if she is recalcitrant. She will arrive panting at the place of execution, the rope around her neck, sometimes blinded in one eye, delivered into the hands of butchers who have been brutalized by their despicable trade and who perhaps will begin to cut her up before she is completely dead. Even her name, *vache* ("cow"), which ought to be sacred to the men she nourishes, is a term of ridicule in French, and certain readers of this book will doubtless find this remark and those preceding it equally ridiculous.

The child belongs to a time and a milieu in which domesticity is an institution; it is understood that Monsieur and Madame de C. have "inferiors." This is not the place to ask whether Aldegonde and Barbara are more satisfied with their lot than were slaves of antiquity or workers in a factory; let us note, however, that in the course of her life, which she has barely begun, the newborn will see the proliferation of types of servitude even more degrading than domestic labor. For the moment, Barbara and Aldegonde would doubtless say that they have nothing to complain about. From time to time one of them, or Madame Azélie, takes a brief look at the cradle, then quickly returns to Madame. The child, who does not yet know (or who no longer knows) what a human face is, sees, bending over her, great indistinct orbs that move about and produce sounds. In the same way, many years later, she will perhaps see bending over her the faces of the doctor and nurses, blurred this time by the confusion of her death agony. I like to think that the dog, Trier, who has been chased from his usual comfortable place at the foot of Fernande's bed, finds a way to edge toward the cradle, sniffs this new thing whose odor he does not yet know, wags his long tail to show his trust, and then returns on his crooked legs to the kitchen, where the tasty morsels are kept.

At two o'clock in the afternoon, all danger of hemorrhage seeming remote, Monsieur de C. went to find his brother-in-law Théobald at Théobald's club, then his brother-in-law Georges, who had come from Liège to spend a few days with Jeanne and who had already received a note informing him of the morning's events. These three gentlemen went to register the birth at the parish hall in Ixelles. Monsieur de C. was perhaps unaware that this building, by no means ugly, had been some fifty years earlier the country house of La Malibran, the celebrated singer whose premature death inspired Musset to compose a poem that Michel and Fernande loved and had more than once recited for each other: "Doubtless it is too late to speak of her still; / A fortnight has passed since she ceased to be . . ." Not far from there, in the Ixelles cemetery, a suicide has been resting for several years, a Frenchman to whom Monsieur de C. recently paid a respectful visit: the brave General Boulanger, lofted to glory by cabaret songs, who let down the deputies of the Right when they were engineering a coup d'état in support of him, in order to rejoin his dying mistress, the tubercular Madame de Bonnemain, in Brussels. Monsieur de C. thinks the worthy general a ridiculous political figure, yet he has nothing but admiration for this faithful lover's death ("How could I have lived eight days without you?"). The moment, in any case, was not one for thoughts of death. The civil-service official duly registered the birth of a daughter to Michel-Charles-René-Joseph C. de C., landholder, born in Lille (Nord, France), and to Fernande-Louise-Marie-Ghislaine de C. de M., born in Namur, spouses, residing in the same house and domiciled at Saint-Jean-Cappelle (Nord, France). The first C of the father's name was the initial of an old Flemish patronymic that was inscribed on official documents but that was used less and less in everyday life, Michel himself preferring the entirely French-sounding name of an estate acquired in the eighteenth century.

This official document is, moreover, almost as full of errors as a text written by a scribe in antiquity or the Middle Ages. One of Fernande's given names is entered twice by mistake; in the record of the name and status of the witnesses, the baron Georges de C. d'Y., resident of Liège, manufacturer (I don't know what business he was director of that year, but I know that later he became involved with a concern that imported French wines), despite his very legible signature, is given the same last name as his brother-in-law Théobald de C. de M., who lived in Brussels and was not a baron. In addition, by a confusion probably resulting from informal usage, Georges is entered as the granduncle of the newborn; he was actually Fernande's first cousin and the husband of her oldest sister. Small blunders, or simply inaccuracies, but of a kind to drive generations of scholars mad when the document in question is more important than this one.

The physician who had been chosen to replace Dr. Dubois declared the state of the new mother satisfactory, all things considered. The next two days passed without incident: Jeanne and Fräulein looked in on Fernande briefly each morning upon their return from Mass at the Carmelite church, which Mademoiselle Jeanne would not have missed for anything in the world. On Thursday, however, a slight fever gave Madame Azélie some cause for worry. The next day Monsieur de C. decided to begin keeping a record of the patient's temperature and pulse, taken morning and evening by the nurse. He took up at random a visiting card bearing side by side, almost absurdly, the arms of the two families and began by writing down the previous day's date, trying to recall exactly Fernande's temperature and pulse for that day. Neither he nor Madame Azélie could remember them. His list was as follows:

June 11	8:00 a.m.		
	8:00 p.m.	3 ...	
June 12	8:00 a.m.	38.7	pulse 100
	4:00 p.m.	39.9	p. 120
	8:00 p.m.	39.	p. 100
	noon	38.2	p. 108
	4:00	38.7	p. 106
	10:00 p.m.	39.	p. 120
June 14	8:00 a.m.	38.5	p. 108
	10:00 p.m.	39.6	p. 110
June 15	8:00 a.m.	38.2	p. . . .
	noon	38.2	p. . . .
June 16	8:00 a.m.	39.6	p. 130
	noon	38.3	p. 108
	4:00	40.3	p. 130
	9:00	40.4	p. 135
June 17	8:00 a.m.	39.7	p. 134
	noon	38.7	p. 124
	4:00	37.2	p. . . .
	5:00	39.6	p. 134
June 18	8:00 a.m.	38.6	p. 130
	4:00	39.6	p. 133

Fernande died on the evening of June 18, of puerperal fever accompanied by peritonitis. The only day of the month that Monsieur de C. did not include in his list is the thirteenth, even though the pulse and temperature are both given for that date. Perhaps it was superstition that prompted him to omit that numeral.

That eventful week was marked by a few incidents of lesser importance. The first was the baptism. It took place without any pomp at all in the dull parish church of Sainte-Croix, built in 1859 and somewhat altered since the time I am writing about, doubtless to make it harmonize, after a fashion, with the architectural plan of the imposing Radio and Television Center next to it. It was in this parish that Michel, two and a half years earlier, had married Fernande. Aside from the priest and his acolyte, the only people present were the godfather, Monsieur Théobald; Mademoiselle Jeanne, the godmother (supported as always by Fräulein and by her chambermaid, whom she called her two canes); and Madame Azélie, who held the baby and who was impatient to return to her patient's bedside, where Monsieur and Barbara were taking her place for the moment.

The little girl received the names Marguerite, after the beloved German governess, who had been called Margareta before everyone began addressing her as Mademoiselle Fräulein;

Antoinette, a name that, along with Adrienne, belonged to the detestable Noémi, whose commonly used first name seemed decidedly old-fashioned and a bit grotesque; Jeanne, after Jeanne the Invalid, and also to some extent after a friend of Fernande's who bore this name and who was destined to play a fairly important role in my life; Marie, after she who prays for us poor sinners at all times and in the hour of our death; and finally Ghislaine, as is often the custom in the north of France and in Belgium, Saint Ghislain being thought to guard against childhood illnesses. The ritual boxes of sugared almonds had been ordered in advance and would be delivered as soon as the baby's first name had been inscribed in italics in silver on each cream-colored cover ornamented with a mother and child by Fragonard. Barbara kept hers for a long time. Some years later I sucked thoughtfully on those sugar-coated almonds, those white pebbles, at once hard and crumbly, that dated from my baptism.

A more remarkable incident, at least in the eyes of Monsieur de C., took place the following day. Fernande, in one of those moments when she found the strength to wish for something, sought spiritual guidance. She remembered having several times prayed before the relics displayed at the Carmelite church, where she had gone with Jeanne. In cases of serious illness, those relics were sometimes brought to the homes of the sick who requested them. She asked Monsieur de C. to solicit this favor for her from the superior of the convent.

She did have some relics closer to hand, however. On a console table in a corner of the conjugal bedroom, where she liked to say her prayers alone, there stood on a pedestal a seventeenth-century crucifix from the chapel of the château at Suarlée, where she had grown up. This pedestal and the arms of the crucifix were inset with little monstrances: through a thin piece of curved glass one could see fragments of bone displayed on a ground of faded red velvet, each furnished with a thin ribbon of parchment indicating to which martyr it had belonged. But the ink of the Latin inscriptions had faded, and the martyrs had again become anonymous. All that was known was that some grandfather or other had brought back this sacred treasure from Rome and that these bits of bone had come from the dust of the Catacombs. Perhaps the fact that the names of the saints were unknown, or perhaps the fact that this somewhat lugubrious object, with its soft-figured Christ of silver and its slightly nicked edges of shell, had become too familiar to her, weakened Fernande's faith in its effectiveness. The relics venerated by the Carmelites, in contrast, were believed in the parish to be miraculous.

A young monk came that very day. He discreetly entered the pretty room on the second floor. Drawing the reliquary from a fold in his robe, he placed it on the pillow with infinite care and respect, but Fernande, having relapsed into her agitated torpor, did not even notice the arrival of this longed-for aid. Then, kneeling, the young Carmelite recited some Latin prayers, which were followed by a silent orison. Monsieur de C., who also knelt, more for form's sake than from conviction, watched him pray. After a long moment, the visitor in the brown habit rose to his feet, gazed pensively at the sick woman with what appeared to Monsieur de C. to be profound sadness, gently took back the portable reliquary, tucked it away again, and headed for the door. Monsieur de C. accompanied him as far as the street. It seemed to him that the sadness of the young monk was not caused only by compassion for the dying woman but that, having doubts himself about the power of the relics he brought, he had hoped for a sign, a sudden improvement which would have dispelled his guilty doubts, and that he departed in low spirits. Perhaps Monsieur de C. invented all this.

The second visit was that of Noémi. Out of affection for Monsieur de C.'s son, who was still called "little Michel" despite his tall frame and his nineteen years, she had disapproved of her son's second marriage, and even more of Fernande's pregnancy. The telegram announcing the happy news had provoked her customary gesture of vexation, which was to slap her thigh with the flat of her hand, a mark of vulgarity that irritated her son. "Little Michel has been cut in two!" she had exclaimed, signifying by this metaphor that her favorite would inherit only half his father's property. In the end, however, she did come to Brussels, doubtless because as a woman—especially an old woman—she was curious and could not resist the urge to visit the scene of a recent birth, and also to some extent because Monsieur de C., for whom this whole episode was proving quite costly, had asked his mother to lend him several thousand francs. She would bring them herself and would thus taste the pleasure of exchanging, as always on such occasions, a few sharp words with her son. Despite her age, she went to the Belgian capital from time to time to do some shopping, Paris being decidedly too far and Lille offering too limited a selection. The only inconvenience was that, on the way back, customs charges were levied on certain articles. But she usually managed to avoid paying anything.

Hardly had she stepped out of the hired carriage than she could infer Fernande's condition. Indeed, the street in front of number 193 had been covered with a thick layer of straw, so as to muffle the noise of passing vehicles. Such a precaution, always taken in cases of grave illness, had already informed the neighborhood that the new mother's condition was critical. Barbara opened the door to Madame Mère, who refused to make herself comfortable in the little ground-floor drawing room or to relinquish her parasol. She took a seat on the bench in the vestibule.

Forewarned, Monsieur de C. recognized from the second-floor landing his mother's corpulent but shrunken silhouette, and the manner in which she pressed to her belly, as if to guard against thieves, her black leather purse ornamented with the fancy coronet of a count, which annoyed Michel, though he himself in weak moments sometimes allowed tradesmen to address him as "Count." Approaching the elderly lady, he immediately gave her a straightforward report of the situation: there was no longer any hope of saving Fernande. However, the fever had abated somewhat, and a brief visit with the patient could do no harm. At the moment, she was fully conscious and would be touched by this attention on the part of her mother-in-law.

But the old woman had smelled death. She frowned, and clutching her bag more tightly, she said, "You don't think I might catch something?"

Monsieur de C. restrained himself, merely assuring his mother that puerperal fever was a danger she need no longer fear. Madame Mère, huddled on her bench, refused to stay to dine, and Michel did not press her, since Aldegonde, who had tended Fernande part of the night, had just about extinguished her cooking fires. The dowager climbed back into her waiting carriage, headed to the railway station, and thence sped home to Mont-Noir without further delay. She claimed later that, in her agitation, she had forgotten to give her son the expected loan.

Not long afterward, Fernande received one last visit, but this time there was no question of exchanging a few words with the person or of greeting him with a smile. It was the photographer. He made his entrance with the tools of his sorcerer's art: plates of glass sensitized to fix for a long time, if not forever, the way things looked; the camera obscura constructed like an eye, compensating for lapses of memory; the tripod, with its black cloth. In addition to the last image of Madame de C., this unknown man preserved for me bits of decor, thanks to which I re-create that forgotten interior. At Fernande's bedside, two five-branched candelabra hold only three burning candles apiece, lending an indefinable air of gloominess to that scene which would otherwise be merely solemn and calm. The mahogany headboard stands out against the bed curtains; glimpsed to the left, a second, identical bed, which is carefully covered by a ruffled spread and in which, assuredly, no one has slept this night. I'm mistaken: looking more closely at the photo, I see a dark shape on one corner of the spread—the forepaws and nose of Trier, who is curled up on his master's bed and whom Monsieur de C. no doubt found it considerate and touching to allow there.

The three women had laid out Fernande with the greatest care. She gives, above all, the impression of being exquisitely clean: the trickles of sweat and the seeping lochia have been washed away and dried. A sort of temporary hiatus seems to have set in between the dissolutions of life and those of death. This deceased of 1903 is wearing a batiste nightgown trimmed with lace at the collar and cuffs; a veil of diaphanous tulle imperceptibly covers her face and haloes her hair, which appears quite dark against the whiteness of the bed linen. Her hands, entwined with a rosary, are joined together atop her belly, which is distended by peritonitis; the sheet bulges with the swelling, as if she is still waiting to give birth. She has become what one sees of the dead: an inert, closed mass, insensible to light, warmth, and physical contact, no longer either inhaling or exhaling air and no longer making use of it to form words, no longer taking in nourishment and excreting part of it afterward. Whereas in portraits of her as a girl and as a young woman Madame de C. presents a face that is no more than pleasant and delicate, at least some of her deathbed photographs give the impression of beauty. The emaciation caused by her illness, the calmness of death, the absence now of any desire to please or to create a good impression, and perhaps, too, the skillful lighting in the photograph—all improve the features of this human face, emphasizing the slightly prominent cheekbones, the deep arches of the brows, the delicately curved nose with its narrow nostrils, and lend her a dignity and firmness that no one previously would have thought existed. The large, closed eyelids, giving the illusion of sleep, impart to her a softness that would otherwise be lacking. The curving lips have assumed a bitter expression, with that proud line which the dead often have about the mouth, as if they have won a difficult victory. One can see that the three women have carefully arranged the freshly ironed sheet in large, almost sculptural pleats extending the entire width of the bed and have fluffed up Madame's pillow.

That week friends and acquaintances received two items in the mail, almost at the same time. The first was a small envelope discreetly edged with a fine blue line and ordered, like the boxes of sugared almonds, in advance. A piece of matching paper bore the notice, printed in equally celestial italics, that Monsieur and Madame de C. were delighted to announce the birth of their daughter, Marguerite. The second was brutally bordered with a wide black band. Fernande's husband, daughter, stepson, mother-in-law, brothers, sisters, brothers-in-law, aunt, nephews, nieces, and cousins wished to make known, with the deepest sorrow, the irreparable loss which they had recently suffered. The burial would take place on June 22 at ten o'clock, in the vault belonging to the deceased's family, at Suarlée, following a funeral Mass, which would not preclude another Mass that would be celebrated eight days later in Brussels. Carriages would be waiting at the Rhisnes station, where the funeral procession was to begin as soon as the 8:45 a.m. train arrived from Brussels.

That ceremony took place as planned; whether it was raining or sunny, I do not know. The mother-in-law and the stepson remained at Mont-Noir. After a breakfast that was somewhat hurried but perhaps a bit more copious than usual, the mourners went at the appointed time to the station in the Quartier Léopold. At Rhisnes, coachmen who had come from Namur, and for whom this funeral represented a good day's work, were waiting with their carriages lined up by the side of the road; from time to time the horses would bend their heads to snatch a succulent mouthful of grass. Fernande was lowered into the vault adjoining the exterior wall of the village church; a railing separated the plot from the rest of the cemetery. After three years and three months with Monsieur de C., she was returning to her kin. The little family plot with its identical crosses was already the dwelling place of her parents and of two brothers and a sister who had died young. Following the service, Monsieur de C. exchanged a few words with the priest, who drew his attention to the humbleness of his church. It was indeed fairly ugly, not very old or else badly restored, its interior walls plastered a brownish yellow. But what bothered the priest most was the lack of stained-glass windows in the chancel. A beautiful window depicting Saint Fernand, on the side nearest the burial plot, would surely be a touching memorial to the deceased. The widower drew out his checkbook.

Dear Departed

Some months later he received at Mont-Noir a photograph of the newly installed window, which he thought hideous. An obsequious letter from the priest was enclosed. The window certainly enhanced the chancel of the church, but, in contrast, the plain window on the left side now looked worse than ever. It could perhaps be ornamented, so as to make a matched pair, with a stained-glass image of Saint Michael. Monsieur de C. threw this letter away.

Throughout those event-filled days, no one had a great deal of time to devote to the baby, who was often given cold milk that had not even been boiled and who thrived on this diet. Only once did she become the topic of serious discussion. In one of those moments when Fernande regained consciousness, becoming aware of her condition and of what was going on around her, she gave her husband the following instructions in the presence of Mademoiselle Jeanne and Fräulein:

"If the little one ever wants to become a nun, don't let anyone prevent her."

Monsieur de C. never told me about this, and Jeanne had the discretion to avoid mentioning it. It was otherwise with Fräulein. Each time I prepared to spend several days visiting the woman I knew as Aunt Jeanne, Mademoiselle Fräulein would tirelessly repeat to me my mother's last words, which made the poor old German woman, whose caresses and boisterous teasing I already found irritating, unbearable to me. From the age of seven or eight, it seemed to me that this mother of whom I knew almost nothing, whose picture my father had never shown me (Mademoiselle Jeanne did have a photograph of my mother, along with many others, on her piano, but she hardly took the trouble to draw my attention to it), encroached unduly on my life and liberty, trying to push me too obviously in a particular direction. The idea of entering a convent appealed very little to me, but I would doubtless have been just as rebellious if I had known that on her deathbed she had planned my future marriage or named the school I was to attend. Why were all these people interfering? I balked, imperceptibly, resisting like a dog that turns its head when shown a collar.

On further thought, it seems to me that my mother's instructions were prompted by something other than the piety which Fräulein so admired. Everything convinces me that neither her childhood, with its reveries and emotional effusions characteristic of her time, nor her marriage and the full life that Monsieur de C. tried to give her had completely satisfied Fernande. Seen from the midst of her sufferings, which must have been frightful, her brief past doubtless seemed paltry to her. Her immediate pain crossed out, as with a black line, whatever happiness it might have held here and there, and she wished to keep her child from following a course that for her had turned out badly. In one sense, those few words constituted a discreet reproach to her husband, who so firmly believed that he had fulfilled his duty to her and given her everything one owes a woman: she was letting him know that, like Mélisande, who had been about her age, she had not been happy.

Not that Madame de C. didn't have religious feelings; quite the contrary, as I have indicated. It is possible, then, that Fernande in her death agony felt an impulse toward God and that it was not only her own life but all life on earth that appeared to her vain and artificial in the dim light of death. Perhaps in wishing for her child what seemed to her the tranquil life of the convent, as her memories showed it to her, Fernande was trying to keep ajar for her daughter the only door known to her that led out of what was formerly called "the century" and toward the only transcendence she could name. I tell myself that, late in life and in my own fashion, I have embraced religion, and that Madame de C.'s desire has been realized in a way she doubtless would have neither approved nor understood.

More than fifty-three years passed before my first visit to Suarlée. It was in 1956. I crossed through Belgium after leaving Holland and Germany, having just been to Westphalia, in order to breathe the atmosphere of Münster for a book I was working on. I had chanced to arrive in that gloomy city on a patriotic and religious holiday: the occasion was the resumption of services in the restored cathedral, which had been half destroyed by bombardments in 1944. The ancient center of the city was decked with huge oriflammes; speeches blared from loudspeakers. The area around the cathedral, which in the sixteenth century had witnessed the lunacies of John of Leiden and the bloody repression of the Anabaptists, was filled with a crowd bitterly preoccupied with the memory of its own sorrows and with the pride of having restored its own ruins. I myself, the American woman friend who accompanied me, and our Dutch driver all had equally bitter memories of the year 1944; they were not the same as those of the Westphalians. We felt like intruders, made ill at ease by the solemnity whose importance to that German city we fully understood but in the midst of which we were yesterday's enemies and today's strangers. We quickly left Münster.

In The Hague the newspapers were full of the kidnapping of Ben Bella, the latest sensational turn of plot in the North African melodrama. A few days later, announced with great

fanfare by the radio and the press after clumsily covert preparations, the unfortunate Suez episode began. In a large city in
Flemish Belgium, I witnessed the chauvinistic euphoria of a
group of official-looking Frenchmen as they toasted the
victory—over whom it was no longer very clear. Some English
industrialists, glimpsed a day or two later, echoed this bellicosity
with a British accent. There was already talk of a black market,
and Belgian housewives were hoarding kilos of sugar. The
shrewdest people bought lead foil to cover their windows, as
protection against atomic radiation. Meanwhile, the Soviets
were able to fortify their buffer zones, taking advantage of the
fact that the West had turned its attention elsewhere. I arrived
in Brussels as the news erupted that Russian tanks were surrounding Budapest. Further darkening the picture—which
was, to be sure, already fairly gloomy—our jovial taxi driver
exclaimed: "The Russians are tossing phosphorous bombs there!
Those things really burn! What a show!" The good man was
carried away like everyone else, not, of course, by enthusiasm,
for he was afraid of the Russians, but by that almost joyful
excitement that three-fourths of all people feel at the sight of
a raging fire or a splendid railway accident. Invited to the home
of a well-bred elderly lady, since deceased, I heard another
version of things. The mistress of the house detested the Soviets,
as was proper; but she took a dim view of the Hungarian revolt.
"A workers' rebellion!" she exclaimed contemptuously; and one
felt that, loyal to the end to fine principles, wherever they might
lead, she believed for the first time in her life that the Kremlin
was right. In all this brouhaha, the recent drama of French
Indochina, foreshadowing even more somber dramas, had already been forgotten. However, on arriving in Paris and crossing
the street to see the interior of Saint-Roch again, I found there

a priest and several women in mourning who were still praying for the dead of Dien Bien Phu.

Before leaving Brussels, I had been to pay my respects to the Brueghels in the Musée d'Art Ancien. The half-light of a gray November afternoon was already drowning *The Census at Bethlehem*, with its docile peasants scattered about on the snow; *The War of the Good and Bad Angels*, the latter with their sub-human maws; *The Fall of Icarus*, which shows him plummeting from the sky while a farmer, uninterested in this first airplane disaster, carries on with his plowing. Other paintings in other museums seemed to appear behind these: *Mad Meg* howling her just and useless fury in the midst of a village in ashes; *The Massacre of the Innocents*, mournful counterpart to *The Census*; *The Tower of Babel*, showing the chief of state respectfully being received by his workers, who are erecting for him that heap of errors; *The Triumph of Death*, with its rows of skeletons; and perhaps the most appropriate of all these allegories, *The Blind Leading the Blind*. Brutality, greed, indifference to the sufferings of others, madness, and folly held sway over the world more than ever, exacerbated by the proliferation of mankind and supplied for the first time with the instruments of ultimate destruction. Even if the current crisis resolved itself after destroying only a limited number of people, other crises would come, each aggravated by the aftereffects of the ones preceding. The inevitable had already begun. The museum guards who came to announce closing time, pacing the halls with their military tread, seemed to herald the shutting down of everything.

My short stay in Namur was a pleasant distraction. It was my first visit; I saw all the tourist attractions. I conscientiously toured the cathedral, which contains the heart of Don John of Austria and is thus linked with the mortuary chapel of the Escorial, where his body was brought. I visited the Church of Saint-Loup, a Baroque masterpiece, the "funereal boudoir" admired by Baudelaire, who was overwhelmed there for the first time by that "wind of imbecility" which he had long felt approaching. I climbed to the Citadel, a lofty site where little Fernande must have been taken to admire the view and which in ancient times must have known the tread of the warriors, women, and children of the Celtic tribes seeking refuge from Caesar's troops. I went to the Archaeological Museum to see the little Gallo-Roman bronzes and the heavy jewels dating from the barbaric invasions. The afternoon was devoted to Suarlée. I shall speak here only of my visit to the cemetery.

The family plot had become crowded since the day Michel had laid his wife to rest. Jeanne, Théobald, and Octave, the last of whom died insane, were there. The married sisters were not in evidence, having been buried with their spouses in other cemeteries. The epitaphs, which had been shallowly incised, were difficult to read; they made me think nostalgically of the beautiful firm characters of classical inscriptions, which perpetuate through the centuries the memory of any obscure and forgotten person. I gave up trying to determine whether or not Fräulein had been granted a place between Fernande and Jeanne. I doubt it. It's all very well to love and honor an old governess, but family is family.

Despite all my efforts, I did not succeed in establishing a rapport between those people lying there and myself. I had known personally only three of them, the two uncles and the aunt, and I had lost touch even with them before my tenth year. I had traversed Fernande; I had nourished myself for several months on her substance, but the facts I had gleaned were cold knowledge to me, as if they had come from a textbook. Her grave affected me no more than that of an unknown woman whose death someone might describe to me briefly and in passing. It was even more difficult for me to imagine that Arthur de C. de M. and his wife, Mathilde T., about whom I knew less than about Baudelaire and John of Austria's mother, could have borne within them some of the elements of which I am made. Yet beyond this gentleman and this lady enclosed in their nineteenth century are ranks of thousands of ancestors extending back to prehistory and then, losing all human resemblance, to the very origin of life on earth. Half the amalgam of which I consist was there.

Half? After that process of reblending which makes each of us a unique creature, how could one calculate the percentage of moral or physical traits I had inherited from them? I might as well have dissected my own bones to analyze and weigh the minerals that compose them. If, moreover (as I believe more firmly with every passing day), it is not blood and sperm alone that make us what we are, every calculation of this sort is false from the start. Nevertheless, Arthur and Mathilde were at the second intersection of the lines that connect me with everything. Whatever our hypotheses about the strange shadowy realm from which we come and to which we return, it is always bad to eliminate from our minds the simple, banal facts—these being so strange themselves that they do not seem to apply to us altogether. Arthur and Mathilde were my grandfather and grandmother. I was Fernande's daughter.

Furthermore I realized, as I reflected on those graves at Suarlée, that I was relating those people too closely to myself. If Arthur, Mathilde, and Fernande were almost nothing to me, I was even less to them. During my mother's thirty-one years and four months of life, I had occupied her thoughts only slightly more than eight months at the most. I had been for her, first, an uncertainty; then a hope, an apprehension, a fear, and for several hours a torture. In the days that followed my birth, she must sometimes have felt for me stirrings of tenderness, of surprise, perhaps of pride, mingled with the comfort of being, or believing herself to be, safely through that dangerous episode, when Madame Azélie had displayed to her her new baby girl all freshly dressed. Then the rising fever had swept everything away. She did, as we have seen, give a moment's thought to the fate of the child she was leaving behind, but it is clear that her approaching death concerned her more than my future. As for Monsieur Arthur and Madame Mathilde, both deceased, one ten years and the other twenty-seven years before their daughter's marriage, I had been for them merely one of those vague grandchildren referred to in the nuptial Mass, whom, it is hoped, the couple will live long enough to see one day beside them.

My palms resting on the iron railing were stained with rust. Generations of weeds had flourished since the day that gate had reopened to admit the last arrival, Octave or Théobald, I'm not sure which. Of Arthur and Mathilde's ten children, seven had been buried there; of those seven, there remained in that year 1956 only one offshoot, namely me. It was, then, up to me to do something. But what? Two thousand years earlier, I would have made an offering of food to the dead, who would have been buried curled up like fetuses ready to be born—one of the most beautiful symbols of immortality that mankind has ever devised. In Gallo-Roman times, I would have poured milk and honey at the base of a columbarium full of ashes. During the Christian era, I would sometimes have prayed that those people would enjoy eternal repose, at other times that, after a few years in Purgatory, they would be vouchsafed heavenly bliss. Contradictory wishes, but doubtless ultimately expressing the same thing. Such as I was, and assuming those people were somewhere, I could do no more than wish them good luck on the inevitable road all of us travel. And this, too, is a way of praying. To be sure, I could have had the iron railing repainted and the ground weeded. But I was leaving the following day; there was no time. Besides, the idea didn't even occur to me.

About two weeks after Fernande's death ("Doubt-less it is too late to speak of her still; / A fortnight has passed since she ceased to be . . ."), her family and close friends received in the mail one last item referring to the young woman. It was something known as a *souvenir pieux*: a small religious card that could be inserted between the pages of a missal. On the front of the card would appear a sacred image, accompanied by a prayer or several prayers, each of which might often have at the end, in tiny letters, the precise hours, days, months, and years of indulgence that their recitation would procure for the souls in Purgatory. On the back would be a plea to remember the deceased before God, followed by some quotations from the Scriptures or from devotional works, as well as by some eja-culatory prayers. The *souvenir pieux* for Fernande was unpre-tentious. The prayer, which in those days the stationer-engraver often suggested to bereaved families, was full of banal unc-tuousness: it had been recommended to the faithful on July 31, 1858, by Pius IX as appropriate for comforting the souls in

Purgatory, but it dispensed with any sort of computation based naïvely on the clocks and calendars of the living. On the back, followed by ejaculatory prayers that assured the dead the usual indulgences, appeared two phrases for which no source was given but which I assume were written by Monsieur de C.:

We should not weep because she is no more; we should smile because she existed.
She always tried to do her best.

The first of these thoughts I find quite moving. In the pitiful arsenal of our consolations, this one is among the most effective. The widower meant that the young woman's life was a fact, a good in itself, however brief it may have been, and that death in no way annulled it. But Monsieur de C.'s usual precision is missing from this aphorism. One may smile out of pity, one may smile out of contempt, one may smile out of skepticism just as often as out of tenderness and love. Monsieur de C. may at first have written "We should rejoice that she existed" and then found the word "rejoice" too strong for an expression of grief; or perhaps he was carried away by his love of symmetry. The second phrase is equally perplexing. Michel surely felt that to say of someone that he had done his best was the highest praise one could bestow. The expression echoes Van Eyck's motto, *Als ik kan*, which I have always wanted to make my own. But the phrase "She always tried to do her best" doubles back on itself in a confused way, creating the impression that Fernande had only partly succeeded. Among the friends and relatives who read this encomium, some must have seen in it a resemblance to those letters of recommendation that a good man who dislikes lying gives to a person who is leaving his service and in whom he can find no particular talent to praise.

The phrase can be either condescending or touching. Monsieur de C. intended it to be touching.

The knifelike pain of his loss was, moreover, becoming dull. He was heard to say to one of his brothers-in-law that, after all, giving birth is the special duty of women: Fernande had died on the field of honor. This metaphor is surprising coming from Michel, who, far from demanding that Fernande produce children, had conceded me to her, in a manner of speaking, so as not to thwart her maternal urges. Neither was he the type of person who believes that God imposes on all couples the duty to procreate. But the metaphor, which must have seemed to him to sound good coming from the mouth of a former cuirassier, no doubt arrived in the nick of time in one of those moments when one is at a loss for words. The reality had been a hideous chaos: Monsieur de C. enclosed it, after a fashion, within a commonplace of which Théobald and Georges undoubtedly approved.

He was extremely busy that week. Dr. Dubois, on the occasion of his hasty departure, had forgotten his forceps and apron in a corner of Fernande's room. Monsieur de C. had them wrapped with paper and twine and brought them himself to the doctor's house. A maid answered his ring. He tossed the parcel through the half-open door and departed without a word.

He went next to the real-estate agent and put the house on the avenue Louise up for sale. He himself recrossed the border, returning to Mont-Noir with his little daughter, accompanied by Azélie the nurse, whom he had persuaded to stay in his service till the end of the summer to train Barbara in her new child-care duties. Aldegonde and the gardener were let go, with generous compensation. Michel brought along the horse,

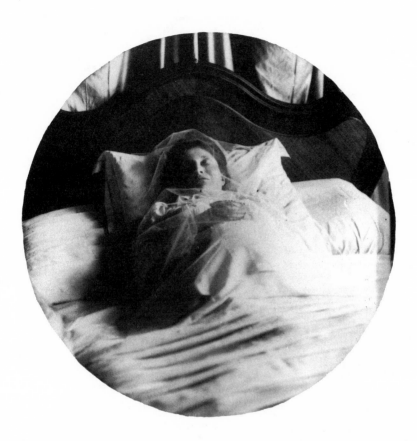

Fernande on her deathbed

SOUVENEZ-VCUS DANS VCS PRIÈRES

DE

DAME

Fernande de CRAYENCOUR

Née de CARTIER de MARCHIENNE

ENFANT DE MARIE

DÉCÉDÉE A BRUXELLES

le 19 juin 1903, dans sa trente-deuxième année, Munie des Sacrements de Notre Mère la Sainte Église.

———

Il ne faut pas pleurer parce que cela n'est plus, il faut sourire parce que cela a été.

Elle essaya toujours de faire de son mieux.

Miséricordieux Jésus donnez-lui le repos éternel.

Doux cœur de Marie, soyez mon salut.

Jésus, Marie Joseph, faites que j'expire en votre sainte compagnie.   100 j.

Mon Jésus miséricorde.   100 j.

Pompes Funébres, 6, rue du Parchemin, Brux.

Fernande's *souvenir pieux*

who would roam the fields at Mont-Noir, and Trier, so named because he had been born in Trèves, who had accompanied Michel and Fernande on all their travels and as a result was even more of a memento of the deceased than the baby herself.

The books, too, were taken back. Monsieur de C. would gladly have kept the enormous table from the library, on which his favorite books and those of Marguerite's mother (this was how the deceased was henceforth referred to) had been piled side by side. But its great weight and the need to call in a professional mover discouraged him. It was the same with the helmeted Minerva, who in the end remained in place on her green marble pedestal, indifferent as always to the transactions of purchase and sale.

Before leaving, Monsieur de C. ran one last errand. He paid a visit to the antiques shop where Fernande had bought several objects and returned one which she had purchased on trial. The shop owner, an old Jew with gentle, delicate features, was a man of taste; in the course of their previous encounters, Monsieur de C. had taken great pleasure in exchanging a few words with him—perhaps the only man with whom he had enjoyed conversing during his stay in Brussels. This time, he limited himself to explaining briefly that he wished to return something. The antiques seller noticed that his customer was in mourning, and made discreet inquiries. Monsieur de C. told him what had happened.

"And the child?" asked the old Jew, after offering the usual condolences.

"The child lives."

"A pity," said the old man softly.

Monsieur de C. echoed him.

"Yes," he agreed. "It's a pity."

I take issue with the assertion, commonly heard, that the premature death of a mother is always a disaster or that a child deprived of its mother feels a lifelong sense of loss and a yearning for the deceased. In my case, at least, things turned out otherwise. Not only did Barbara take the place of my mother until I was seven; she *was* my mother, and it will be seen in a later volume that my first wrenching separation was caused not by the death of Fernande but by the departure of my nurse. Subsequently, or at the same time, my father's mistresses or quasi-mistresses, and later his third wife, provided me with an ample share of motherly and sisterly relationships: the joy of being coddled or the sadness of not being, the still-vague need to give tenderness in return for tenderness, admiration for a beautiful lady, in at least one instance love and respect, in another that consideration tinged with annoyance that one feels for a good person with no great talent for serious thought.

Yet the point here does not have to do with me; it has to do with the fact that, but for this accident, Fernande might perhaps have lived thirty or forty years longer. I've sometimes tried to imagine her life. If the separation that Michel envisaged had taken place, Fernande would have joined that somewhat drab group of abandoned women who were not rare in that milieu. She was not the type to console herself by taking a lover, or would have done so only with the deepest remorse. If, on the other hand, my birth had strengthened their marriage, it is unlikely that they would thereby have recovered their delightful harmony. Time would doubtless have instructed Fernande, would have taken away her languors and melancholies typical of a woman of 1900; yet experience shows us that most people change very little. Influenced by her, or irritated by her, my adolescence would have inclined a bit more toward submission or toward revolt, and revolt would almost inevitably have gained the upper hand around 1920 in a girl of seventeen. Had Fernande, unlike most women in her family, lived to be very old, I can envision only too well her last years as a pensioner in a convent or as a resident in a Swiss hotel, and the fairly infrequent visits I would have paid her, out of duty. Would I have loved her? It is impossible to hazard an answer to such a question when the people concerned are unknown to us. Everything leads me to believe that at first I would have felt for her an egoistic and absentminded love, like most young children, then an affection based above all on habit, marred by quarrels, increasingly weakened by indifference, as is true of so many adults who love their mothers. I write this not to be unpleasant but to confront things as they are.

Today, however, my current effort to recapture and recount her history fills me with a sympathy for her that I have not felt heretofore. She is much like those characters, imaginary or real, that I nourish with my own substance to try to make them live, or live once again. The passage of time has, moreover, inverted our relationship. I am now more than twice as old as she was on June 18, 1903, and look at her as at a daughter whom I am trying my best to understand, without completely succeeding. The same effects of time account for the fact that my father, who died at the age of seventy-five, seems to me now less like a father than like an older brother. To be sure, I had a similar impression of him even when I was twenty-five.

During that month of June, Monsieur de C. surrendered himself to a ritual which was even more poignant than the one that had taken place at Suarlée and which I would call, for lack of a better term, the occultation of relics. With Jeanne's approval, the deceased's lingerie and dresses had been given to the Little Sisters of the Poor to be sold for the benefit of their flock. What remained were the odds and ends that always persist, even for those people who are by nature most inclined to divest themselves of everything. Monsieur de C. made up a little box of Fernande's remaining possessions: a deeply affectionate letter that she had written him before their marriage, notes from her sisters, the brief records he had kept during her illness, little remembrances from her schooldays, awards, classroom exercises and good reports, and finally a notebook, which I have since thrown away, in which Fernande, already married, indulged in a fairly lamentable literary effort. It was a romanesque novel set in an old Breton manor (Madame de C. knew nothing about Brittany) and entirely concerned with describing a second wife's jealousy of her husband's first spouse, whose ghost haunts her. In it, Monsieur de C. took the form of a sportsman endowed with British elegance. I do not judge Fernande by this little piece, which testifies above all to her need to romanticize her own life.

Michel also put into this box all the photographs of his

wife, taken both during her life and after her death, and the snapshots taken during their travels. He slipped into a carefully labeled envelope the locks of hair that Marguerite's mother had had cut off the day before her confinement. While examining these around 1929, I noticed that that fine hair, so brown it looked black, was identical to mine.

Other capillary relics inspired me with horror. They were heavy bracelets plaited of reddish-brown hair which must have come from Fernande's mother or one of her grandmothers. These coils of almost metallic stiffness no longer had anything in common with the organic matter secreted by the human skin, no more than artfully tooled leather bears any resemblance to the skin of a flayed animal. I got rid of them by selling them for their golden clasps. A coffer of morocco leather contained, in addition to some souvenirs from long-ago formal balls, one of those coral necklaces that one buys in Naples and that Madame de C. had doubtless picked out as she was leaving some restaurant on the via Partenope or returning from a carriage ride on Posillipo. Its fragile branches had been reduced nearly to crumbs in their cocoon of tissue paper. The more valuable jewels, which had been stored in a bank safe, I either sold on a day when funds were low or had reset, transforming them to such an extent that Madame de C. would not have recognized them. A wedding ring lay hidden at the bottom of the coffer; it, too, was eventually melted down, that type of ring being sacred only when left on the finger of the dead. Some holy medallions I gave away—to whom I no longer remember. The reliquary of ebony and shell found refuge in a convent.

A few other bits of flotsam rounded out the collection. A volume of Bossuet, his *Meditations on the Gospel*, a gilt-edged Garnier edition half-bound in red leather, bore an inscription in angular gothic characters indicating that the book had been a birthday gift to Fräulein from one of her dear little girls, Zoé. On the inside cover, a bookplate engraved with the family's coat of arms (seven silver lozenges) reveals that Fräulein, who doubtless preferred devotional works in German, had donated that book to the small library at Suarlée. These *Meditations* had kept the fresh appearance of books that are seldom read. In contrast, a two-volume *Missal of the Faithful*, published in Tournai by Desclée, Lefebbre, and Company in 1897, had been much used, to judge by its worn sheepskin binding; a crown surmounting the initials of Fernande's maiden name mars the cover with vanity. The *Missal* contains a perpetual calendar that I consult from time to time. Occasionally, too, I reread in it the noble Latin prayers that Fernande imagined would be recited till the end of time and that the Church today has cast aside. On a small *carnet de bal* shaped like a lady's fan one could still read, written in pencil on its ivory blades, the names of Fernande's dance partners; I deciphered a few of them. Two fancy-leather articles from Paris must have been gifts from Michel. One, very reminiscent of the Belle Epoque, was a visiting-card case ornamented in elegant Japanese style with enamel irises against a background of violet and sea-green. The vogue for such cases having had its day, I put in it little cards on which I had copied verses or thoughts that were dear to me around 1929 or that helped guide me through life. This viaticum took its place among the keys, the pen, and all the accessories that clutter a lady's handbag. Frayed, stained with ink and lipstick, it eventually went the way of all objects. The second article, a much finer one, was an Empire-green coin purse made of leather so polished it appeared to be lacquered. A golden peacock and its fan-shaped tail formed the clasp and edge. Though it was made more for gold louis bearing the image of *La Semeuse* than for our nickels and our grimy bills, my antipathy for objects lying abandoned in the back of a drawer prompted me, around 1952, to use it. I lost it two years later on an outing in the Taunus mountains. If objects that have gone astray end up by rejoining their deceased owners, Madame de C. would be pleased to learn that her daughter had also strolled along the roads of Germany.

The little box sealed by Michel has fulfilled its duty, which was to make me muse about all that. Those pious odds and ends, however, would cause us to envy animals, who possess nothing apart from their lives, which we so often take from them; they would also cause us to envy sadhus and anchorites. We know that such knickknacks were once treasured by someone, that they were occasionally useful, and that their chief value lay in the extent to which they helped define or enhance the image that person had of himself. But the death of their owner renders them worthless, like the playthings one finds in tombs. Nothing shows better the insignificance of our human individuality, which we prize so highly, than the rapidity with which those objects that support it and sometimes symbolize it are, in their turn, outmoded, outworn, or lost.

THE TOUR
OF THE
CHÂTEAUX

I shall now take advantage of the momentum acquired in the foregoing pages to set down what little I know about Fernande's family and about her early years. For the plunge into her ancestral past, I shall make use of the meager facts I've gleaned from genealogies and from works by local scholars. For more recent years I shall rely on remembrances of Fernande transmitted by Michel. The history of my paternal background, whose details are more familiar to me, and my father's history, which I can glimpse in the anecdotes I heard him tell and retell, are more closely related to my own, and the same is true of the descriptions of the locales and regions where I spent my childhood. They are inseparable from my own memories and will be set down at a later date. What follows here is, in contrast, largely foreign to me.

If one can believe local accounts, the Quartier family (this is the way the name was spelled until the mid-seventeenth century) was long established in the Liège region. A certain knight named Libier de Quartier, married to one Ide de Hollogne, was *maître à temps* of the city of Liège in 1366, a title that means something like "consul," the city in the fourteenth century having two *maîtres*, one taken from the "lineages" and the other from the "trades." This family, in the end, went the way of most old families: it died out—or would have, had not a certain Jean de Forvie, who in 1427 married one Marie de Quartier, taken up its name and coat of arms. Thus grafted onto a new trunk, the Quartiers continued to prosper in that strange ecclesiastical principality, under the jurisdiction of the Holy Roman Empire, that was Liège before 1789. These people married prudently, within their caste; their dowries doubtless consisted of fertile estates and the assistance of fathers and uncles influential with the prince-bishop or in the city. Their landed wealth prospered under the sun: "Forvie" remained part of the family name until the end of the eighteenth century; "Flémalle" made its appearance in 1545; but it was not until 1714 that Louis-Joseph de C. (the family could henceforth use that initial, which was more seemly than the preceding one, the letter *Q* having some rather crude associations in French), lord also of Souxon, of a place called Mons, and of the pale of Kerchrade, inherited from an aunt the seignorial rights over Flémalle-Grande, former seat of the knightly order of Saint John of Jerusalem.

Various members of the family served, successively or simultaneously, in official capacities: noble alderman, high alderman, mid- and lower-level court officers, chief magistrate, perpetual delegate to the States of Liège, financial secretary, privy counselor to His Holiness the Bishop Maximilian Henry of Bavaria, privy counselor and treasurer to His Holiness the Bishop Joseph Clement of Bavaria, canon landowner of the Collegiate Church of Saint John and of Notre-Dame d'Huy. Five served as burgomaster of Liège in the eighteenth century, three of them holding this office twice. A century earlier, that honor would have entailed some risk: five burgomasters of Liège perished on the scaffold in the seventeenth century, and a sixth was assassinated. The former were members of the reform party. Fernande's ancestors, for their part, supported the miter. But even so, public offices were not sinecures. Around 1637, a noble alderman suspected of having participated in the murder of Burgomaster La Ruelle was torn apart by rioters, who, it is said, drank the unfortunate man's blood and ripped his body with their teeth.

There would be hardly any point to evoking the history of a family if it did not offer us a window onto the history of a small state of old Europe. Ecclesiastical city founded, we are told, by the legendary Saint Hubert, cradle of the family of Charlemagne, whom, rightly or wrongly, we have naturalized as French like us, passionately involved in that very French endeavor the First Crusade, enriching our *chansons de geste* with its legends—Liège from a slight distance gives the impression of being a great city of France. Everything leads us to believe it: that Walloon tongue, so close to our *langue d'oïl* (people in Liège were wrong to take offense when I told them that, while exchanging a few words with a local farmer, I had thought myself transported to the thirteenth century); its "mad populace" referred to by Commynes, that choleric, high-spirited man, pious and anticlerical, proud of his city, "where they said as many Masses per day as in Rome," but living untroubled for five years under the sentence of excommunication pronounced by his bishop; the very French appearance of its lovely eighteenth-century mansions; the music of Grétry and, later, of César Franck; the blaze of enthusiasm inspired by the Declaration of the Rights of Man; and finally the escapade of Théroigne de Méricourt. We are inclined to see, in the poor neighborhoods of Liège, an extension of the Faubourg Saint-Antoine, and in Liège itself that chief town of the *département* of Ourth which the Revolution made of it.

That is one of the panels of the diptych. The other has as background the regions of the Moselle and the Rhine to which Liège owed its precocious splendor around the year 1000—its ivories, its enamels, its illuminated Gospels, supreme efflorescence of the Carolingian and Ottonian renaissances. That art which communicates with antiquity via Aix-la-Chapelle and, beyond that, Byzantium, is undeniably an imperial art. The grand style of Saint-Barthélemy's baptismal fonts, which were sculpted around the year 1110, seems four centuries ahead of its time or a millennium behind. On the one hand, it foreshadows the draped figures and the masterly nudes of Ghiberti; on the other, the muscular back of the legendary philosopher Crato, who is depicted in the act of being baptized, harks back to the bas-reliefs of Augustan Rome. This work by a certain Renier de Huy, who sculpted in the classical style, reminds one irresistibly of a philosopher of the Liège region who thought in the classical manner a century later and was as a result burned at the stake in Paris in 1210, on the site of what is now Les Halles, for having taken his inspiration from Anaximander and Seneca: the pantheist David de Dinant. *Quis est Deus? Mens universi.* Almost certainly, the distant ancestors of the Quartiers had no connection with that sculptor or that heretical genius. At most they were wonderstruck by the superb skill of the former and outraged by the ideas of the latter (if indeed they were familiar with them at all). Nevertheless, I evoke this exceptional work and exceptional destiny because too often people know nothing of those great veins originating in antiquity and running through what seems to us, wrongly, the monolithic Middle Ages.

The Tour of the Châteaux

Situated between the Cologne of Albert the Great and the Paris of Abelard, communicating with Rome and Clairvaux through the comings and goings of clerks and churchmen, Liège remained until the end of the thirteenth century a stage on the highways of the spirit. Exhausted subsequently by two hundred years of civil war, already swelling with the social unrest of its seventeenth century, the city squandered its Renaissance and is linked to it by no more than the slender thread of a few Italianate artists. French elegance had an early influence on the upper classes, just as Enlightenment ideas would later inflame the liberal bourgeoisie that was gradually coming into being. But although Jean-Louis, Louis-Joseph, Jean-Arnould, and Pierre-Robert spoke Versailles French (albeit not without a slight Walloon accent) at the court of the prince-bishops of the House of Bavaria, until the last days of the ancien régime the manners and the ambiance would nevertheless be the pleasantly old-fashioned ones of the little principalities of Germany.

These people of good family, who would have felt demeaned by any connection with commerce or banking, were or (more important) wished themselves to be exclusively landholders, men of war, and men of the Church: in the Middle Ages, their sword-bearing noble canons scandalized Commynes. Like all nobility under the Holy Roman Empire, they were infatuated with their titles, coats of arms, and genealogical trees—pretty toys that were equally precious, certainly, to the French nobility but that they had not learned to speak of with a smile, as good taste obliged one to do in France. Notwithstanding their alliances with a wealthy bourgeoisie that wanted only to blend with them, they formed a caste tied by self-interest to a particular status quo, maneuvering in front of the lower classes like an army before its adversary. Other Belgian cities give the impression (partly false, moreover) that despite their ferocious battles of party and class, the nobility, the patricians, the bourgeoisie, and the trades occasionally put up a united front. As great rebel lords, the Gueux felt they had the support of the poor people of Flanders and took pride in this; Count Egmont was mourned by the people of Brussels. These brief impulses toward union were lacking in the prince-bishops. The eternal game of tug-of-war between the great and the small, the constant appeal to foreign allies by one or the other, the expenditure of intelligence and energy solely for destructive ends make Liège's history a perfect example of the tumultuous political unrest that characterizes three-fourths of the political history of all city-states, including the mistakenly celebrated political histories of Florence and Athens.

In 1312 the tradesmen of Liège imprisoned and burned alive two hundred knights in the Church of Saint-Martin, thus committing their Oradour. In 1408, after various incidents, Bishop Jean de Bavière threw into the Meuse the leading tradesmen, their wives, and the priests who had taken their part. The wealthy looked for protection to the dukes of Burgundy, in whose courts the feudal system was already mantling itself in that fantastic sunset splendor for which the Hapsburgs would inherit such nostalgia. The poor, on the other hand, would become pawns for Louis XI to advance and to sacrifice as necessary on the chessboard of the Occident. When Charles the Bold forced the fox of France to join in sacking rebellious Liège, and poor folk fleeing to the lonely wilds of the Ardennes died "of cold, hunger, and exhaustion" or were murdered there by turncoat nobles eager to return to favor, Libert de Quartier and his wife, Ivette de Rutinghem, doubtless approved of such housecleaning methods. Or perhaps, on the contrary, they deplored the Burgundians' destruction of the profitable "iron mills" scattered throughout the forest, the earliest incarnation of the heavy industry that would later develop there.

When disorder erupted in the following century, the ecclesiastical principality remained loyal to its foreign master and profited handsomely as a result. The pikes of the Walloon guards were possibly forged in Liège, and those of the soldiers of William of Orange as well, contraband being in every age a quasi-official activity of arms manufacturers. The overworked lower classes seem to have stuck to their labors without trying to emulate the mass uprisings of the other Low Countries; the fate of the Flemish, moreover, was sufficient to give them pause. The plague of heresy seems to have been less virulent in Liège than elsewhere. Such spoilsports as the Anabaptists, whose doctrines appealed to the downtrodden everywhere, were quickly suppressed; the widow of one of these rebels made her way to Strasbourg and there married a certain Calvin. When in 1585 Jean de Quartier married Barbe du Château, daughter of a city commissioner, the recapture of Anvers and L'Ecluse by Spanish troops must have been the subject of joyful comment among the men at the marriage festivities; the women, I imagine, were busy helping the bride with her toilette. Some thirty years later, in contrast, when Jean's son married Isabelle de Sclessin, likewise daughter of a city commissioner, foreign intrigues and the high cost of living provoked unrest; the Protestants of the United Provinces and the Very Christian King, in his desire to play a trick on the Holy Roman Empire, bought off the protesting lower classes, but the leaders of these have-nots came to a bad end, and the negotiators of the Treaty of Nimègue refused to receive their emissaries. The bishopric finally gained the upper hand—a position it would maintain for the next century.

Dear Departed

Under the aegis of the prince and his functionaries, Liège in the rococo period, wallowing like the rest of Europe in absolutism and the good life, passed its days busily and relatively peacefully, despite the disdain that the "Grignoux" in their dress coats or smocks occasionally directed at the elegant "Chiroux," who sported swallowtail hairdos and black satin breeches. The old presyndicalist flame of the trades, which in any case were devouring one another, was quite dead, and the tradesman class itself was being replaced by a proletariat that did not yet know its own name. The only conflagrations that the burgomasters in Fernande's family had to prevent or extinguish were the very real ones that were always to be feared in that city of smiths and weapon makers. This fact doubtless explains why buckets made of boiled leather, stamped with the city's arms and with their own, modeled on those that were passed from hand to hand when a fire ravaged the workshops and sheds and threatened the mansions of the wealthy, were regarded as an emblem of their office. I was shown some of these during a visit to one of the tribal châteaux; but one can assume that Louis-Joseph, François-Denys, Jean-Arnould, Pierre-Robert, and Jean-Louis also did their best to smother any new ideas from France that flared up among lower-class hearths.

As is the case everywhere, self-interest still obliged great and small to live together in a sort of hostile symbiosis, whether they liked it or not. The bishop would have been an extremely minor prince without the yield of his arms manufactures, and Jean-Arnould, his treasurer, would not have known how to replenish his coffers. But the subsistence of the workers depended to an equal extent on a healthy business atmosphere—that is, on the course of world events: on purchases of muskets for the Seven Years War, pistols like those with which Cartouche murdered travelers and Werther blew out his brains, or fine daggers with chased handles that gentlemen sported in the salons of Brussels. In an age when manufactured products, hard currency, and the tripling of the population were already touted as remedies for every ill and when Voltaire echoed public opinion in criticizing the Church, whose holy days deprived the laborer of work time, the benefits of industry, including that of firearms, became an enduring lay dogma. Jean-Arnould and Pierre-Robert did not gainsay it.

In the course of time, and as a result of circumstances, these noble functionaries came to differ less and less from prosperous bourgeois. The wind from France would sweep away their feudal rights, but the landowners' wealth had long depended on leases granted to the farmers as much as, and more than, on revenues (payment in kind or in work) dating from an earlier age. For a long time, too, the well-to-do had been investing their money in commerce and industry and engaging in speculation through the agency of their bankers. It was the use of coal, increasingly common from the eighteenth century on, that little by little transformed the still semi-artisanal factories into large-scale industry. We can be sure that the first members of the nobility who discovered treasures of coal beneath their idyllic but unproductive fields and pastures were just as pleased as the Texas farmer and the Arab prince who today reap the profits of their oil wells. The time would soon come when, in a Belgium enamored of business, Baron de C. d'Y. would call himself a manufacturer, when Monsieur de C. de M. would take pride in the title of engineer, and when distinctions of nobility, still highly prized, would serve to ensure the most adroit a good position in business circles.

In the opening years of the eighteenth century one of my distant granduncles, Louis-Joseph de C., with the aid of his wife, Marguerite-Pétronille, daughter of Gilles Dusart, Grand Recorder to the aldermen and Supreme Recorder of Liège, transformed into a modern and pleasant dwelling the remains of a residence at Flémalle that had once belonged to the knights of Saint John of Jerusalem. It is interesting to imagine them settling thus, like animals in the abandoned burrow of a distantly related species, in one of the empty shells of those great monastic and military orders whose peak years already belonged to the remote past. Thierry de Flémalle, Conrad de Lonchin, Guillaume de Flémalle (dubbed the Champion), the Order of Saint John, and the Chapter of Saint-Denys were even more distant in time from Louis-Joseph than he is from us. The pre-Romantic fascination with the Middle Ages that would later become the vogue had not yet completely emerged, and the word "Gothic," until recently a term of scorn, was just beginning to stir people's imaginations. It is unlikely that Louis-Joseph and Marguerite-Pétronille were ever disturbed in

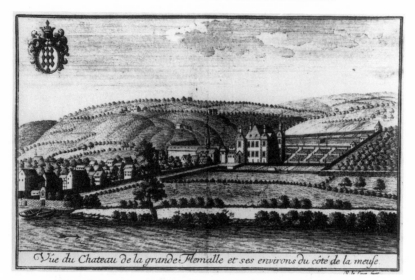

Vûe du Chateau de la grande Flemalle et ses environs du côté de la meuse.

View of the château of Flémalle-Grande and its environs, as seen from the Meuse. Engraving from *Délices du pays de Liège (Delights of the Liège Region)*, 1718

their slumbers by ghosts of knights emblazoned with red crosses.

A picture of Flémalle, cut by a vandal from the lovely volume *Delights of the Liège Region* of 1718 and inserted in an old frame of gilded glass, was among the assorted objects left by Fernande. It shows a turreted château which, as is frequently true in the Low Countries, appears to predate by a hundred years the time of its actual construction; the local masons lagged behind those of France. The gardens, in contrast, like all the gardens of that time, are modeled on the parterres of Versailles. In the angles of the high wall that borders them to the north, a relic perhaps of the days when the knights owned the estate, old watchtowers can still be seen. From there the gardens spread over the hillside and rejoin the Meuse, making a rustic transition through orchards, fields, and vineyards. The château is flanked, or buttressed, by a massive barn and a chapel that has retained its medieval air. A perfectly straight road leads to the river; on the bank, two dozen tall houses with peaked roofs and in some cases half-timbered walls constitute the village of Flémalle-Grande. Two or three tethered skiffs rock gently on the water. People would borrow them when they wanted to cross the river to the Abbaye du Val Saint-Lambert, which in those days, of course, did not include the immense factory complex it does now. People would also use them for fishing or for hunting migratory birds on a little wooded island known as Crow Island. If, on the other hand, one were to cross the groves and grassy slopes of the hills protecting the château and village to the north, in a few miles one would reach Tongres, ancient capital of Belgian Gaul, and, farther on, the Limbourg border of the states of the prince-bishop.

Let us look for a moment at this cluster of dwellings by the water, which, for the eighteenth-century engraver, merely added a picturesque element to the scene. Older than Louis-Joseph's château or the knights' residence that preceded it, they already existed, lower and roofed with thatch, early in the second century of a time that had not yet heard of the Christian era, when a veteran soldier, whose honorable discharge engraved in bronze was later dredged up from the Meuse, came there to live out his days. This legionnaire, originally from Tongres, had served in one of the garrisons of the island that subsequently became England; his discharge dates from the first months of Trajan's reign. I like to believe that his unit, returning from overseas, disembarked at Cologne, the military center of lower Germany, around the time the general received news of his accession as emperor—news brought at full gallop by his nephew Publius Aelius Hadrianus, a young officer destined for a brilliant future. One imagines him sitting on the riverbank, surrounded by naked children lolling in the high grass, an old man recalling once more the familiar scene: the cheers of the troops, warmed as was fitting by gifts of beer and money; the officer, still drunk with speed, telling of the ambush that enemies had set for him near Trèves, on the banks of the Moselle, and that he had foiled with the quickness and vigor of his twenty years . . . According to travelers who from time to time made a detour by way of Cologne, that young man was now emperor; his profile had been seen on coins recently minted in Rome. Trajan, heaped with honors, was dead . . . This man from Tongres had perhaps even visited the Imperial City, on the occasion of some victory over other barbarians, enemies of his own . . . If so, he described, with many exaggerations, the lofty, flat-roofed buildings, the great temples, the streets crowded with carriages, the shops that sold everything, the beautiful girls too costly for his soldier's purse, the savage contests between men and beasts, men and men, beasts and beasts, which are the finest spectacle he has ever seen. The old veteran, slightly numb, gets to his feet with effort, thinking that nowadays he would no longer have the strength to carry the heavy gear of a legionnaire; he has forgotten what little Latin he learned from his centurions. Soon he will hear on the soft ground of the towpath, in the black of night, the hoofbeats of the Hunter and the baying of the hounds that drag the dead to the land of the beyond . . .

I digress here less than one might think: antiquarians when the whim took them, as the wealthy were in those days, Louis-Joseph and his heirs must have examined with interest the poor relics unearthed by their gardeners' spades. They reverently handled those rusty coins and those shards of red pottery, with their stereotyped but exquisite reliefs—the remains of vessels from which the humble folk of the Gallo-Roman world ate their beans and their barley gruel. They quoted relevant Latin verses learned in school, slightly mangled by lapses of memory, uttering here and there a commonplace on the passage of time or the fall of empires and even of principalities. That is what I in my turn am doing here; but it is better to offer commonplaces on these matters than to turn one's head away and close one's eyes.

If Marguerite-Pétronille fulfills her duties as chatelaine properly, she will go down to the village from time to time bearing old linens, a little wine, and soothing broth for some invalid or a woman in childbirth, raising her skirts high in the narrow, muddy streets, where sows root among the filth and chickens perch on the dungheaps. Louis-Joseph occasionally makes his silver-headed cane ring on the threshold of a peasant more prominent than the others—someone who is on a small scale in Flémalle what that nobleman is on a large scale in Liège and whom it is politic to honor in this way. Small industry has taken hold in Flémalle while awaiting the large: Jean-Louis has invested in a needle factory and has sanctioned the opening of a quarry. Between village and château have been woven ties of resentment, of hatred (we shall presently see an example), sometimes also of mutual advantage, of benevolence—even of a sympathy transcending class boundaries, as when Madame confides her troubles to her maids, or of a stronger inclination born of the flesh itself, if perchance Monsieur should sleep with a pretty girl. Everyone prays together in church, though of course Louis-Joseph and his wife sit apart in their own pews emblazoned with their family crest.

Together everyone follows the procession on Corpus Christi, each with his particular rank and place, along lanes strewn with sweet-smelling flowers. In summertime, orchards and gardens bloom for rich and poor alike; then come the grape harvest and the making of an inferior wine that Monsieur likes a good deal less than Burgundy. In the fall, the barnyards of both château and village echo with the squeals of dying pigs, and the good smell of ham rises from all the kitchen hearths. Venison, the product of cynegetic exploits that nourish many a conversation, is served at Monsieur's table on silver platters; except for such handsome tableware, people eat just as heartily in the houses down by the water, where the venison comes from poaching and inspires just as many boasts and good stories. We are in the land of Saint Hubert; but the hunter who was converted by the sight of a weeping stag bearing the crucified Christ between its horns has become, by an inversion whose irony no one appreciates, the patron saint of hunters and their hounds, a bit the way the crucifix, in a court of law, has come to be placed over the judge's bench instead of over the accused, where it should be. Good form obliges Monsieur and Madame to have their food prepared by a French chef well versed in sauces, but the scullions and kitchen girls are of local stock, and tidbits from above readily make their way down below. Over dinner, at the château, the curé laments that he has had to dissolve the rustic brotherhood of Notre-Dame-de-la-Chandelle, whose revenues, spent entirely on lavish feasts, no longer led to anything but debauchery and scandal, and Monsieur and Madame join him in deploring the piggishness of the villagers.

The prince-bishop has surely troubled himself more than once to visit his privy counselor, a courtesy made all the easier for him since his own summer residence at Seraing, today the site of the Cockerill factories, is nearby; the first locomotive manufactured on the Continent will take shape there in a little less than a century. Neither His Holiness the bishop nor his trees nor the birds in his gardens, where blast furnaces will soon be flaming night and day, have any inkling of this, any more than they suspect that giant prehistoric beasts once wandered the area, leaving in the river's mud their footprints and their bones, which are only slightly more deserving of being called "fossils" today than that locomotive of 1835. Moreover, distinguished visitors are common in this century, when Spa, the Monaco of that rococo principality, draws the cream of society to its thermal cures and above all to its gaming establishments, from which His Holiness collects a tithe. One may reasonably imagine that some notable traveler coming from or going to Paris by way of Namur stopped at Flémalle to rest his horses, and received refreshments and compliments from the burgomaster or privy counselor of those days.

The most famous of these wayfarers traveled incognito, or nearly so. Around 1718, there is Peter the Great, progressive monarch, regal despite his brown cuffless and collarless garment and his unpowdered wig, but with his face occasionally distorted by a twitch that momentarily gives him a wild and terrible aspect. The burgomaster will be obliged to conduct a tour of the city's workshops, omitting no detail. Peter takes advantage of his travels to further the industrialization of his country; this carpenter-autocrat who will send his own son (deemed too conservative) to death seems more like the men of the hammer and sickle than like his own timid descendants, who will perish in a cellar in Ekaterinburg. Around 1778, there is the count of Falkenstein—that is, Joseph II—liberal monarch, another great visitor of factories and workhouses, who is equally exhausting for his hosts but who is preoccupied above all by the follies of his sister Marie-Antoinette and the inertia of his fat brother-in-law. A bit later, there is the count of Haga—"*chi molto compra e poco paga,*" as his Italian creditors sighed—otherwise known as Gustave III, connoisseur of arts and pleasures, who, wherever he goes, is heading toward the masked ball at the Stockholm Opera where he will be cut down, struck in the belly through his domino by Anckarström's bullet and supported by his favorite, von Essen. Among those travelers who at least pause at Flémalle to admire the fine view, I would like to be able to number a certain knight of Seingalt, alias Giacomo Casanova, who passed through Liège several times, the first time at top speed, suffering from venereal disease and intent on reaching Germany and finding a good doctor; later, in an even greater hurry, seeking to keep his new mistress, a seventeen-year-old from Brussels, out of the clutches of her pursuing family.

But enough of these visitors who are merely plausible. Chroniclers assert that the château was twice occupied by foreign troops during the eighteenth century, though it is unclear whether this was during the War of the Spanish Succession, that of the Polish Succession, that of the Austrian Succession, or the Seven Years War; neither is it known whether the occupiers were Austrians, Prussians, Hanoverians in the service of the British crown, or Frenchmen. But it was the age when warriors wore lace: those gentlemen who were billeted in the château no doubt behaved irreproachably. Perhaps there were Hanoverians to join Madame in sight-reading a bit of Rameau on the harpsichord, or chivalrous, tipsy musketeers to make the young ladies dance in the park's avenues, which a Louis-Joseph or a Jean-Denys had just laid out and which they imagined would eventually be age-old. As for lesser folk, in the days of Fanfan La Tulipe they were accustomed to brigandage and to girls' being more or less raped.

Concerning another Louis-Joseph or a Jean-Baptiste, son or grandson of the rebuilder of Flémalle (the texts I have in hand contradict one another, and reconciling them would take more research than the information is worth), tradition tells us three things: widowed, he took holy vows and became canon landowner—which means paid from ecclesiastical revenues—of the Collegiate Church of Saint John; he was highly educated; his peasants detested him and gave themselves a holiday lasting several days when he died. His taste for learning reveals less about him than one might think. Certainly, it is a simple matter to try to reconstruct the library of Jean-Baptiste (if that was his name), whether at Flémalle or at the house he must have had in the city, closer to his church. It would have contained all the Latin authors and perhaps a few Greek ones, though the latter more probably in Madame Dacier's translations; whatever a canon needed in the way of theologians and Church Fathers, Leibniz and Malebranche if Jean-Baptiste was a thoughtful man, but surely not Spinoza, considered far too impious; all the great writers of the age of Louis XIV, flanked by heraldic treatises and some travel narratives. Of contemporary writers, perhaps Fontenelle and the *Odes* of Jean-Baptiste Rousseau, the worthy books of Voltaire, such as *The Temple of Taste* or *The History of Charles XII*, and surely his *Tragedies*. If the canon had a weakness for spicy literature, and if Catullus and Martial did not satisfy him, no doubt Piron, and *The Maid of Orleans* in some elegant binding bearing a serious title on the spine; but probably not *Candide*, which was unquestionably beyond the limits. And certainly these good books, including the erotic ones, frequently helped shape minds that were free of the prejudices of their age, minds that learned to think for themselves and, if necessary, against themselves. One could not do any better than some of those men of taste, who assuaged their sorrows with Seneca or studied "the subtleties of the human heart" in Racine. But more often, these same readings were merely proof of a proper education, enabling a man to cite Horace or Molière over dinner, to crush a sensible remark beneath an unassailable authority, and to discuss genealogy and local history with the assurance of an expert.

The hate that the peasants felt for Jean-Baptiste is not of great significance either. Perhaps he was a greedy or brutal master, with a nobleman's arrogance and a churchman's calm insolence, or, conversely, a decent man but cold and aloof, lacking that openness which makes genial scoundrels likable. However that may be, my heart goes out to the dying man who could hear through his open window the shouts of laughter and the raucous songs inspired by his approaching end. Jean-Baptiste seems to have quarreled not only with his peasants but also with his family, for he willed Flémalle to his two "housekeepers." That word, when used in relation to an eighteenth-century canon, evokes charming creatures in discreetly revealing fichus and sleek-fitting stockings, bringing their good master his morning chocolate; but the Demoiselles Pollaert were perhaps well beyond the canonical age and steeped in virtue. In any case, their name appears only briefly in the list of Flémalle's owners; the natural heirs, by one means or another, regained possession of the château. It would be nice to think that, in exchange, the ladies received compensation sufficient to buy a little white house bowered in honeysuckle or to win themselves husbands from the ranks of their former admirers. But that is uncertain.

The estate soon left the family, however. François-Denys, burgomaster of Liège in 1753, had no children by his wife, Jeanne-Josèphe, daughter of the president of the Supreme Council of Gueldre. At his death, he left the château to the Benevolent Society for Children of Providence and of Saint Michael, perhaps out of philanthropy, perhaps to spite the cadet branch of the family. The Revolution was approaching: the assets of the Children of Providence and of Saint Michael were combined with those of the Civil Almshouses of Liège; the latter resold the estate. It subsequently passed to two families in succession; then the powerful Compagnie des Charbonnages (Coal-Mining Company), which henceforth controlled the region, acquired what was left of it. I've been told that in 1945 refugees from the east camped for an entire winter in the abandoned château, sleeping on the parquet floors, shivering before the armorial mantelpieces, which were stone cold, or warmed at best by small fires made of a few sticks of dead wood gathered in the ruined garden.

When I visited Belgium in 1956, the memory of the engraving that remained in my possession inspired me with a desire to see Flémalle. A taxi took me from Liège through working-class suburbs, along an interminable street, gray and black, devoid of grass and trees—one of those streets that only custom and indifference make us think habitable (by others) and whose like, the accepted setting of twentieth-century labor, I had of course seen in dozens of countries. The lovely view of the Meuse was obscured: heavy industry interposed its hellish landscape between the river and the workers' dwellings. The November sky was a sooty canopy. After exchanging a few words with some of the local people, the driver stopped the car before the yawning gate of a derelict garden. A heap of flagstone and rubble in the center indicated that a house had recently been torn down. There remained only a single and surprising fragment. Resting on a bit of flooring that itself overhung a crumbling retaining wall, a graceful staircase rose toward a vanished second story. The steps were gone, but the railing with its eighteenth-century ironwork was intact. Several weeks earlier the château had been consigned to a demolition expert. Whatever could be sold and taken away had been removed; this railing had evidently been left in place until the antiques dealer who had bought it could arrange for its delivery. I arrived on the day of the closing, and what greeted me was this scene from Piranesi, this truncated staircase climbing airily toward the sky. The canon, if he had had a mind suited to his calling, would surely have seen this as a symbol.

Most old estates die a sad death. Stripped of its gardens and its park, this one reminded me of one of those thoroughbreds that are reduced to the state of hacks before being led off to the glue factory. I was told that the garden would be converted into a municipal square, but squares that have been voted into existence by the city governments of our day have an odd way of turning into parking lots. I mourned not the destruction of a house and the quincunxes of a garden but the destruction of the land, ruined by industry as by the effects of a drawn-out war, the death of the water and the air, which were as polluted at Flémalle as in Pittsburgh, Sydney, or Tokyo. I thought of the inhabitants of the ancient village, exposed to the sudden floods of the river, which had not yet been tamed within its banks. They, too, in their ignorance, had fouled and abused the land, but the lack of advanced techniques had prevented them from going very far in that direction. They had emptied into the river the contents of their chamber pots, the carcasses of the cattle they had slaughtered, and the wastes from their leather making; they had not poured into it tons of toxic and even deadly chemicals. They had killed too many wild animals, felled too many trees; but those depredations were as nothing compared to ours, for we have produced a world in which animals and trees can no longer live. Certainly they suffered hardships that the naïve progressives of the nineteenth century believed had been eliminated forever: they starved in times of famine, only to stuff themselves in times of plenty with a gusto

81

we can hardly imagine; they did not nourish themselves with artificial foods laced with insidious poisons. They lost a tragic number of young children, but a kind of balance was maintained between the natural environment and the human population; they were not afflicted with the overcrowding that causes world wars, devalues the individual, and rots the species. From time to time they suffered savage invasions; they did not live under the perpetual threat of atomic destruction. They were subject to the force of circumstances, but not yet to the cycle of over-production and senseless consumption. Not more than fifty or even thirty years ago, this transition from the precarious exis-tence of beasts of the field to an existence of insects swarming in their nest seemed to everyone to be a mark of undeniable progress. Today we are beginning to think otherwise.

In 1971 I decided to take a trip to Liège, to see in one of its museums the bronze certificate of that Flémalle veteran and at the same time to revisit some of the local sights. On this occasion it was a warm day in May, already anticipating the summer. A quarter of an hour before we arrived at the industrial district, the driver advised rolling up the car windows to keep out the stinking yellow fumes blanketing the sky, which, as everyone knows, are irritating when one is not used to them. Road repairs prevented us from driving through Flémalle, but I was told that a project to deindustrialize the area was under way. The reason was not ecological concern but rather one of those mergers that are, in our day, what the great concentrations of territory in the hands of feudal lords were in the Middle Ages. The dragons spitting fire on the far riverbank had de-voured the weaker ones opposite. The Vieille Montagne coal-works, not far from Flémalle, had been shut down, and its vacated buildings looked like the enchanter's ruined castle at the end of one of the acts of *Parsifal*. Seen from a distance, this area, blighted by the greed and shortsightedness of four or five generations of businessmen in the nineteenth and twentieth centuries, remained on the whole what it had been in the days of the old engraving *Delights of the Liège Region* and even, doubtless, in the days of the veteran from Tongres: a precarious human border between the river and the lofty hills. But the nearly indelible traces of industrial attrition remained.

The decision to make extensive use of certain carbon fuels has, during the last two centuries, launched humans on an irreversible course by placing at their disposal sources of energy which their avidity and their violence have quickly abused. Coal from forests that died millions of centuries before mankind began to think, oil born of the decomposition of bituminous rocks or slowly produced by billions of microscopic flora and fauna—these are what have transformed our slow-paced adventure into the headlong race of horsemen of the Apocalypse. Of these two dangerous adjuvants, coal triumphed first. It so happens that my paternal land, the Lille area, and the two sites linked to the memory of my mother's family, Flémalle-Grande and Marchienne, were disfigured by it at an early date. Flémalle, formerly one of the "delights of the Liège region," presented me that day with a sample of the errors that we, like sorcerer's apprentices, have committed.

I$t was likewise at the beginning of the eighteenth century that my distant forebear Jean-Louis de C., born in 1677, cousin of the owner of Flémalle, contracted a marriage that gave him a foothold in Hainaut. He took as his wife the daughter of a certain Guillaume Bilquin, or de Bilquin (the "de" does not appear on his tombstone), lord of Marchienne-au-Pont, of Mont-sur-Marchienne, and of Bioul, ironmaster, bailiff of the forests of Entre-Sambre-et-Meuse. In what is perhaps a too flattering portrait, this wealthy man is depicted as quite handsome, with his flowing wig and satin robes in the style of the Grand Siècle. According to family legend, his ancestors had also been iron-masters, a noble profession, and one of them is said to have fashioned a cuirasse or a sword for Charles V. That is possible. Charles of Ghent equipped himself primarily at Augsburg, but from time to time he doubtless gave commissions to weapon makers in the Low Countries. Bilquin's wife, Marie-Agnès, somewhat plump-looking in her brocades, came from a family that had been firmly rooted in Hainaut and Artois since the early Middle Ages. This was the Baillencourt family, lords of

Landas; since the time of Lothair, their name had appeared in various cartularies, or church charters. A more recent ancestor had added the sobriquet "Courcol," allegedly received on the battlefield at Crécy, that little pool of blood-soaked mud which we glimpse in the dim distances of the Hundred Years War. The name of that place of defeat, where French knights trampled their own foot soldiers by mistake, is to today's average Frenchman hardly more than the name of a soup. Yet those forgotten battles regain their life and color when one sees at Tewkesbury Abbey, in Gloucestershire, the tomb of Sir Hugh le Despenser, who fought at Crécy, and the kneeling effigy of Hugh's son Edward, who fought at Poitiers, his hands joined in prayer throughout the past six hundred years. With his bright black eyes painted on the stone and his mustache framed by his chain-mail helmet, Edward—whose image, Sacheverell Sitwell aptly noted, evokes in us "the shock of the suddenly revealed past"—displays the cruel eagerness of a wildcat, a trait seen in many a feudal countenance. It is in the company of such men of prey that one must imagine Baudoin de Baillencourt, dubbed Courcol, whom we picture as blue-eyed and rather thickset.

The heiress of the Bilquin and Baillencourt-Courcol families brought her husband a dowry that included not only large tracts of land but also a nearly new château, built or rebuilt at Marchienne in the seventeenth century. For Jean-Louis, burgomaster and councillor of Liège (in keeping with the family tradition), it was doubtless merely a pied-à-terre. But his descendants made it their residence and ended up by adding "Marchienne" to their name. The Jean-François-Arnould who next inherited it, and whose wife was the daughter of a chief magistrate of Binche, must have been preoccupied all his life with the question of whether or not he would be invited to Beloeil by the prince de Ligne, the most elegant and cultured man in the Belgian provinces, or invited to slaughter wild birds with His Highness Charles de Lorraine, governor of the Low Countries, at his Mariemont estate. At Mariemont, Jean-François-Arnould would have been presented to the good Charles's aged mistress, Madame de Meuse, known as La Pelote ("the Ball of Wool"), who graced Mariemont with her presence and received perquisites of forty thousand francs a year at a time when the annual earnings of a mason amounted to two hundred. This worthy prince, cruel only to thrushes and quail, suffered from abscesses on his buttocks and leg, as we know from his diary. The abscess on his leg finally dispatched him; he died, mourned by all, in 1780. Thus ended the rococo period in the Austrian Low Countries, leaving the same cloying aftertaste as the still lifes of the lesser Flemish masters of that day, with their fruit, their *fois gras en croûte*, and their animal carcasses reposing on vermeil platters and Turkish rugs.

In 1792 the master of Marchienne was Pierre-Louis-Alexandre, a forty-year-old whose wife, Anne-Marie de Philippart, seems to have been a good ten years younger than he and already the mother of five children. Dumouriez's army, galvanized by the precedent of Valmy, crossed the border. The château, a strategic site, was immediately occupied; it was there that Saint-Just, commissioner to the armies of the North, composed most of his reports and his letters to Robespierre. The sans-culottes, whose belief in the revolutionary cause was soon bolstered by the strictness of the young commissioner, could do no more than repeat in their turn, on those plains and riverbanks, the sweeping back-and-forth movement that French royal armies and their adversaries had been tracing for several centuries. But the republican ideology lent an air of novelty to that invasion. The old world was crumbling: His Holiness the

Bishop of Liège had prudently left his palace in the city for his fortress of Huy on the Meuse; the news from Paris froze the blood of those who retained ties of affection or self-interest to the ancien régime; for two years Pierre-Louis and Anne-Marie lived the strained existence of heads of an enemy-occupied household. A panel in the chapel concealed the hiding place of a priest who had refused to swear loyalty to the new constitution; food and water were passed to him secretly when his wastes were taken away, and members of the household may have joined him at night for prayers. Citizen Decartier must have found it necessary now and then to venture a complaint to the French officers and the formidable commissioner regarding damages caused by the troops; Anne-Marie no doubt had her hands full preventing indiscretions by the children, protecting her maids as best she could from the Frenchmen's advances, and perhaps tending in secret, aided by a single servant, some Austrian soldier wounded at Jemappes or Fleurus and hidden away in a barn.

Like a number of French men and women of my generation, I worshipped Saint-Just when I was very young. I spent a good deal of time at the Musée Carnavalet contemplating the portrait of the Exterminating Angel by an anonymous artist who had endowed him with the somewhat languid charm of Greuze's subjects. That handsome face framed by flowing locks, that feminine neck enveloped as if from modesty in an ample cravat of fine linen, counted for a great deal in my admiration for Robespierre's cruel friend. I've changed since then: admiration has yielded to a tragic pity for this man who seems to have been eroded away before he could find fulfillment. At the age of eighteen Saint-Just engaged in the classic pranks of a young man from the provinces who sows his wild oats in Paris; confined in the Petit-Picpus at the request of his alarmed mother, he wrote *L'Organt*, the century's dullest erotic novel, a clumsy imitation of all the forbidden books read on the sly in school. At twenty-two, in his hole at Blérancourt, he eagerly followed from a distance the first stages of the Revolution. At twenty-four he became, in the intellectual sense of the term, the Infernal Consort of the Incorruptible: he who advised, exhorted, incited, and supported—the lightning accompanying that smoky cloud Maximilien d'Arras. His dry, specious arguments helped cost Louis XVI his head; he likewise rolled into the basket those of the Girondists, the Dantonists, the Hébertists; he executed Camille Desmoulins, the Parisian gamin who had been his friend and in many ways his opposite. Commissioner to the armies of the Rhine and of the North, responsible for eliminating all who were doubtful or lukewarm, he struck as coldly and efficiently as he spoke. At twenty-six, elegant despite his thirty-six hours of agony, impeccable in his finely tailored dress coat and pale gray breeches but ominously shorn of his flowing hair and his ear hoops, his handsome neck bare of its fine linen, he stoically awaited his turn on the scaffold between his colleague the paralytic Couthon and his god with the broken jaw, Robespierre.

These demonic destinies are worth contemplating, but demonism is not always a sign of human genius or sublimity. Nothing in this gifted boy indicates the slightest inclination to transcend the sectarianisms of the decade, much less of the century. His speeches, which are embellished with striking paradoxes and which constrict the facts within a corset of formulas, add to his beauty: in the eyes of writers, they make him the ideal image of the young political genius. The methods he advocated are those we have seen, ad nauseam, become harsh and finally useless in all regimes termed "strong": the skillful fostering of suspicions favored by a state of war, which is in turn indispensable for the promulgation of extreme measures, so that he was cynically led to advise Robespierre "not to emphasize our victories too much"; concentration-camp tactics leading to the debasement and destruction of enemies of the regime; the abolition of those slender guarantees with which a society protects itself against its own injustice, accompanied by the assurance, which fools always accept, that these odious measures are necessary. When the author of *L'Organt*, dining at the Frères Provençaux at the time of Marie-Antoinette's trial, remarked that, after all, the foul accusations against the queen would serve "to improve public morals," his youthful mouth exhaled that odor of false virtue which was the noxious breath of the Revolution. His vision of ideal humanity—for which he was prepared, according to a friend, "to sacrifice a hundred thousand heads, including his own"—was, to be sure, fashioned after the republican heroes of Plutarch, seen from a great distance and very approximately, but also after the outmoded dramas of Marie-Joseph Chénier and the Roman novels of Monsieur de Florian. Any man who dies young wears his youth like a mask on history's stage. No one can tell whether, in Saint-Just, a statesman would have emerged from that adolescent infected with violent ideologies and conventional rhetoric—just as, from the little Corsican captain who fired on the mob crowding the steps of Saint-Roch on 13 Vendémiaire, it is difficult to deduce the man of the Consulate and the Code, the man of Tilsit, and the man of Saint Helena. But at that age, despite the inevitable compromises with his conscience, Bonaparte was still virtually unblemished politically; before him lay the entire expanse of his future. Saint-Just, in contrast, died with his reputation in ashes.

Which does not mean that we can deny him all greatness. From the perspective of myth, more profound than that of history, he had the greatness to incarnate the Nemesis that kills and then obliterates the human avatar it has chosen to carry out its executions. His supreme virtue was courage, which is surely neither the rarest nor the highest of human virtues but without which all the others dissolve or turn to dust. His gambler's audacity blazed out on that sultry summer night spent at the Committee of Public Safety, when, before his colleagues' very eyes, he worked interminably on the speech calling for their indictment, and boasted of it—yet not a soul had the nerve to stab him or to strike him with a chair. His boldness, which led him as commissioner to expose himself coolly to the Austrians' bullets, stood him in good stead when the rabble of Robespierrists were surrounded in the town hall; the melodramatic engraving that shows him supporting the wounded Robespierre is probably accurate in crediting him with this gesture. Finally, and above all, the devotion of one man to another is always a noble phenomenon, even if the attachment concerns two complementary fanaticisms; it is impressive to see this brilliant boy, haughty to the point of insolence, take and keep (to all appearances voluntarily) a secondary position to Robespierre—that touchy, indecisive, stubborn man whom we nonetheless accord the respect unshakable convictions always inspire.

"You whom, like God, I know only through miracles," he had written to Robespierre at the beginning of their association. Saint-Just kept silent during the brief but interminable interval that separated their arrest from their death, and doubtless there was nothing more to say. Looking down from the pinnacle of his silence, did he pass judgment on the little group surrounding him, typical in their diversity of the functionaries of all dictatorships? The vile Simon, ex-cobbler and ex-jailer; the worthy Lebas, his comrade in the armies of the Rhine, who was already dead, having escaped the guillotine by suicide; the drunkard Hanriot, in part responsible for the final fiasco, lying deep in a coma resulting either from wine or from his wounds; Couthon, more sickly than ever, whom the soldiers had roughly dragged from the closet in which he was hiding; Augustin de Robespierre, likewise dying, who deprived Saint-Just of the palm of loyalty by deliberately having himself imprisoned with his brother; and the fifteen other supernumeraries who would die obscurely in the wake of these leading players. "You whom, like God, I know only through miracles . . ." Did he have doubts about Robespierre and take for the first time the measure of his fallen idol? Until the end, he played the role of Saint John to this nebulous Messiah. As Robespierre lay crumpled on that table at the Committee of Public Safety—the table at which they had sat as they governed France—did Saint-Just suffer to see him awkwardly gather up bits of paper and put them in his mouth to remove broken teeth and clots of blood? Did he mourn for a world whose pleasures he had known and in which his ambitions and opinions might one day have led him to oppose his unfeeling and incorruptible friend? Saint-Just wrote somewhere that death was the only refuge of the true republican, and we must not allow the rhetoric of the statement to obscure the intensity of this view that had become very much his own. He did not exempt himself from the bloody solutions he preferred—a preference that allies him more closely with Sade than with Robespierre. One imagines him among that pitiable group, confirmed and immured in the disdain for humanity which penetrates his revolutionary harangues, coldly keeping his courage, rejecting one after another every idea and emotion that might prevent him from persevering to the very end.

Certainly, when I was at the romantic age, I would not have found it unpleasant to imagine that tender feelings had existed between the handsome Saint-Just and Anne-Marie, my great-great-grandmother. A rudiment of good taste prevented me from doing so. Not that I so readily accept today the legend of Saint-Just's chastity, dear to left-wing idealists in all eras. It is not so easy to renounce pleasure when one has been its devotee; throughout his turbulent life, the young proconsul might well have sought diversion here and there in lovemaking, just as he did in riding horses. But even if Anne-Marie did have rather lovely eyes (as provincial eyes go), it is doubtful whether the wife of an aristocrat of the Austrian Low Countries would have made him feel that voluptuous emotion which young mothers surrounded by their children conventionally inspired in roués of the period. To Anne-Marie, on the other hand, this dandy in his tricolor scarf must have seemed spattered with blood—as in fact he later was, in the tumbril, when loathsome pranksters filled a bucket at a butcher shop on the rue Saint-Honoré and flung its contents at Robespierre. If my great-great-grandmother had had an urge to deceive her Pierre-Louis, it would more likely have been for a white uniform. But Saint-Just seems closer to me at Marchienne than my vague forebears. I like to imagine him galloping along on a mount requisitioned from Citizen Decartier, reveling in the boundless energy of his youth—just as he was to do in the Bois de Boulogne on the morning of 9 Thermidor, to clear his head after a sleepless night, carrying in his pocket the folded pages of the speech on which he would stake his all, and never dreaming (or dreaming quite the opposite) that on the morrow he would perhaps be laid to rest, cut in two pieces, in the cemetery of Errancis.

Once the turbulent years had passed, Anne-Marie resumed the interrupted course of her childbearing. This hiatus makes me suspect that Pierre-Louis had sent his wife away from the occupied château and that what little I have tried to reconstruct of my ancestor's life amid the sans-culottes is nothing but fabrication pure and simple. However that may be, four children were added to the five she already had; one of them, Joseph-Ghislain, born in 1799, was my great-grandfather. His oldest son, my grandfather, left Marchienne for good around 1855, but children from a second marriage remained there, and their descendants were still living in the château toward the end of the Second World War.

As a child, I visited Marchienne only once, and can remember nothing about it except flower beds and shrill-voiced peacocks. I went back there in 1929 during a long stay in Belgium, which I had not visited in twenty years and where I renewed ties with my mother's family, until then merely a legend to me. My Great-aunt Louise received me graciously but with a shyness that was typical of many well-bred Englishwomen of her day. Born in London, Louise Brown O'Meara was entirely or partly of Irish descent. Those who were fond of her maintained that she was of good family; the malicious declared (an assertion which, to be sure, does not necessarily refute the first) that Emile-Paul-Ghislain, my great-uncle, had met and married Louise at Brighton when she was only a young governess. The dates on file at the registry—unless they were intentionally transcribed falsely—contradict other, even more spiteful insinuations concerning the birth of their first child. "An honorable man, he had married the woman he loved," wrote a naïve family biographer, going almost as far. The initial years of this romantic marriage were spent on an estate of Emile's in Holland, where, temporarily separated from friends and family, he sent letters extolling the joys of marriage to his somewhat misogynistic cousin, Octave Pirmez.

His son Emile chose a career in the diplomatic service. Conservative by nature, without even needing to bolster his conservatism with political principles, in protocol a member of the old school, greatly liked in the best circles of Washington, he made two brilliant marriages there, both childless. I may seem to be describing a Norpois, but there was in that half Irishman, half Walloon an appetite for life that is not discernible under the impeccably gracious veneer of Proust's diplomat. He liked pretty girls, good food, and fine painting. The last two qualities made his London residence an agreeable refuge for members of the Belgian government-in-exile between 1940 and 1945. A rather crusty man, unpopular with at least some of the family, he displayed the caprices of one who always does precisely as he wishes. He was minister in China just after the Boxer Rebellion, and when Tz'u Hsi's government agreed to pay reparations for the embassies that had been damaged or destroyed, he had his own rebuilt to look like Marchienne. Not only were the plans identical, but bricks and roof tiles were shipped from Belgium in numbered crates. This odd edifice still exists and at present seems to have been leased by Belgium to the Burmese embassy, until such time as the government of China retakes possession of it. The interior of this curiosity was quite up-to-date. Emile de C. de M. once persuaded two young princesses of royal blood to accept a dinner invitation, though they had never until then been outside the walls of the Forbidden City. There was an anxious moment over the coffee when these aristocratic women withdrew discreetly and failed to return. The host set up a search for them. They were found next to one of the ultramodern flushing devices, repeatedly pulling the chain and each time releasing a gurgling little cascade that harmonized with their delighted laughter. That dinner party was one of Uncle Emile's social triumphs.

This man who led such a full life died in London in 1950, doyen of the diplomatic corps, and there received impressive funeral rites which paid tribute to a species of man that was fast disappearing, as well as to the war-torn country he had so long represented. I learned from one of his colleagues that in the months preceding his death he was assailed by bitter regrets; it seemed to him that all his life he had been merely a cardboard bureaucrat, a bemedaled puppet whose strings were controlled by protocol and who performed against backdrops that soon would no longer exist. This regret in itself proves he was more than that.

His younger brother, Arnold, who never aspired to anything higher than to oversee, in an easygoing way, the estate of Marchienne and another that he owned in the Low Countries, was a genial man of the world. He was separated from his wife, who came from his social set and who was gifted, or afflicted, with clairvoyance. Their son, Jean, my junior by several years, enchanted me with his fondness for wild animals. He had tamed a fox, which followed him on a lead, its neck adorned with a blue velvet collar. This creature, with its intelligent eyes and its bushy tail the color of a maple leaf in autumn, accompanied him obediently but in that oblique, slinking fashion which one sees in puppies being trained to the leash.

The 1907 Baedeker assures the traveler that Marchienne's fine collection of paintings is well worth seeing. The collection was no longer at the château in 1929, and I imagine it was then adorning Emile's embassy. Immense family portraits, done with a romantic realism reminiscent of Courbet, graced the walls of the Second Empire drawing room: gentlemen with walking sticks strolling down tree-lined avenues, horsewomen leaning gracefully against the flanks of their mounts. In one corner a Baillencourt-Courcol of the eighteenth century, Bishop of Bruges, provided a touch of the ancien régime. Aunt Louise placed on my lap a cardboard box full of miniatures. My eye was caught by the image of a young woman in a white muslin dress, small in stature, with the coloring of a Portuguese or a Brazilian, her curly black hair held in a transparent white cap. On the back, in faded letters, was the name of the subject: Maria de Lisboa. My hostess knew nothing about her except that she was not one of my direct forebears; it seems, rather, that she was related to the family by a second marriage. If I mention her here, it is because I have sometimes thought of using her name and face in a novel or poem.

Aunt Louise served tea on the terrace, with an elegance that reminded me of England. The peacocks and rose bushes that I remembered from my childhood were still there. I do not intend to reprise here the theme elaborated at Flémalle—that of air, water, and soil polluted by what our ancestors sincerely believed to be progress, an excuse we no longer have. Yet the fate of Flémalle-Grande was threatening Marchienne. On the far side of the ornamental pond, beyond the already diminished grounds of the estate, factory chimneys vomited their offering to the industrial powers, whose founding shares had probably augmented Emile and Arnold's portfolio. Discreetly, before pouring out the tea, Aunt Louise used a corner of her embroidered napkin to wipe the Sèvres cup, on which several black specks had just settled.

In 1956 Marchienne was on my list of places to revisit in Belgium. The grounds, which had become a public park, seemed to me somewhat shrunken, but one must always take into account the tendency of memory to inflate things. It was well maintained, with a hint of bureaucratic coldness about it. The château enjoyed one of the fairest destinies that can befall an abandoned dwelling: it had recently become a public library. The rooms on the ground floor had that look of stingy upkeep typical of buildings under municipal care, but the card catalogues and the shelves full of labeled books marred their beauty somewhat less, perhaps, than the fine Second Empire furniture had formerly. I saw neither the Chinese boudoir, done all in ormolu and Martin lacquer, nor the chapel where Jean had long ago shown me the priest's hiding place, having to move aside to do so some displaced grave markers arrayed against the wall. Those sculpted or incised effigies were now stored in the parish church, where they had joined other, more recent monuments, still set in their places; I noticed that of Guillaume Bilquin and his heiress, née Baillencourt-Courcol, in their spare seventeenth-century elegance, a monument decorated with little columns and white urns on a black ground. One or two memorial slabs stranded there had been executed in the grand, severe style of the early fifteenth century; others displayed the ornate style of the late Gothic, or of a Renaissance imitating the Gothic. The little dogs curled up at their mistresses' feet lent an appealing air to these bits of flotsam. An inscription on the grave marker of a certain Ide de C. made me wonder if it didn't come from the old chapel at Flémalle, but my knowledge of heraldry was too slight to enable me to find my way through the thicket of banderoles and eroded escutcheons.

A middle-aged woman who had come to the library to return a book either recognized me or heard my name spoken. She had formerly been my Aunt Louise's chambermaid. From her I learned all the latest news of the family, in the fullest sense of the term. Madame had died before the war, and I refrained from mentioning the details that certain malicious persons, clearly set in their obstinate dislike of the Irishwoman, had provided me concerning her declining years. Aunt Louise, according to them, had been seized with a nostalgic longing for the whiskey of her homeland. Watched over by Arnold and Jean when they were there, and the rest of the time by elderly housemaids who intercepted unauthorized purchases, she turned to more discreet stimulants, mentholated alcohol and vanilla, of which innumerable empty bottles were apparently found in her room. The woman with whom I was speaking would no doubt have rejected these rumors indignantly. Even supposing they were true, one would have to be excessively prudish to be scandalized that an old woman who feels life slipping away from her should comfort herself as best she can, even if the means she chooses are not, medically speaking, the best. Mentholated alcohol with its knife-edged chill, the black essence of vanilla, and even bitter whiskey, to my palate the most unpleasant of the three, become talismans against death, as ineffectual as all of them are.

Sitting beside me on a bench in the park, my informant

continued her narrative, which was, to be sure, brief. Monsieur Jean had left the diplomatic post he held in 1940 to enlist in the Royal Air Force, an expedient often taken by Belgian patriots in those days when their country was torn between remaining neutral and participating in the war. Subsequently joining a Resistance group, he had been killed in 1944 by a stray bullet. His little daughter had survived. I learned later that she had married—about the time this conversation took place, I believe—and that she had died in an automobile accident shortly afterward. The family name and this particular branch would have died out along with Jean if Uncle Emile toward the end of his life had not had the name transferred to some distant relations. Names live on forever.

Not long before his death, Arnold, feeling somewhat adrift, had resumed living with Jean's mother, who in the interim had become a professional clairvoyant. She was to return to this line of work in her widowhood and, I'm told, distributed cards that displayed in the bottom left corner her hours of consultation. This detail was imparted to me during a reception in a large Belgian city by a young writer then in vogue who was moved to laughter by this outcome. But I, who wondered if in those years an Irish banshee might not have been heard wailing beneath Marchienne's walls, was moved to pity at the thought that that mother gifted with second sight had perhaps shared the fate of all prophets, which is to know, and yet be powerless to prevent, the future.

In 1824, at the age of twenty-five, my great-grandfather Joseph-Ghislain obtained confirmation of his patent of nobility from William I of Holland, to whom the Congress of Vienna had entrusted Belgium so as to afford it better protection from the perpetual designs of the French. At that time a number of Belgians took this precaution, made necessary by the many changes of regime. Six years later, when the revolution of 1830 divorced Belgium from Holland, we find Joseph-Ghislain a colonel in the militia and burgomaster of Marchienne, where he died in his forties after two marriages, of which only the first concerns us here. In the beginning of that tumultuous year 1830, at the château of La Boverie, at Suarlée, not far from Namur, he had married a twenty-year-old heiress named Flore Drion. From this union, soon severed by death, was born my grandfather Arthur.

Not until quite recently did I do some investigating into the history of the Drions, a good family of local patricians, part aristocratic and part bourgeois. "Our line lacks men of war," the current family representative, a writer, said to me. It did

100

include, however, four or five lieutenants or standard-bearers who served under the Spanish Crown. It also included one Récollet, a missionary sent by Clement XI to China, where, as his monk's habit obliged him to, he took the Franciscans' side in the dispute over Rites and was allegedly assassinated at the instigation of the Jesuits. In 1692, when Louis XIV made an appearance at the siege of Namur with great pomp, celebrated so prosaically by Boileau, the head of the Drion family at that time had the honor of welcoming the king to his estate at Gilly as an overnight guest. The era of fierce nationalisms had not yet dawned: this loyal subject of Charles II found it natural to receive, with all marks of respect, an enemy monarch. The King of France, who probably did not care to sit at table surrounded by provincial visitors, requested that only members of the immediate family be present at the evening meal. Descending to the drawing room, he beheld a crowd of people. "Sire, those are but my children and grandchildren," said the hospitable patriarch. His grandson Adrien, another patriarch, had the more galling distinction of being among the six citizens of Charleroi ordered to pay, within two hours, a tribute of ten thousand francs each to the Jacobins who occupied the city in 1793, an obligation almost as agonizing as being guillotined.

Not long afterward, tradition claims, a member of the family gave a dinner for Ney the day before Waterloo; and a little girl sitting that evening at one end of the great table believed for the rest of her life that she remembered seeing perspiring couriers on exhausted horses bearing urgent messages from Napoleon to the marshal. The head of the Drion family today, who has the scruples of a historian, points out that Napoleon at that time anticipated certain victory and had no reason whatsoever to send orders and counterorders to Ney. For my part, I am always inclined to put faith in a child's memories and would willingly concede that the emperor, even if sure of the next day's outcome, might have dispatched to Ney some of those imperious missives he was in the habit of sending. Still less does the learned Drion of our own day admit that the fumes of his forebear's wine could have clouded Ney's head somewhat on the day of the battle. But these stories have their value: they help us appreciate the extent to which every family, from century to century, has felt itself involved in the vicissitudes of war in that country which was continually being overrun.

Nearly all those old lineages had a policy, either tacit or explicit, regarding marriage. The most ambitious of them, whenever possible, took wives of a higher social status than their own, thus facilitating the rise of the next generation; others, like the Quartier family, seem to have selected from a narrow circle in which the same lineages intersected again and again. The Drion sons appear to have often chosen brides who were from bourgeois or quasi-rustic families but who were doubtless provided with large dowries, and perhaps also endowed with hot blood and a measure of lower-class vigor; in any case, the longevity enjoyed by members of this family makes a strong contrast with the rather brief lifespan typical of the Quartiers. Through those Maries and Marie-Catherines, daughters of Pierre Georgy and Marguerite Delport or of Nicolas Thibaut and Isabelle Maître-Pierre, through those Barbe Le Vergers and Jeanne Masures, I feel as if I am in direct contact with the solid village life of Hainaut.

An affinity for science and letters was common in that milieu, as well as (it is said) a certain independence of mind. "Everything bad in the Pirmez family comes from the Drions," a member of the former declared not long ago to a member of the latter, in the course of a shooting party that was evidently not remarkable for its cordiality. If he was thinking of a dangerous love for arts and letters, he was exaggerating somewhat. My Great-great-aunt Irénée Drion—mother of the romantic Octave Pirmez and his brother Fernand, nicknamed Rémo, who lived his radicalism and died of it in the bosom of a traditionalist family—was well known all her life for the firmness of her principles. On the other hand, one finds among Octave and Rémo's paternal forebears some worthy minds open to enlightened ideas, and even a few restless souls with a taste for Hindu sutras and Swedenborg.

In 1829 one Ferdinand Drion, fifteen years a widower, and the proprietor of glassworks, nail factories, and coal mines, died at the age of about sixty on his Suarlée estate. Shortly before his death, this good father had taken care to divide his diamonds personally among his four daughters, who ranged in age from seventeen to twenty-two. A certain Madame de Robeaulx, the dead man's sister, married successively to three Frenchmen— of which the last, age twenty-five, wed her when she was already in her sixties—served as mentor to the young girls. This undoubtedly charming woman had sent her nieces to be raised in Brussels, at the Hôtel de Marnix, which had become a pension for noblewomen exiled from Paris by the Revolution. These pious educators, nearly all of whom belonged to the world of the prewar aristocracy, and several of whom had lost parents to the guillotine, instilled in their young charges the fine manners of the ancien régime. The Drion demoiselles were considered desirable matches, each one having a coal mine as dowry. The subject of their toilettes must have taken up a good deal of the conversation that autumn and early winter at Suarlée, where the four young ladies lived, chaperoned by Madame de Robeaulx. Indeed, it was necessary to order not only mourning clothes (Papa having died in October) but also bridal trousseaux and maid-of-honor gowns. In February, at Suarlée, Flore married Joseph-Ghislain de C. de M. In June she undoubtedly danced at the wedding of her sister Amélie and Victor Pirmez, former member of King William's guard of honor and son of wealthy landowners of the region. In April of the following year, Irénée was betrothed in her turn; she married Benjamin Pirmez, Victor's brother, and thus prepared to make her mark on Belgian literary history, less by the several essays that later appeared under her name than by means of two of her sons. This time, Flore did not dance at the wedding. Four days earlier at Marchienne she had given birth to her son, Arthur, my future grandfather. She died three days after the wedding. That same night Irénée, who was then in Paris on her honeymoon, had a nightmare announcing her sister's death.

The following autumn, in November, Zoé, the youngest, barely past the six months of mourning prescribed for a sister, took as her husband a young justice of the peace, Louis Troye, son of one Charles-Stanislas (former delegate to the Estates-General of the Low Countries) and a man with a fine administrative career ahead of him. He was governor of Hainaut from 1849 to 1870. Two decades later one of the couple's daughters, Mathilde, married her first cousin Arthur, thus giving me two Drion sisters as great-grandmothers.

In the spring or early summer of 1856, Arthur de C. de M., apparently after spending several months at Mons with his father-in-law, Governor Troye, came to Suarlée to settle permanently there with his wife, Mathilde, and their firstborn child, little Isabelle. Mathilde was expecting another baby; in November, at Suarlée, she gave birth to a boy, christened Ferdinand, who died when very young. If I can judge by customs that still existed in my own childhood, Monsieur Arthur and Madame Mathilde must have passed through the iron gate beneath an arch decorated with boughs and welcoming banderoles; this, at least, was the practice in French Flanders around 1910, even if the homecoming in question took place after a mere three-month absence. Of Arthur, who was quite a dandy, there exists a contemporary formal portrait showing him in dress coat and cravat of fine linen; this portrait and its companion, depicting a slender Mathilde in hoopskirt and low-cut bodice, tell us little about their subjects. A rather good painting of Mathilde executed some years later shows with less pomp an attractive young woman with a pink and white com-

plexion and thick coils of reddish-blond hair that enabled me
to identify the hair of the bracelets I had got rid of years before.
Her face is gay and a bit mischievous. That evening, the young
couple must have retired early to the master bedroom, where a
fire had probably been laid, despite the season, to ward off the
icy chill of long-uninhabited dwellings. Arthur had acquired
Suarlée from his mother, Flore, and the house had doubtless
not been occupied since her marriage, in any case not since her
death. The servants surely took their time opening hatboxes
and carpetbags and unpacking provisions, amid that picnic atmosphere which always prevails on moving day; little Isabelle
slept soundly. Monsieur Arthur was to live at Suarlée thirty-
four years. Mathilde would die there seventeen years later,
fourteen months after the birth of her tenth child.

Suarlée, or rather the château of La Boverie, where my
grandparents lived out their days, has been gone for three-
quarters of a century. A faded photograph showed me its main
building flanked by turrets and its outbuildings set at right
angles. Inside, to judge from the few relics that remain, Arthur
and Mathilde had stocked it abundantly with modern furnishings—folding screens of rosewood, and ebony cabinets done
in elaborate fretwork. But every old house has surprises in store:
when, fifteen years ago, I climbed the concrete steps of the
seaside-style villa that replaced the manor house of days gone
by, the proprietor's daughter who let me in, an amiable woman
who deplored the bad taste of the late nineteenth century,
hunted up an album containing a photo of the attics of the old
mansion, taken at the time of its destruction. Its beams reminded me of the ridgepiece of a cathedral. Beneath those joists
crisscrossed like branches, the remains of oak groves where
herds of swine had wandered in the Middle Ages, the children
of Monsieur Arthur and Madame Mathilde or, prior to them,

the little Drions in lace pantaloons had no doubt played on rainy
days—hiding from the maids, scaring one another, making believe they were lost in the forest, where their cries would echo
like those of the birds. I handed the album back to Mademoiselle
de D., regretting, as she did, the demolition of that lovely
woodwork.

Let us try to conjure up that house as it must have been
between 1856 and 1873, not merely to carry out the experiment
(always valuable) that consists in reoccupying, so to speak, a
corner of the past, but above all to attempt to distinguish in
that gentleman in his frock coat and that lady in her hoopskirts,
who are now scarcely more in our eyes than specimens of the
humanity of their day, that which is different from us or that
which, despite appearances, resembles us—the complicated
play of causes whose effects we continue to feel. First of all,
Arthur and Mathilde are good Catholics, as these are defined
under the long papacy of Pius IX, in this land where a jesuitical
and rococo piety continues to flourish, characterized by both
the dogmatic severities and the almost worldly amenities of the
Counter-Reformation. The newspaper subscribed to is a Catholic paper; Advent and Lent, Christmas and Easter, All Saints'
Day and All Souls' Day keep the rhythm of the cycle of seasons
and that of family feast days. High Mass in the morning, vespers
in the afternoon, and the evening service at the end of the day,
all in the village church, as well as the various attentions to
one's toilette that are necessary for attending these rituals, take
up a good part of every Sunday—assuming that the announcement of some splendid religious ceremony with music has not
caused the family to hitch up the horse and carriage and set
out for Namur. This Catholicism, for the property-owning
classes, has not yet become quite the rallying point or even the

offensive weapon that it will be later; nevertheless, one is a Catholic the way one is a conservative, and the two terms are inseparable. The fulfillment of one's religious duties is confounded in one's mind with the respect owed established institutions and is often grafted onto indifference or onto a discreet or vague skepticism. It is understood that one departs from this life piously supplied with the sacraments of Our Mother the Holy Church, and families concur in this to such an extent that the formula figures in all death announcements, even if the deceased has passed away very suddenly, without giving anyone time to call a priest, or (a scandal that occurs quite rarely) if the deceased has refused last rites. As we shall see, it is the women who are more consistently sensitive to the gentle balm of prayer.

But religious instruction and theological learning are not emphasized, the latter, indeed, being as little encouraged by the clergy as mystical transports. Monsieur Arthur and Madame Mathilde have probably never met a Protestant or a Jew, types of humanity regarded from afar with distrust. The same holds for the freethinker, a specimen considered more vulgar than impious. It is assumed (so unacceptable is complete lack of belief) that such an individual is nothing but a braggart who will repent at the moment of death. The Gospels are seldom read—one scarcely knows more of them than of those passages recited, often unintelligibly, at the altar. But insipid devotional works abound, and with few exceptions constitute Mathilde's sole spiritual nourishment. One speaks often of the Good Lord, but rarely of the Lord God. This Good Lord, composed of childhood memories and of vestiges of the primitive family, in which the elder of the Tribe has the power of life or death over his sons, is said to be threatening when thunder peals; He takes care of the good and punishes the bad, even if experience proves

just the opposite; His will, furthermore, serves to explain little
domestic mishaps as well as great catastrophes. He has made
the world in His image, which eliminates in these bourgeois
Christians nearly every impulse toward social progress or reform. Midway between folklore and myth, a bit frightening and
a bit indulgent, He is hardly distinguishable, in the children's
eyes, from Saint Nicholas, who is likewise adorned with great-
coat, crown, and beard, and who brings them sweets on the
sixth of December if they've been good.

Jesus is seen almost exclusively in two guises: as the pretty
child in the manger and as the silver or ivory Christ on the
crucifix, who retains almost none of the stigmata of physical
anguish that are so striking in medieval crucifixes. Martyred
yet neat and clean, with no streaks of blood or spasms of pain,
He died to save the world, as everyone knows; but only a few
very pious souls, gifted in meditation and closely supervised by
their spiritual advisers, make an effort to discover the meaning
of Christ's tragic sacrifice. The children are ceaselessly reminded of the existence of the Guardian Angel, who watches
over them while they sleep, deplores their pranks, and weeps
if perchance the little boys should "touch themselves." But this
great being of radiant whiteness goes the way of baby teeth,
bibs, and pinafores: he is no longer relevant to the adult, whom
this silent presence, purer than self, hardly preoccupies at all.
It is agreed that Madame Mathilde's dead children are little
angels, but people would think her insane if she imagined herself
seriously consoled by their apparition or protected by their intervention in heaven. The Holy Virgin is the most beloved, the
most frequently invoked of the celestial figures; in these times
her immaculate conception is often spoken of, but for ninety-
nine out of a hundred believers this doctrine means no more
than Mary's physical virginity, and few enlightened priests take

the trouble to try to explain that something different is meant: an immunity against the evil that is inherent or virtual in the mere fact of existing. A prosaic good sense and a simplistic literalism debase these great notions little by little, as deep skepticism and raillery have done elsewhere. Families gladly give their daughters to God (it's impossible to find husbands for them all), but when a son takes holy orders, this is almost always resented as a burdensome sacrifice. It is among the lower classes that having a priest in the family is considered a spiritual advantage and a form of social betterment; the seminaries contain, all else being equal, more sons of farmers than of great landowners. Within the village hierarchy the curé occupies an equivocal position, scarcely higher than that of the doctor and sometimes lower; he is regularly invited to Sunday dinner, but the inhabitants treat this man, from whose hand they receive God, with a certain condescension. His father was, after all, a mere nobody.

But the real gods are those that one serves instinctively, compulsively, day and night, without having the power to transgress their laws, and even without any need to worship them or believe in them. These true gods are Plutus, prince of strongboxes; the god Terminus, lord of the cadastre, who takes care of boundaries; the rigid Priapus, secret god of brides, legitimately erect in the exercise of his functions; the good Lucina, who reigns over birthing chambers; and finally, pushed as far away as possible but ever-present at family funerals and devolutions of inheritance, Libitina, goddess of burials, who concludes the procession. Madame Mathilde is the handmaiden of Lucina. If one remembers that in large families a few miscarriages usually intervene in the succession of births, and if one considers moreover that the convalescence of a lady at this time means six months of bed rest (only peasant women return to work a few days after childbirth, which proves the coarseness of those commoners), then Madame Mathilde has spent more than ten of her eighteen years of marriage in the service of the procreative deities. Ten years spent counting the days as she wonders whether or not she has "taken"; enduring those minor inconveniences of pregnancy that Dolly in *Anna Karenina*, her Russian contemporary, found more trying than the pains of childbirth; preparing the layette of the new arrival by reusing that of the infants, alive or dead, who have come before; and, more discreetly, assembling each time in one of her drawers the articles of her own deathbed toilette, bearing slips jotted with timid last requests, in the event that this time God might want to call her to Him. Then, the ordeal over with, waiting once again "to see something" and looking ahead with fear or desire, or perhaps both, to the renewed conjugal intimacy that will bring her back to the beginning of the cycle. The force that creates worlds has taken possession of this lady in flounces and parasol and will not release her until it has depleted her utterly.

The bedroom in the nineteenth century is the Cave of Mysteries. At night, the wax of the candles and the oil of the lamps illuminate it with their flames, which waver and flicker like life itself and which are no more successful in reaching the shadowy recesses of the room than are the glimmers of our mind in elucidating all that is unknown and unexplained. Window-panes hung with tulle and draped with velvet allow the light of day to enter only sparingly, and the breezes and scents of evening not at all: the English custom of opening the windows at night is considered unhealthy and may in fact be so for delicate constitutions in this damp part of the country. Arthur and Mathilde sleep closeted in their high-ceilinged room, the way their forebears did in their low-roofed huts. The chamber is full of living materials, or materials that were alive at one time: real wool, real silk, the horsehair that makes armchair cushions resilient to human bottoms. Its basins and bowls contain "the waters," as the chambermaids say simply; the exudations and residues of the skin, the animal oils of the soap, float or settle in them. The discreet mahogany night tables store the urine, tinted or pale, clear or clouded, in their recesses until morning; each has its flask of orange-water enthroned on top. Human fragments —baby teeth set into finger rings, bits of hair in lockets—pass the night in dresser-top trays. Trinkets, gifts, and souvenirs clutter the étagères, concretize remnants of past life: dried flowers, paperweights bought in Switzerland in which one can release a blizzard at will, seashells gathered on a summer's day on the beach at Ostend and in which, it is said, the murmur of the sea can still be heard. The fresh water in the ewer and the cut logs ready for the evening fire maintain elementary presences in the room. The water and the sprig of holy palm add a note of the sacred; everyone knows that the round-bellied chest of drawers, covered with a white cloth, will serve as an altar at the moment of extreme unction. The well-tucked-in bed has known the blood of deflowerings and births and the sweat of death agonies, for the fashion of going on honeymoon trips is of recent vintage and that of entering a hospital or clinic to be born or to die has yet to take hold. It is not surprising that the heavily charged atmosphere of this room should be favorable to ghosts. One makes love here; one dreams here, carried off to other worlds where even one's spouse cannot follow; one prays here, under the fixed gaze of those absent or dear departed ones in the daguerreotypes; on days when quarrels arise, the sound of angry retorts is muffled by the thick hangings. And doubtless Arthur and Mathilde do not analyze the elements of their bedroom any more than we analyze our own, a mere sleeping-garage, invaded by the clamor from outdoors and the

din of radios, furnished with metal, synthetic fabrics, and ply-
wood, competing for lovemaking with public beaches and parks
or the back seats of automobiles. But these spouses are vaguely
aware of the solemn nature of this retreat, in which the children
are hardly ever allowed, in which one receives visitors only when
bedridden or in times of emergency, and which it would be
indecent and almost obscene to expose to view with the bed
unmade.

Madame Mathilde does not appear to be a woman who
dislikes love. Does she love (not quite the same thing) her
Arthur? Perhaps she has never asked herself the question. Has
she received him with warmth, with innocent sensuality, with
the respectable satisfaction of a wife, with resignation, perhaps
with disgust or fatigue, or simply with the indifference of long
habit? It is likely that during eighteen years of shared nights,
she will have experienced all these in turn. In any case, if
hostility or fear has at times overwhelmed her, Mathilde has
no recourse. The priest, consulted with a few vague words,
would preach to her in the name of natural law or the will of
God or both. He would even assure Mathilde that this type of
mortification of the senses is the equivalent of another. Zoé,
her affectionate mother, might be concerned about her darling's
numerous pregnancies, but such problems and their solution
are the province of husband and wife; and besides, the Good
Lord blesses large families. As for sensual incompatibilities,
neither the law nor the Church nor one's parents want to know
about them. If she admitted to her mother that Arthur's way
of making love displeased her, Mathilde would seem at once
immodest and a bit ridiculous, as if she were complaining of
his manner of snoring.

But doubtless she loves him, and it is certain that, like
almost all other women, she loves children, and that her own,

the first few especially, have brought her joys often more delightful for a member of her sex than sensual pleasure itself:
the pleasure of washing them, of combing their hair, of em-
bracing those little bodies that satisfy her need for tenderness
and her notions of beauty. She has relished the languor and
indolence of pregnancy and gratefully received the small attentions of her mother, come to assist with the births. On Sundays
she has congratulated herself on having her dear ones, more or
less well behaved, sitting by her in the armorial pew to the left
of the choir. Unless we suppose her to be extremely stupid,
which is always possible, she must nevertheless have had her
worries about the future: so many educations to see to, so many
marriages to negotiate, so many places to find in the administration, like Papa, or in the diplomatic service, so many ample
dowries to give to daughters and to receive from daughters-in-
law, like the one that she herself brought to her Arthur. But
all that is very far away: Isabelle, her oldest, is still only a tall
young girl with long curls. The Good Lord will provide. Then,
too, she is thirty-seven years old; the baby that is on its way
will perhaps be her last; at best (or at worst), she can scarcely
have more than one or two after this. And she drifts off to sleep
with a prayer on her lips.

Monsieur Arthur's reflections on this subject, assuming
that he had any, are less easy to divine. Did he believe that his
duties as a Christian and as a gentleman of good family demanded that he set an example by having a large family? A
model husband, did he never in eighteen years cease to desire
Mathilde, in whom all women were summed up for him? Or,
if his liaison with "a person of Namur," or anyone else, did not
begin until after Mathilde's death, was this his way of keeping
her occupied—by installing her, for years, in this tumult of
procreation? This man, for whom nothing is more sacred than

the familial and social status quo, has doubtless never found anyone to tell him that he is disturbing the balance of that very status. *Proles*: the bit of Latin that he has learned has not led him to ponder the etymology of the word "proletariat." Neither Arthur nor Mathilde foresees that in less than a century this serial (not to say mechanical) style of human production will have transformed the planet into an anthill, despite massacres on a scale found only in the Bible. Keener minds than Monsieur Arthur have nevertheless predicted this outcome, albeit without envisioning all the horror. But Malthus is, for Arthur, nothing but an obscene word: he doesn't even really know who the man is. Doesn't he have sound morals and family traditions on his side? His grandfather, Citizen Decartier, had nine children in revolutionary times. As for Mathilde, she has doubtless never met, as did Tolstoy's Dolly (of whom she decidedly reminds me), an Anna Karenina to explain to her how one can limit pregnancies. If such a meeting were to take place, she, like Dolly, would doubtless recoil in embarrassment and say that such things were "bad." And something inside us echoes her. Yet there is a still worse alternative, and that is to overcrowd the world. And since their religion prohibits them from using all the little tricks that mankind has devised for controlling reproduction, there remains only abstinence, which Arthur and perhaps even Mathilde do not want.

Life gone by is a withered, cracked leaf, without sap or chlorophyll, riddled with holes, frayed and torn, which, when held up to the light, reveals at most the skeletal tracery of its slender, brittle veins. Certain efforts are required to give it once more the fleshy green appearance of a new leaf, to restore to events and incidents that fullness which satisfies the people who live them and which keeps these people from imagining anything else. The life that Arthur and Mathilde lead is full to bursting. Arthur has his leases to dispute with the farmers (they are so demanding), repairs to reject or approve, agricultural machines to supply or replace (the farmers are so careless) if the lease stipulates that this is the responsibility of the proprietor. The improvements in the garden as well as the purchase and care of the horses, harness, and carriages all demand the master's attention, not to mention the maintenance of the château and the judicious purchase of wines for the cellar: Arthur would blush to offer his guests a Burgundy inferior to that which is maturing in the casks on the neighboring estate. The master is known for the splendor of his hunting mounts and his hounds: he would not consider himself a gentleman if hecatombs were not perpetrated every autumn on his lands. The raising of the broods, the choice of gamekeepers, and the latter's connivance with the poachers cause him endless worries. The need to keep his portfolio up to date, the certificates of interest that he detaches meticulously every six months also give him plenty to do. And supporting the most right-thinking candidate in the local elections is likewise not the least of his cares.

Madame Mathilde, above and beyond the physiological tasks that are accomplished in her, has even more varied preoccupations. She descends only rarely to the dark kitchen, whose stairway is dangerous for this woman so often pregnant, but she "makes" the menus and verifies the cook's "book"; she arranges flowers; she is responsible for the hiring and firing of servants (who, in any event, are dismissed as rarely as possible). The children's toothaches and stomachaches, their grievous little transgressions—which are hidden, when possible, from their father—create constant problems for her. Fortunately, this queen bee has found an admirable auxiliary. The young Fräulein, engaged to serve as governess to the girls, gives evidence of remarkable abilities as a manager. What is more, she excels in making fine seashells of butter arranged on dishes of leaves and also, when there are formal dinners, in shaping napkins into bishops' caps, a detail that always elicits a good-natured jest from Monseigneur when he unfolds his at the dinner following a confirmation. Also, when the dressmaker comes from Namur with her boxes, there are the enormous efforts to "harmonize" the shades of a particular fabric and the anxious deliberations over whether a dress is or is not too fancy.

Relatively few guests are received at Suarlée. The advantage of a staid milieu such as this is that social climbing is nearly nonexistent. The idea of cultivating close ties with the prince de C. or the duc d'A., whom one invites to one's home and whom one visits on grand occasions, does not occur to people, any more than they would think of dining with the gardener. An almost equal indifference still reigns (it will soon cease) in business matters; Arthur hoards his money but would never venture into risky speculations; acquisitiveness is fierce only when it pertains to land. But family relationships are what matter the most. Every uncle, great-uncle, brother-in-law, step-brother, second cousin is a person one knows, associates with, and respects to the precise degree prescribed by the particular tie of kinship, just as someday one will go into mourning for him within certain limits, neither more nor less. Faced with some failing in a member of the group—with a disease that would threaten the health of his immediate family and that thus prevents marriages, with an unscrupulous act, with a vice—everyone responds by keeping silent about it or denying it, if silence and denial are possible. If there is a scandal, the response is to abandon the individual in question, who is afflicted with sudden nonexistence, so to speak. The same line of conduct is followed in the case of a "liaison" or a foolish marriage, which, if it is extremely foolish, casts into the void whoever has contracted it. Family visits are events that take the place of pleasure trips, which are out of the question for Mathilde. Sometimes she stays with her kindhearted parents for long periods; in any case, she is there when a first baby Jeanne (dead in infancy) is born, which seems to indicate that the past winter had been spent at Mons. The gentlemen travel about in great style to attend large shooting parties.

In the drawing rooms and dining rooms that one frequents, all is known and appraised—the smallest pieces of furniture, the portraits of common ancestors, the guests around the tables, and the specialties of each cook. Aunt Amélie's gastritis, Mathilde's interesting ailments, the unexpected marriage of Arthur's stepbrother to his Irishwoman are endlessly fascinating subjects. Moreover, people are so well brought up and so prudent that they rarely speak ill of anyone, even among themselves: a discreet commiseration or shocked surprise in response to some reported gossip, with repeated denials of its authenticity, is the only evidence that might betray a particular hostility or resentment. These people who trace their kinship back six generations characterize one another among themselves only by harmless eccentricities or completely exterior details: Uncle So-and-so likes sweet dishes; Cousin So-and-so has a pretty voice. It goes no further than this. A sensual nature (if a person has one) or objections to the habits and opinions of the group (if a person has any) are concealed just as thoroughly as is political dissidence in a totalitarian country today. Independence of mind does not display itself. People agree about everything: differences arise only over questions pertaining to joint inheritances or to hunting rights.

The result is that an odor of stagnation emanates from this milieu, where life, no worse than elsewhere, is nevertheless more sensible than our own in some respects. These ruling classes, who by this time scarcely rule any longer, are gradually ceasing to be the enlightened classes or to pretend to be such. "Artist" is a term of contempt; Arthur knows less about the artistic aspect of a stained-glass window or a religious painting than does the most insignificant Jewish antiquarian or critic of Anglican art. *Midnight, Christians* is the most beautiful moment of the midnight Mass. The only thing retained from Musset's works is his allusion to Voltaire's "hideous smile." Victor Hugo is a dangerous revolutionary who abuses Belgian hospitality: so much the worse for him if he had a few stones thrown at him in the place des Barricades in Brussels. People find it surprising that Governor Troye's old friend the fiery Gendebien, former member of the provisional government, invites to his home these French exiles whose resources and principles are anything but obvious. After each visit to Acoz, Arthur mentions with some irritation the radicalism of his young cousin Fernand, and even the milk-and-water liberalism of his cousin Octave. Aunt Irénée is wrong to invite the exiled Frenchman Bancel to give a literary talk for the sake of pleasing her sons, but at least she has insisted that he speak about Bossuet.

Public spirit, still strong in this milieu among certain members of the older generation, has rapidly faded: the state is felt to be the enemy of family patrimonies. Charity is a virtue that funeral elegies attribute to all the dead without exception, which is already cause for suspicion. In fact, the heyday of Christian charity came to an end with this milieu: the care of prisoners (whom one would be wrong to treat too leniently), orphans, and the insane is henceforth the concern of public institutions, to which they are left without anyone's giving a thought to how these institutions are to fulfill their functions. The Red Cross, which a Swiss idealist is trying to establish, is an innovation that is still viewed rather unfavorably, if only because of its Protestant origins: it will take the war of 1914 to induce one of Madame Mathilde's granddaughters (yet to be born) to devote a part of her life to it. The couple donate to Catholic causes with a carefully rationed generosity, but if Mathilde were to exceed the sum that Arthur allows her for the village charitable society, she would hear herself reminded where well-regulated charity begins and could only agree. When the winter is harsh, firewood and blankets are distributed to the deserving poor; the undeserving poor receive nothing. Mining disasters upset everyone, but Arthur does not dream of using the influence he might derive from his shares as founder to obtain less niggardly pensions for the victims' families and the installation of less primitive safety devices; this is the business of company directors, who must above all think of increasing the return on their shareholders' capital. A fairly suspicious individual, a Frenchman who has written poems condemned for indecency, has described with horror the blinded starlings that can be heard in every corner of Belgium, confined in their cages in shops and rear courtyards, sending forth their sightless trilling. If (as is quite probable) the cook at Suarlée has a cage of this type on her kitchen windowsill, Madame Mathilde, though tenderhearted, has doubtless never protested. Such are the odious effects of habit.

Arthur and Mathilde are privileged but do not realize it. It doesn't even occur to them to congratulate themselves on their wealthy circumstances, which are no more than their due and in which the will of God has placed them. The couple at Suarlée are even less aware of the privilege of living in an age and in a country where for the moment nothing threatens their security. Their forebears had no such luck; their descendants will be infinitely less fortunate. On the contrary, they tremble at the threat of vague revolutions that could arise here just as in France and that one is never sure of cutting off in time. Hardly a day passes when someone doesn't make reference to the malcontents in the country districts. It is true that the age has its share of wars: precisely the amount needed to fill the newspapers and furnish dramatic subjects for the artists of *L'Illustration*. The war in Piedmont seems from a distance to be a lively military outing; at Solferino, that scene of butchery, the scarlet of the zouaves' breeches makes more of an impression than that of the spilled blood. The cannons of the U.S. Civil War thunder on a continent where no one in Arthur's circle has gone or desires to go: a settling of scores between American Protestants. The Mexican expedition is reduced to a romantic tragedy: the handsome archduke, who was executed, and his wife, Charlotte, the Belgian king's daughter, who went mad, stir the hearts of everyone at Suarlée, from the master and mistress to the kitchenmaid. The war in Schleswig-Holstein is a local affair devoid of interest. Sadowa causes more concern: it's monstrous that Catholic Austria should be conquered by Prussia, but Fräulein does not hide her joy at the founding of the North German Confederation.

This joy will become even greater when the German Empire is proclaimed in the Hall of Mirrors at Versailles. In the schoolroom, Fräulein has hung an engraving that depicts the emperor in a red, white, and black cravat. No one has the heart to make her take it down; after all, her master and mistress are not French. Belgium's neutrality, guaranteed by the warring powers, gives people the reassuring feeling that they are on the sidelines. But this time the frightful reality has come too close for comfort; Arthur trembles at tales of landowners taken as hostages and shot. Mathilde pities the Parisians, who have endured cold and hunger. Then the Commune evokes horror, but people calm themselves with the thought that this type of violence is frequent on the part of their turbulent neighbors to the south. The crackling of gunfire at Versailles, a just recall to order, can scarcely be heard at Suarlée on those lovely evenings in May 1871, when Mathilde conceives her last child, Fernande. At about the same time, in a Jesuit school in Lille or Arras, a boy of seventeen (who will one day marry Fernande), weeping with indignation, composes an ode to the Commune's dead and is nearly expelled for his efforts.

I have said that in this milieu devotion is above all the appanage of women. Every morning, when her health permits, at five-thirty in the summer and at six o'clock in the winter, Mathilde slips quietly out of bed so as not to wake Arthur and gets ready to attend Low Mass at the village church. A maid who has risen before her has placed a jug of hot water in the dressing room. As she inserts her last hairpins, Mathilde hardly glances at the mirror, which is still gray in the chiaroscuro of dawn. Even though her interest in fashion has greatly declined, she feels a pang of regret as she puts on her dress: what a shame that crinolines aren't worn anymore; their fullness was such an advantage at certain times . . . She takes up her prayer book from a little table and noiselessly leaves the house, now given over to the servants, who, fortified with a pot of tea, do the dusting and brush the carpets.

The church is separated from the château by nothing more than a meadow; Mathilde prefers to take this shortcut rather than the road. In winter she sets her boots carefully on the clumps of brown grass, doing her best to avoid the snow and the patches of ice. In summer the brief journey is a delight, but Mathilde does not altogether admit that the attraction of the morning Mass is augmented by the pleasure of this uncon-

Mathilde de C. de M., about 1869. Artist unknown.
Collection of Mme Jean Manderbach

Priez pour le repos de l'âme

DE DAME

MATHILDE-LOUISE-ISABELLE **TROYE,**

Epouse de Monsieur Arthur-Ferdinand-Joseph-Ghislain

DE CARTIER DE MARCHIENNE,

Pieusement décédée à Suarlée, le 8 mai 1873,
après une courte et cruelle maladie, dans sa
39e année, munie des Secours de la Religion.

Adieu cher époux, chers enfants, que j'ai
tant aimés, adieu! Mon départ est bien brusque,
bien précipité; Dieu l'a voulu; que sa sainte
volonté soit faite. Priez pour moi. Je vous laisse
en mourant deux grandes choses auxquelles je
tiens beaucoup : l'esprit de foi et l'esprit de
famille.... Conservez et augmentez ces deux
esprits.... Adieu, je prierai pour vous. S. V.

Elle était le bonheur et la consolation des siens;
la bonté de son cœur et l'aménité de son caractère
lui avaient concilié l'affection de tous. JUDITH.

Heureux celui qui prend soin du pauvre et de
l'indigent, le Seigneur le délivrera au jour de l'affliction. Ps. XL, 1.

Soyez toujours prêts... Heureux celui qui n'a pas
attendu le moment de la mort pour s'y préparer.
S. MATTH.

Miséricordieux Jésus, donnez-lui le repos éternel
(100 j. d'ind.)

R.   I.   P.

Namur. — Typ. Lambert-De Roisin.

JESUS REDEMPTEUR

Voici l'agneau de Dieu
qui doit effacer les péchés du monde.

REQUIESCAT IN PACE

Mathilde's *souvenir pieux*

strained walk through the fields. Often, but not every day, before entering the church, she takes a look at the enclosure where her two dear little ones are buried. Out of humility, she refrains from sitting in the pew belonging to the château and takes a place in the nave. Besides, there are very few people. Mathilde, like so many of the faithful at this time, does not read in her missal the translations of the Latin prayers, which she knows by heart anyway; her body, kneeling and rising, follows the Mass for her. She prays spontaneously, perhaps addressing one of the plaster statues that ornament the shabby, ugly church. She prays that it will be fine weather on Sunday, when Aunt Irénée comes, so that the table can be set out on the terrace under the chestnut trees and Arthur will approve her arrangements of flowers and fruit; she prays that her fragile health may improve and that she may be permitted to bear her burden to the end; she prays that she might have the strength to fulfill her daily obligations and that, if her strength should fail her, her weaknesses might be forgiven. Frivolous requests and profound requests intermingle, as do frivolous emotions and profound emotions in life. The former fall away of their own accord—humble wishes quickly forgotten. The latter are to some extent fulfilled even as they are uttered: Mathilde concludes her prayers feeling more at peace than when she began.

She prays for her loved ones, which is nearly the same thing as praying for oneself. She prays that her daughters might find worthy husbands and be good wives to them; that her dear Papa might recover his health quickly in the clear air of La Pasture; that Fräulein, who has recently experienced great personal sorrow, may find solace; that the Good Lord might enlighten her cousin Fernand, whom people call a freethinker (but it is impossible that a gifted young man like him should err in such a way). She prays that her little Jeanne might learn to walk someday; that her Gaston, who is thirteen, might at last learn to read. She prays that Arthur might not be punished for an infidelity that she has learned of recently with indignation and horror—but, after all, who knows if she herself might not be responsible? Since her latest confinements, she has sometimes revealed how tired she is of all that . . . And finally, like so many other devout Catholics of her time, she prays for the sake of the Holy Father—a voluntary prisoner, it is said, but in reality forced by the Freemasons to shut himself up in the Vatican. Whether received or not, these waves of goodwill emanate from her, and one would not dare to say that they serve no purpose, even if the course of the world appears in no way altered. Mathilde, in any case, benefits from sending them: one loves people more when one has prayed for them.

The Mass comes to an end, hurried along somewhat by the curé, who thinks of the farm work that awaits his flock and a bit, too, of the attention he himself must give to his vegetable and flower gardens. Madame Mathilde drops two sous in the poor box and says goodbye to the choirboy who is the son of Suarlée's coachman. She recrosses the meadow, retracing her path step for step, since one must be careful not to tread too much on the hay. Her visit to the church, which has included, without her realizing it, a descent into herself, has for a brief time restored her youth, which she thinks is long gone; life flows in her as it did at eighteen. From time to time she stops to detach a barbed ear of hay that has clung to her skirt and, like a child, makes its seeds slip between her fingers. She even ventures to take off her hat, in defiance of the rules of decorum, to feel the caress of the breeze on her hair. The cows that give the little château of La Boverie its name are grazing or sleeping in the meadow, separated from her by a mere hedge. La Belle Vaque, as the farmer calls her, the best milch cow of the herd, is rubbing herself gently against the thorny enclosure. Scarcely eight days ago, she lowed despairingly when the butcher's cart came to take away her calf, but she has forgotten; she is once more contentedly chewing the good grass. Mathilde murmurs soothingly to her, rediscovering the gestures and intonations of the Isabelle Maître-Pierres, the Jeanne Masures, and the Barbe Le Vergers, her distant forebears. A few paces farther and she stops before the coachman, who is polishing a curb chain at the threshold of the stable; she congratulates him (she has put her hat back on) for the way his son has assisted at the Mass.

The odor of hot coffee and fresh bread drifts from the dining room. Mathilde sets down her book on the vestibule table and hangs up her things carefully on the clothes pegs. Everyone is there. Fräulein is speaking German with her three girls, in a low voice, so as not to disturb Monsieur, who is reading his newspaper. Mathilde glances a bit anxiously at Gaston, but he is eating tranquilly and not bothering anyone. The maid, at the other end of the table, is feeding broth to baby Jeanne, who is sitting in her high chair. Little Octave, seeing his mother enter, runs to her, choking with laughter, explaining some incomprehensible trifle; Mathilde turns him away gently and sends him back to sit next to his brother Théobald, who for his part is well behaved. Perhaps, as she passes behind the chair in which Arthur is sitting, she timidly touches the shoulder of this arid man with the somewhat parsimonious heart; this modest caress thanks him for an obliging word or gesture that he bestowed on her the night before. But there is a proper time for everything: at the moment, Arthur is reading his newspaper. Moreover, he himself feels a bit frustrated: he has just finished reading a remarkable article on the administration of Germany's Bureau of Customs; he would like to talk with someone about it, but women aren't interested in such things.

Mathilde takes her place at the table and draws toward her the coffeepot and the pitcher of hot milk. But a catastrophe occurs: a metal cup falls to the floor, rolls about, and continues to resound before coming to rest against the foot of the table. Mathilde glances sideways at Arthur; he pretends not to have heard. The maid, very red in the face, does her best to sponge up the milk that is trickling along the tablecloth. That girl has once again allowed the child to pick up the cup herself, and as always, a convulsion has thrown the pretty silver mug to the floor . . . But the little one is still so young; perhaps her illness will pass. It is said that there are good specialists in Brussels. Or if not, Lourdes . . . Yes, Lourdes. Mathilde raises the lid of the sugar bowl. Usually, for the sake of mortification, she refrains from taking sugar, but the baby she is carrying within her must be nourished. One lump and then a second fall into the creamy liquid. Mathilde says a silent grace, chooses a slice of whole-wheat bread, helps herself to some butter, and devotes herself seriously to the sweet pleasure of eating.

I think the time has come to introduce Mathilde's ten children, not as she knew them, in the form of "fair-haired babes" (as the bad poetry of those days would have called them), but as adults, settled in the circumstances of their lives. Portraits of a few of them have already been sketched in the early pages of this book, but presenting them as a group will perhaps help me, if not to show certain culminations, or the absence of such (for in a world where all is in motion, nothing truly culminates), at least to discern in these people certain traits that I might rediscover in myself. To be sure, I'm getting ahead of my story, since the few pages that describe these individuals go beyond the framework of Suarlée, but these somewhat spectral aunts and uncles quickly disappeared from my own life and played only a minor role even in my mother's: I would hardly know where to put them if I did not put them here.

I shall devote only a few lines, by way of a memorial, to the two children who died in infancy—the first Jeanne, at the age of one year, and Ferdinand, at four and a half—whom doubtless only Mathilde remembered with any degree of accuracy. Of each of the five daughters who survived, an accordion-folded frame contains an image, carefully separated by its leather border from the neighboring images. Each of these women does, in fact, seem to live in a world by herself, one marked by characteristics that are uniquely hers; their physiognomies differ to such an extent that they would never be taken for sisters. Leaving aside Jeanne, tranquil and a bit cold, as she usually was, and of whom I have spoken and shall speak again, and a fairly disagreeable-looking Fernande (who was photographed, so I'm told, on one of her bad days), I shall devote myself here to detaching from their frame the portraits of the three older women. Isabelle, known as Isa, the eldest, is first and foremost a lady. She is shown to us already aged. A light mantilla falls about her thin, fine-boned face and covers her hair, which might be blond or already gray—it's impossible to tell. The clear, bright eyes are smiling with a kindness that is tinged with melancholy. This is how Aunt Isabelle looked when I saw her once or twice in my early childhood; already she was suffering from the heart condition that would cause her death a few years later, and was so quickly fatigued that I scarcely had time to sit down in the drawing room, swinging my little legs, when I was told to get up and say goodbye to my aunt.

Isabelle had married her cousin, the baron de C. d'Y., whom we have already seen witnessing my birth certificate. She had three children, of whom the oldest kept the line and the family traditions alive; a daughter, quite sickly, died when she was about twenty; the youngest, the robust Louise, who devoted herself to good works from a very early age, was one of the heroic nurses of the Great War. Brusque, jovial, and authoritarian, this strong, blue-eyed blonde was adored by her patients and feared but venerated by the staff of her hospital. After the Armistice, she spent the rest of her life directing the radiography unit in a Catholic institution for cancer victims. She died from the dangerous rays she worked with. In 1954 I saw her briefly, lying in one of the rooms of her own hospice, surrounded like a queen by relatives and friends who had come to pay court to her; the religious chants that could be heard in the corridors formed a sonorous background. Her favorite nurse was caring for her, an aide-de-camp assisting her leader to the end. The recent success of one of my books, which she had never read, delighted Louise, because it was obviously an honor to the family. She would have said as much, and no more, of her own medals and military crosses.

The second sister, Georgine, appears as a majestic young woman in a tightly laced corset and generous décolletage; she wears her hair in short, gathered curls, closely following the lines of her head, a style that gives a counterfeit classical look, like that of a Greek statue, to Queen Alexandra's contemporaries. Her face, with its regular features, expresses nothing. This photograph was taken in Vienna in the days of waltzes, during a visit that Georgine made to the city with her husband, who was the son of a Namur banker and a descendant, it is said, of an old family of merchants from the Low Countries. He was a freethinker who every Sunday accompanied his wife to the door of the church and came again to fetch her when the Mass was over. It is also said—and this was considered even more scandalous—that he sometimes whiled away the intervening time at a café.

This lovely woman was, by the age of forty-eight, nothing more than a ruin. A chambermaid used to lead this visitor—slightly stooped, partially blind, weakened by diabetes—toward one of the rattan armchairs in the little winter garden where Jeanne would receive guests. Georgine's loose teeth could scarcely manage to chew the most crumbly biscuits; her hair, still black, framed her sallow face with its thin bands. To me, she was less a sick woman than the terrible symbol of Sickness itself. Only her chestnut-brown eyes, which gaze so fixedly from the image taken by that Viennese photographer, shone with a brightness at once gentle and keen, looked upon people and objects with a sort of inquisitive coquettishness. I no longer remember a single word of the two sisters' conversation, and since I know nothing of Georgine's temperament or her personal life, the only thing that remains to me is the ever-vibrant gaze in that ravaged face.

Jean, her son, settled with her on the outskirts of Bruges, so as to give his ailing mother the chance to breathe more invigorating air than that of Namur. There, he married a woman of good standing in local society, who is today just as decorated with crosses and ribbons (but from a different war) as Cousin Louise was after 1914. He would have lived the tranquil life of a wealthy bourgeois of Bruges had it not been for two periods of enemy occupation, the first of which forced him into khaki fatigues and onto the roads of France. He observed the second one from his sickbed and died around 1950, leaving no descendants.

I spent more time with his sister Suzanne, a young Cybele, though slightly heavy, endowed with the same brown eyes as her mother, whom I can still see visiting the pine groves of Mont-Noir; the handsome setter who followed her about contributes a great deal to these memories. Some twenty years later I met Suzanne again, on an estate in the Ardennes; she had married late and was now the mother of a little girl. She came there only in the summer, spending the rest of the year with her husband in North Africa, where Monsieur de S. had a large agricultural business. Suzanne, it seemed to me, had become hardened; there was an element of harshness and of colonial indifference in that house in the Ardennes. A hyena brought from Africa paced back and forth in an enormous cage, following the gestures of the humans with its mistrustful eyes and howling savagely throughout the night.

The portraits of Zoé, Fernande's favorite sister, interest me all the more because I never saw their model. The first shows a young woman in a plaid dress, holding in her firm grasp some object or other, perhaps a book. Her abundant hair, done up in disorderly fashion, gives the impression (probably erroneous) that Zoé has had it cut short. She looks out of the frame as if waiting for someone—a Monsieur D., no doubt, whom she will marry in 1883 and who seems to have been one of those people it is a mistake to wait for. The face, with its boldly structured planes and highlights, has something of that strangeness of proportion by which da Vinci defined beauty. A later photograph shows a woman of about forty, looking nervous and constrained, with the bright, somewhat glassy-eyed gaze that Jeanne and Théobald also wore at times. We shall see further on how life had treated her.

There is no photograph to help me describe the three boys in their early youth. I shall therefore not try to imagine a portrait of the eldest of my uncles, who died sixteen years before I was born. Gaston is an enigma such as one often encounters in the obscure recesses of families. Born at Suarlée in 1858, dying at Suarlée in 1887 at the age of twenty-nine, he seems to all appearances never to have existed. And yet this Gaston, who is not even a ghost, had become almost from the cradle, as a result of the death of a brother only slightly older than himself, the eldest of a traditional family; as such, he must have been showered with special attentions; he must have inspired hopes and plans for the future. But there is no vestige of him in the

few letters and numerous oral accounts of those years that have
been imparted to me. Not one recollection of boyhood or schooldays, not a single reference to a girlfriend or fiancée or to a
marriage arranged and broken off, not the slightest indication
as to the career or occupations of this man, who, as we have
seen, was already nearly thirty when he died. His sisters and
brothers, who could scarcely find themselves together for an
hour at a time without speaking of their childhood, and Fräulein, so unbearably talkative when it came to reminiscing about
what from a distance seemed to her the good old days, never
made the least mention of him, with the exception of a fairly
somber detail, true or false, concerning his death that Fernande
confided to my father. This silence seems even more unusual
when one considers that Jeanne and Fernande were, respectively, nineteen and fifteen at the time of his death, which
appears to have been a fairly pitiable one, and when one thinks
of what a large role an older brother usually plays in the lives
of his younger sisters, whether he be hated or loved. If Gaston,
like Jeanne, had been an invalid, this fact surely would have
been mentioned. But nothing at all was said about him because
(and my hypothesis was confirmed later by a reliable source) he
was mentally impaired.

Théobald and Octave have left me with quite distinct memories. The former came fairly often to visit his sister Jeanne; I
saw him there about a dozen times, but that thick-witted, grumbling gentleman was not the sort who would please a little girl
of six. I have spoken elsewhere of the easy life he was able to
make for himself in Brussels. In his last years, he took rooms
in the house of the former maître d'hôtel of his club; this con-
summate servant and his wife waited on their lodger hand and
foot. It was around this time that Théobald, who clearly was

fond of his comforts, observed that the sizable fortune he had inherited from his father was nevertheless inadequate and decided that it would help him if he withdrew from his capital an annual sum that each year was slightly greater than the preceding one, so as to compensate for the interest that shrank proportionately as a result. He immersed himself in lengthy calculations, such as he had doubtless not done since the days when he was preparing to take his engineering exams, and came to the conclusion that with a bit of prudence he could reach both the end of his life and the number zero in his assets column at one and the same time.

That is precisely what he did. He was no doubt aided in this endeavor by the prognosis of his disease, a form of gradually worsening paralysis whose insidious course he had already been noticing for some time. When I was about twenty, having been quite out of touch with my maternal family for more than a decade, it occurred to me one fine evening between Christmas and New Year's that it would be polite to send good wishes to this uncle, whose address I had just rediscovered. He answered by sending me good wishes in turn, written on a calling card, and this laconic but ceremonious exchange continued for some years. Each time, a phrase more or less the same appeared in spidery characters at the upper left: "Greetings to you. Paraplegia unchanged." On one occasion the note, in a hand that had become almost illegible, indicated a variation: "Paralysis in its final stages." I received no further word, not even an announcement of his death.

But a few months later a letter from the maître d'hôtel and his wife informed me that this loyal couple had paid a visit to Monsieur at the cemetery of Suarlée. It was summer; on his grave, they had noticed a white butterfly fanning its wings. This spontaneous rebirth of the myth of Psyche left me wonderstruck—occurring, as it did, in connection with an old bachelor from Brussels.

Octave performed, with less success, the same calculations as his brother. In between his journeys, he often came to drink his sister Jeanne's watery tea. This man of average height and fine features, his trousers impeccably pleated, his butter-colored gloves placed on the arm of his chair, was more pleasing to me than his older brother, but the rather untamed little girl that I was in those days nevertheless did not put complete trust in any grown-up person. My aunt and her brother commented on the family news, chatted about the weather, and most of all quibbled about shared memories. Unless I'm mistaken, there was never, in my presence, any discussion of his travels, which he so prosaically recounted in the little book he devoted to a few of them. The world no longer expected great things from this inconsequential globe-trotter, pale tracing of his uncle and namesake Octave Pirmez, who, for his part, had built a reputation by publishing his diaries of Italy and Germany and his meditations on life. But for Jeanne and Fräulein, this comforting visitor was royalty; he was accorded the enormous, unconditional importance and affection that they thought everything from Suarlée deserved. Besides, lack of literary merit was not something that would have bothered the two women.

What was there behind that smooth white face with its black goatee—that face that reminded me of the masks in the Musée Grévin? Wanderlust, which in the language of the family became known in a friendly way as his "fidgets"? An eccentricity that was somewhat "hurly-burly" (a funny word picked up in a London pub, a bit too risqué to repeat in front of Jeanne)? Girls accosted in the hallway of a Parisian cabaret? Casual love affairs in a rooming house or in the hollow of a haystack? Certainly debts, which Jeanne was doubtless not unaware of. The dull fear of something indefinable that he could not name and that would one day swallow him up? Or perhaps nothing at all? The immense disparity between what two well-bred people say when chatting at the tea table and the secret life of the senses, glands, viscera, the mass of suppressed worries, experiences, and ideas, has always been a source of amazement to me. It had not yet become so in the days when, sitting on the ground on a cushion, I contemplated the narrow, glossy half-boots of my Uncle Octave. But a child's ear is quite sensitive: here and there I noticed silences or tail ends of conversations that were prolonged with excessive care. And soon, with a courteous word for everyone present, my somewhat peculiar uncle would take his leave.

Since traveling was expensive, it was about this time that Octave decided to use his brother Théobald's scheme to solve his difficulty; but he was mistaken about the date of his final departure. In 1920 or thereabouts he was found at two in the morning wandering the alleyways near the Grand-Place in Brussels, in a bedraggled state and unsure of where or who he was. Taken to the police station, he gave his name but could no longer remember his address, which was that of a third-rate hotel. He was asked whether he had any family; he answered no, all those people were dead. Clearly they were, for him. But two days later an official, furnished with the report of the doctor who had examined the mentally disturbed gentleman, appeared before Jeanne, whose name and address had been located in the directory; she alerted Théobald and the remaining nieces and nephews. It was agreed that everyone should contribute to a fund that would enable the unfortunate Octave to take up residence in the mental asylum at Geel, an antiquated institution sanctified by pious and poetic legends, on the edge of what had formerly been the picturesque plain of Campine. At Geel, those who are deranged but harmless traditionally live with the owner, whose life and work they share. I don't know how much time the inoffensive Octave spent there, cutting fodder for the cows and digging up potatoes. Perhaps he took pleasure in it; possibly he found there the security that had certainly been cruelly lacking in his life. I vowed to myself that if ever I revisited Belgium I would seek out Octave in his retreat at Geel. But when I came to look up my Belgian family in 1929, I failed to keep my vow. This omission, which could hardly have been the result of simple forgetfulness, seems to indicate that in those days I felt a certain fear of conversing with the deranged man. I have often regretted it since.

A critic once observed that I like to present the characters in my books from the perspective of approaching death and that this point of view deprives their lives of all meaning. But every life has meaning, even if it is only the life of an insect, and the belief in its importance, enormous at any rate for the person who has lived it, or at least in its uniqueness, increases rather than decreases when one has seen the parabola make its loop or, in rarer instances, the flaming hyperbola describe its curve and sink below the horizon. Without in the least wishing to compare my maternal uncles and aunts to meteors, I realize that the trajectory of their lives teaches me something. But it goes without saying that I did not find the common denominators I sought between these people and me. The similarities I thought I discovered here and there unravel as soon as I try to define them precisely, ceasing to be anything other than like-nesses such as those that link all creatures that have existed. I hasten to say, at this point, that the study of my father's family has brought me scarcely anything more in this regard. What survives, as always, is the infinite pity for the little that we are and, contradictorily, respect and curiosity for these fragile and complex structures, poised as if on pilings at the brink of the abyss, and no two of which are exactly alike.

But the portrait of the brothers and sisters of Suarlée obliges me to make several more detailed remarks. I realize first of all that Mathilde's abundant fertility was not the fashion for the succeeding generation: of the eight surviving children she left, only four daughters had children in their turn, for a total of nine; and only three of these, unless I'm mistaken, had descendants. Certainly there is something praiseworthy in this return to moderation, whatever its cause. Yet I find it impossible not to note some occasional failures and lacunae. Mathilde's fertility, seen from a certain point of view, makes one think of the overabundant flowering of fruit trees that have been attacked by rust or by invisible parasites, or that a depleted soil can no longer nourish. The same metaphor perhaps applies to the undue proliferation of humanity that is taking place today.

Fourteen months after Fernande's birth, Mathilde died suddenly, after a period of excruciating agony. A few unpublished lines by Octave Pirmez which recently came to light reveal that the poor woman, stricken with croup, had had to undergo a laryngectomy. A miscarriage ensued, which the hapless Mathilde did not survive. Her *souvenir pieux* alludes merely to "a brief, cruel illness." Since details regarding the physical circumstances of illness and death are rare in this type of document, these few words are enough to show the extent to which Mathilde's rapid end had disturbed or impressed her immediate family. On the small black-bordered card, which Arthur or Fräulein must have ordered from a stationer-engraver in Namur, the Lamb of God appears lugubriously posed amid the instruments of the Passion. I do not know whether it was the widower or the grieving governess who deemed this image particularly appropriate for the departed innocent.

The same *souvenir pieux* attributes to the dying woman solemn last words that one hopes were borrowed from some pious novel describing the death of a mother of a family rather than uttered by the expiring Mathilde: *"Farewell, dear husband and dear children whom I have loved so much! Farewell! I take leave of you too abruptly, too hastily. But God has wished it so; may His will be done. Pray for me. In dying, I leave you two great things, which I prize highly: the spirit of faith and the spirit of family . . . Preserve and increase these two spirits . . . Farewell; I shall pray for you."*

If these affected farewells were actually uttered by Mathilde, Arthur was doubtless the only one to hear them. The lovely month of May was just beginning; Isabelle, Georgine, and Zoé, the three oldest daughters, were probably at their pension in Brussels or with the Dames Anglaises of Auteuil, devoting their time, with or without enthusiasm, to accumulating good grades in anticipation of the distribution of prizes at the end of June. Given that their mother's passing was so sudden, it is doubtful that the girls could have been brought back to Suarlée in time to receive these admonitions. Gaston the Simple would not have understood them at all. Théobald and Octave, who were nine and seven respectively, were perhaps already at the school of Notre-Dame-de-la-Paix in Namur; if they were indeed at the château in May, they would have been warned not to make too much noise, so as not to disturb Mama, who was ill. One would like to think that the foregoing discourse was not addressed to them. Jeanne was doubtless in her baby carriage at the edge of the lawn, securely fastened in with straps, in view of her skill at crawling away from wherever she had been put, with the ingenious persistence of crippled children. As for Fernande, she was sleeping in her cradle, as her own daughter would later be doing in an analogous situation. Louis and Zoé Troye, Mathilde's affectionate parents, were doubtless not present during their daughter's final moments; the former governor, weakened by the disease that was to get the better of him some two years later, would have had difficulty hurrying over the considerable distance that separated Suarlée from his own estate of La Pasture, and it is unlikely that Zoé would have come without him. Surely Arthur and Fräulein were virtually the only witnesses to that death agony, along with the château's servants and the two people professionally associated with the act of passing, the doctor and the local curé, who with the notary formed a funereal trio at the deathbeds of the nineteenth century. But it is unlikely that the notary would have had any functions to perform for Mathilde: everything she had belonged to Arthur.

In contrast, there must have been a fair number of people at the funeral. The dead woman's father and mother would now have had time to make the brief journey; it is likely that her sister Alix and Alix's husband, Jean T'serstevens, came from Brussels. Aunt Irénée and her son Octave, both of whom were still in mourning for their beloved son and brother Fernand, known as Rémo, would have arrived from Acoz; Irénée's other son, Emile, ordinarily detained in the capital by politics and the worldly life, perhaps came with his young wife. Arthur does not seem to have maintained very regular relations with the residents of the château at Marchienne, which he had left to settle at Suarlée eighteen years before; but his half brother Emile-Paul no doubt put in an appearance, accompanied by his young Irish wife. Relieved of her thick red coils of hair, which devolved upon Fernande, Mathilde once again made the journey from the little château to the village church, but this time the cortege led her by way of the road; the familiar path across the meadow was not taken. Fräulein adopted mourning for the rest of her life, in honor of Madame.

We know nothing of Arthur's feelings, but it is always a shock to be deprived so suddenly of a companion with whom one has lived for twenty years. He was left with eight children. Remarriage was not essential for him, as it had been for his father. Perhaps the "Woman of Namur," a quasi-mythical person whom Fräulein would vilify to the end of her days, already existed, discreetly maintained in a modest house on a convenient street in that provincial town. If not, the liaison would be established before very long. In the decidedly dull life that my grandfather had lived since his marriage, this lackluster adventure was probably the only capricious element, the only freely made choice. Less severe than Fräulein, I have not the heart to reproach him for it.

TWO TRAVELERS BOUND FOR THE REALM IMMUTABLE

Entrusting his ailing mother for one day to the care of his brother Emile, who had come to spend a few autumn weeks at Acoz with his wife, herself unwell, Octave Pirmez called for his horse to be saddled at daybreak. He intended to pay a visit to La Pasture, near Thuin, where his Uncle Louis Troye lay gravely ill and where he hoped to see the old gentleman again while there was still time.

In the pages that I draw on here, he himself described that journey. I shall attempt to fill the gaps in his brief account with the aid of excerpts from his other works, to enter into the thoughts of this distant relation of mine, so as to experience along with him the events of a certain day ninety-seven years in the past. This visit to my dying great-grandfather is one of those family duties that Octave considers himself obligated to perform; it satisfies, as well, his passionate fondness for contemplating the end of things. To this temporarily sedentary traveler, those fifteen leagues represent, whether or not it is his intent, a break in the routine that is hemming him in ever more closely; he will fill them with as many impressions and images as he would an outing in the Tyrol or a stroll along the Amalfi corniche.

Avoiding Charleroi and its smokestacks, he follows the road that winds through the Sambre valley. Marchienne, where in years past he stayed several times with his cousin Arthur, makes him think pityingly of Mathilde's widower and of his lonely existence at Suarlée with his little children. But this requires a bit of an effort on his part: he has never had any real liking for Mathilde's husband. Glimpsing the ruins of an abbey, its tumbledown walls surrounded by barren October fields, he thinks back to those religious and poetic Middle Ages whose most minor legends he finds deeply moving. It was here that Rémo . . . The memory of his young brother, who died a violent death three years ago at the age of twenty-eight, is never far from his thoughts, but in the autumn sunlight the pale Shade turns golden, once again resembling the splendidly tanned Rémo who returned to him from his travels in the Orient . . . Three years . . . But the colchicums in the grass, a cluster of blue asters amid those gray and brown tints, a chevron-shaped flock of migrating birds high in the air attract the attention of his restless mind, which despite himself is swayed by the slightest breeze. He searches for the words he will use to describe them in the letter he plans to write this evening to José de Coppin, their young neighbor here in the country, whom he has made his confidant and companion. In the courtyard of an inn where he stops to water his horse, a handsome face makes a deep impression on him (he will say nothing of this to José); he asks a woman for directions and is intrigued by her piquant local speech, in which he detects vestiges of Old French; little girls gathering firewood remind him of the coming winter, so harsh for the poor. As always, each time he turns toward the outer world, life is there, with its unpredictability, its intrinsic sorrow, its deceptive sweetness, and its almost unbearable plenitude.

But he forces himself to retrace Louis Troye's career step by step, because it is to see him one last time that he has undertaken this journey. Octave, whose father died when he himself was about twenty, has transferred to his uncle (who is also his godfather) a portion of his filial emotions; he feels a deferential and slightly distant affection for him, as is considered fitting within their family. He tries to imagine his Uncle Louis's childhood, then his studious adolescence, on the banks of this same river, amid the same countryside, shortly after the cannonades ended at Waterloo. Louis's father, Stanislas Troye, head of the *département* of Jemappes under Napoleon and then a deputy in the Kingdom of the Netherlands, was one of those functionaries who in times of unrest assume responsibility for the daily business of government, a more important concern than fluctuations in regimes . . . But it is from his mother, Isabelle Du Wooz, that he has apparently inherited his perfect manners, which are simply the manifestation of a genuine refinement and nobility of mind . . . Octave is less at ease when it comes to evoking the bitter parliamentary struggles that were raging in Brussels in the days when Belgium, recently separated from Holland, was still a new country on the map of Europe: Louis Troye, a young deputy from the district of Thuin, took part in these now-forgotten disputes . . . Octave recalls the general outlines of the life that his uncle subsequently led as magistrate and administrator, in particular during the twenty-one years he spent at Mons as the governor of Hainaut. Rémo had less admiration for this career, which seemed to him no more than that of an exalted clerk: he was always keenly aware of the injustice that lurks deep within what we call justice, and saw in the most legitimate routines of the state a superficial order that he considered merely a mask for chaos. A world in which twelve-year-old children work twelve-hour days in the mines of Borinage and see daylight only on Sundays was of no interest to him. Louis Troye, in contrast, was one of those men who choose to do the best they can within society as it exists.

Certainly the governor of Hainaut needed more than a little savoir-faire in those days, when every act was still a precedent and when recent industrialization was aggravating the conflicts of interest that were always strong in that nation of hotheads. Hainaut's proximity to France made it vulnerable to the annexationist designs, real or alleged, of "Napoleon the Small," who from time to time seemed to pick quarrels with the Belgians. Rumors were circulating in high places: the French emperor had secretly proposed to Holland that Belgium be separated into two zones, of which he would occupy one; he had made much too detailed inquiries about the number of troops in the forts along the border. Yet Napoleon III also wanted to preserve the established order in France, and that dangerous country was at the same time a friendly country: there was thus a middle ground to be sought between mistrust and an excessive benevolence toward the French liberals in exile. That Louis Troye knew how to navigate through all this is proved by his having been awarded the Legion of Honor.

There were also purely local clashes: that day in Mons when the Radicals laid siege to a convent; the turmoil precipitated in the countryside by the crimes of the Black Gang, and the almost overly harsh repression that followed. On these occasions Louis Troye seems to have been both adroit and humane. In addition, he knew how to be firm. It was at Mons that the regime's most scandalous trial took place—that of the comte and comtesse de Bocarmé, convicted of having assassinated an ailing brother-in-law whose money they stood to inherit. Lachaud came from Paris to plead their case, and the court sessions were so stormy that the governor of Hainaut, the president of the Chamber of Deputies, and a general in uniform thought it necessary to sit on the dais next to the judges. The aristocracy of the country reacted just as that of France and the Low Countries had done during the notorious trial of a certain comte de Horn, in Paris, slightly more than a century earlier: their aim was not to save the unfortunate man but to obtain commutation of his punishment, which was considered degrading for all the noble families related to him. But the governor stood firm, as did the authorities in Brussels. It may be that this *grand bourgeois* took a certain pleasure in resisting such an outpouring of feudal sentiment. The count was executed in the public square of Mons, in full view of the closed and shuttered windows of the Royal Circle and the other titled nobility. Rémo was only a child at the time. Later, despite his horror of the death penalty, he undoubtedly defended his uncle's actions.

At Marbaix-la-Tour, a little village near La Pasture, everyone knows Monsieur Octave. The news he receives concerning the governor is bad. Arriving at the château, he is filled with anxiety: the window blinds in his uncle's room, on the second floor, have been lowered. Has he arrived too late? But Zoé has noticed his arrival from the window of the little drawing room, where she has taken refuge to get a bit of rest; she comes to open the door for him herself. Her poor Louis is very ill but still has all his faculties, thank heaven: he will be happy to see his nephew. Zoé, who once was beautiful, seems softened and swollen by age, sorrow, and fatigue; her charm now consists solely in an extraordinary gentleness. Since the death of her daughter Mathilde (two years ago last May), she has worn deep mourning, which gives her the appearance of a widow before the fact. She informs the visitor that last week her Louis received extreme unction with the greatest piety; there was even some hope that his condition might improve, but this did not come about. The Good Lord surely intends to call the sick man to Him. Octave, who believes or who strives to believe, listens respectfully but wonders if his Uncle Louis's feelings are on the same level as those of his wife. He recalls having written somewhere that in the face of life and death there are only two worthwhile attitudes: Christianity and stoicism. It is above all for his uncle's stoicism that he admires the man.

Zoé hands him over to Bouvard, who has been Louis Troye's personal valet for forty years. Together they go upstairs. Octave, always touched to see the loyalty of one man toward another, notices the deeply furrowed face of the elderly domestic, who for months now has spent every night caring for his master. This old servant seems to him almost closer to Louis than the good Zoé herself.

Noiselessly Bouvard opens the blinds at one of the windows and helps Monsieur sit up against the pillows. Then he discreetly leaves the room. The sick man cries with a sort of vivaciousness:

"What joy, my dear Octave, to see you before I die! Yes," he continues in a weak voice, *"I never doubted that your heart was the equal of your intelligence . . . In any event, I would have sent word to you . . . But perhaps it would have been presumptuous of me . . ."*

Octave, embarrassed, casts about for excuses. How could he have waited so long to visit this dying man, who is so dear to him and who wishes so much to show his affection for him? Does his uncle have some last request that Octave will perhaps lack the strength to fulfill? Louis Troye, who is fond of literature and who respects his nephew as a distinguished writer, realizes that his words of welcome could be construed as a reproach and continues speaking in those slightly solemn tones that seem to have been obligatory in the nineteenth century:

"Your visit, dear nephew, flatters me beyond measure. Like the affectionate care that is lavished on me here, it touches me more than all the honors I have received in my life . . ."

He stops, reflects, then adds hesitantly:

"For it seems to me I have indeed had some honors bestowed on me . . ."

Octave must have been struck by these words, since he took the trouble to write them down. For my part, I like the fact that a dying man deemed eminent by his peers might already be sufficiently removed, or sufficiently detached, from his past to wonder whether he ever received any honors or not.

"Ever since I took to my bed," continues Louis Troye, resuming a more personal tone, *"death has ceased to hold any surprises for me . . . It no longer frightens me . . . But I would gladly have spent a few more years with my loved ones."*

The visitor feels called upon to respond with reassuring platitudes. His uncle interrupts him.

"No," he says, *"my pain eases for a moment only to begin afresh, worse than before. Death will be a deliverance for me. And besides, perhaps I shall see my dear daughter once again . . ."*

Neither the little girl with whom he once played on the manicured paths nor the young woman, nearly always thickened by pregnancy, who would come with her husband to visit Aunt Irénée (he used to escape from the drawing room with the excuse that he was going to compose a poem for them) ever claimed a great deal of Octave's attention. But the insignificant Mathilde is suddenly ennobled in his eyes, because the hope of seeing her again in heaven is a consolation to this dying man. Will

Octave, who has so often asked himself whether he will see Rémo again, reveal to his Uncle Louis that he puts faith in such reunions in the afterlife? *"We believe in immortality,"* he has written in one of his books. *"If we did not, we would fall asleep peacefully, thinking that God has wished it so."* It is a statement characteristic of the man who wrote it, in that it affirms, with perhaps greater conviction than he feels, the opinion expected of him and then turns back almost timidly to the hypothesis that is doubtless the one he prefers. If to die means to sleep, could it be that the reunion with loved ones is but the dream that accompanies this last sleep? Fortunately, Louis Troye does not expect his nephew to confirm or refute his supposition: he has closed his eyes.

Octave, who has always admired his uncle's commanding presence, raises his eyes to the formal portrait of the governor that is hanging in a corner of the spacious room, like a mirror designed to reflect him as he once was. It depicts Louis Troye as still young, in a uniform adorned with the marks of his office. The face, with its chiseled features, is imbued with an almost Grecian serenity. Letting his mind travel back almost thirty years more, the visitor thinks fondly of the lovely drawing executed by Navez, the most gifted student of the elderly David, who was then living in exile in Brussels; it showed the charming Louis, like a child in a classical bas-relief, hugging his little pet goat . . . All that, to come to such an end . . . But the poet is moved by this last form that the dying man has so painfully assumed, and he finds handsome in its turn this gaunt torso in the fresh shirt, already damp, which Louis has donned to receive his nephew, this face reduced to its bare essence, this bony forehead and these hollow temples, fortress of a mind that refuses to surrender. Louis Troye, who has reopened his eyes, inquires politely about his sister-in-law Irénée's migraines, and

Zoé Troye, née Drion

Louis Troye, governor of Hainaut from 1849 to 1870

about the chronic afflictions of his niece, Emile's wife, who has come to spend a few autumn days at Acoz. The visitor is well aware that these trifling ailments can hardly be of interest to a man on the brink of death. Louis Troye is simply remaining true to his guiding principle, which is to think more of others than of oneself. It occurs to Octave, with a pang of something like bitterness, that his intimacy with his uncle is fading to almost nothing. He has taken little advantage of the rare opportunities to speak frankly with him, to compare his own experiences with those of this man who has lived life so fully. At no time has he ever revealed to him the apprehensions, doubts, fears, and personal misgivings that are the very fabric of his existence. Is it too late to ask his advice? If he could at least speak to him for a moment of the book he is writing about Rémo . . . But what right does he have to bother the dying man with problems that he himself does not always dare to confront? In any case, Zoé enters the room at that moment, fearing that the conversation has already lasted too long. She invites her nephew to accompany her on a stroll through the grounds.

"*Consilium abeundi,*" says Louis Troye with a smile, a classicist to the end. "*You are advised to take your departure, my dear Octave. Do as your aunt proposes. You shall come back again later to see me before you leave.*"

Octave and Zoé take a walk around the pond, where clumps of dead leaves have gathered in the shallows. Zoé talks incessantly. She speaks of the way her two children, Alix and Mathilde, along with Octave, used to play with their hoops on these banks. She reminisces about those tumultuous days of 1848, in Brussels, shortly before Louis took office as governor at Mons; Octave had sought refuge at his uncle's house, the good priests at the Collège Saint-Michel having judged it advisable, in case of riots, to send the students back to their families. But fortunately the masses had not allowed themselves to be led astray, like those in Paris, by rogues and rabble-rousers . . . One recollection leads to another: she describes yet again the stirring days of 1830, when she lived with her sister Irénée, then recently engaged to Octave's father. The two young ladies, strolling through the grounds at Suarlée, had heard the thunder of the cannons coming from the direction of Namur; braving the dangers of the road crowded with men in peasant smocks brandishing pikes, they decided to take refuge with their sister Amélie, recently married, my dear Octave, to your Uncle Victor. Does one ever know what to expect when the masses get involved in politics? Frightful images of insurrection hover before the young women's eyes . . . When they arrive at the Pirmez residence, what a surprise it is to discover that Victor himself, former member of King William's bodyguard, is making bullets for the rebels . . . Shortly afterward, order having been restored, it is Joseph de C. de M. (father of that Arthur who perhaps did not always know how to make our poor Mathilde happy) who gallantly conducts the young ladies to Brussels, to witness the enthronement of the King of the Belgians . . . Our Flore, already in an interesting condition, stayed at Marchienne . . . The excellent woman sadly evokes all her dear departed in turn: Flore, so beautiful and so wise, whom the Good Lord gathered unto Him when she was only twenty-one; Amélie and her Victor; the worthy Benjamin, your father, such an enthusiastic hunter and such a fine musician . . . And last, taken so suddenly from us, our dear Mathilde . . .

The soft voice of the elderly lady wearies Octave, who has heard these matters discussed many times, more pointedly and precisely, by his mother, Irénée. He wonders if Zoé will take it upon herself to mention Rémo. But no: she refrains, as he expected she would. They return to the château. Aunt Zoé now speaks of Poléon, the young ladies' cat. She also remembers with emotion that she and her three sisters each year would break open their money boxes to buy a complete new outfit for some poor little girl of Suarlée. At the front door, Zoé congratulates herself for having had this good conversation with her nephew. She offers him some refreshment, which he accepts. A short while later, he goes upstairs to say farewell to his uncle.

But this time Louis Troye does not even try to raise himself on the pillows. He contents himself with clasping his nephew's hand for a long moment in his own, and it seems to Octave that this pressure has expressed all and that it does not matter whether certain things were said or not. He sets out once more on the road to Acoz.

The route is identical to the one followed that morning, but the countryside seems altered as the day comes to its end, cold and windy. The trees, which earlier looked so lovely in their golden finery, are now no more than beggars whose last rags are being torn away by the repeated gusts. The clouds cast their shadow over the fields. Rémo is accompanying his brother once more, but he is no longer the handsome funerary Hermes of that morning, a smile on his pale lips; now he is the bloody specter that figures in so many German ballads. As if his uncle's death agony has suddenly brought him back to the center of that other agony, Octave thinks again of his brother's last moments as they were described to him by the servants. It happened at Liège, in a house near the quais, at the very edge of the city; the balcony gave a pleasant view of the gently rolling hills. In the drawing room, an object that Rémo had brought back from Germany was lying on the table: a sophisticated music box that played quite accurately one of the young man's favorite melodies, a passage from *Tannhäuser*. That morning, after returning from a long walk, Rémo carefully rewound the mechanism and then went into the next room, leaving the door open so as not to miss any of the delicate stream of notes. An instant later, the brutal noise of an explosion drowned them out. The servants who came running found their master covered with blood, standing before the mirror and leaning against it, watching his image as he grew deathly pale. The bullet had pierced his heart: he fell before the last notes of the passage had sounded.

To Octave, Rémo is a martyr. What sorrow had crushed that young man, who was so fulfilled, so intoxicated by his travels and his reading, and more violently free than Octave could ever be—a *"radiant soul"* he silently compares to his own, which is more like a gentle twilight? *"The sorrow that is felt by all great souls in distress, on the fringes of this wretched world."* Rémo was torn by indignation and pity at an early age. The student at Weimar and Jena, the admirer of Fichte and Hegel, the ardent reader of Darwin, Auguste Comte, and Proudhon, the passionate adolescent who could spend hours discussing Swedenborg and Indian philosophers with a young physician friend, was also enamored of Schopenhauer. *"I was no more than a living thought,"* he said, evoking his own brief past. *"It seemed to me I was a traveler ascending a mountain. When I turned around, I saw the vast sea of tears that had been wept by so many unfortunates who no longer exist."* Rémo feels the need to be of use to the living while there is still time, and it is this that has impelled him to political action. From childhood, he fiercely took up the defense of the weak, the oppressed, and the maligned. In later years, he refused to become one of those travelers who want only to wring the beauty out of things, delighting in places and people as they pause between two coach rides or two boat crossings. Gay Algeria and the majestic pyramids impressed him less, when he was in Africa, than the miseries of slavery; at Acoz, the portraits of Wilberforce and Lincoln graced his room. In

Italy, where Octave was intoxicated with life and above all with dreams, the degradation of the southern regions, the fear and cunning evident on the faces in the Land of the Plow, the voracious swarms of beggars, the bodies left to rot where they fell, from the battle of Aspromonte to the battle of Mentana—all these overshadowed what had previously been closest to Rémo's heart: the search for the sites and landscapes of Virgil. *"You seem to have seen the Land of the Plow only under its poetic aspect,"* he wrote sternly to his brother, *"and to have taken the author of the* Georgics *as your sole guide. Tacitus would have served you better."* In that sun-drenched land, *"all was luminous, except man."*

In Greece, which he visited as others make pilgrimages to the Holy Land, he rediscovered the great men of Plutarch and also the palikars, whose exploits had intoxicated him as he sat reading about them under the trees at Acoz not long before. But an act of piracy committed against a certain boat owner—who he was determined should have justice, apprehending the bandit himself in an isolated inn on one of the Cyclades—brought him into contact with the Mediterranean's eternal world of thievery, as well as with the remains of heroes and the vestiges of gods. Returning to his native land, he denounced those who profited from *"man-made hells,"* those who exploited children and *"disapproved of compulsory education but who said not a word against compulsory war."* After the fact, but only after the fact, Octave understood that the *"vengeful hatred"* which Rémo henceforth felt toward the world sprang from *"the fermentation of his need for justice"* and was *"the obverse of a violent love."*

Octave thinks back to the days when he felt the full heat of that dark flame. It was in Paris, where the two brothers had been reunited. Rémo had little liking for "that great glittery city" where he had made many a long stay. On occasion, however, he would plunge with delight into the throngs of people, the way one plunges into ocean waves, but only the opportunities to hear fine music compensated for the noise and the crowds, which quickly became unbearable to him. Wagner had already conquered him; in his younger days, he had belonged to a small group of admirers who had passionately defended the composer of *Tannhäuser*, which the members of the Jockey Club, by passing the word around among themselves, had greeted with a concerted and derisive clamor; to facilitate this pleasant task, they had distributed silver whistles engraved with the title of the detested opera. *"People are bored by the orchestral passages and yawn through the arias." "It was virtually un-French not to laugh."* Stupidity as bold as brass . . . In his rooms on the rue des Mathurins-Saint-Jacques, near the Gallo-Roman ruins that Octave had said were those of the palace of Julian the Apostate (another tempestuous student), Rémo would annotate those cherished scores before taking advantage of the rare occasions to hear the Master's work. The passage from *Tannhäuser* beats once more in Octave's head. But Rémo, he recalls sadly, had in the end rid himself of that passion, which he had come to consider a *"luxury." "Don't you realize,"* he pointed out to his brother, *"what a sacrifice it was for me to turn my back on poetry and the arts? . . . Sometimes I try to soothe myself by contemplating beauty, but the sight pierces me like a sharp pain; I conceal it within me until it flows forth in tears."*

1869 . . . August 1869 . . . Two more strangers stroll by the quais and colonnades of the Louvre, almost without seeing them, then beneath the trees of the Tuileries gardens, which in those days still lay in the shadow of the central part of the palace that was soon to be reduced to ashes. They are deep in one of those immense metaphysical debates that leave nothing in their wake but mental exhaustion and a feeling of subsided ardor. These Walloons adrift in the big city are, unwittingly, becoming an integral part of an eternal Paris that is ceaselessly being renewed, from the medieval scholars debating universals (David de Dinant is not far off, screaming in the flames) to the young men of our own day exchanging their thoughts on Heidegger or Mao. They are temporary citizens of a city in which ideas have been more debated, perhaps, than anywhere else in the world.

In contrast, the more visible Paris of La Païva, Hortense Schneider, and the thunderous Thérésa, the sacrosanct trinity of the street corner, the operetta, and the cabaret, means nothing to them, and neither do the ostentatious displays of the Second Empire, then in the grip of euphoria. Their walk takes them to the brilliantly illuminated Champs-Elysées, still blue in the summer evening's last light, crowded with people who stroll about or nibble ices and who in just a few months will be enduring the humiliation of Sedan and eating rat pâté during the siege. Octave, anxious perhaps to soothe this tormented young man, remarks on the air of happiness animating the scene, on that blend of vivaciousness and ease which exists nowhere else, on those comforts of a civilization cushioned by well-oiled springs, its surface overlaid with an exquisite patina—all of which, strictly speaking, constitute the pleasures of life. Rémo shakes his head. To him, this happiness is nothing but indolence and cowardly inertia, willfully ignorant of the world's ills and of the inevitable tomorrows in store. He points out to his older brother the arrogant or foolish appearance of some fellow sipping his absinthe or iced coffee, the malignity of certain sly smiles, the futility of these people who judge everything by appearances and either put on airs or do their best to conceal what they truly are. Suddenly Octave sees Rémo's gaze soften as it lights on a gloomy-faced stranger in the crowd, a bitter, tattered bohemian who, though dirty and penniless, seems to him less removed from reality than those other complacent souls.

"The feeling of being useful—I must have this in order to live." Knowing that his opinions were too liberal for existing periodicals and that his articles would never be accepted for publication, Rémo had founded in Belgium, with the aid of a fellow combatant, a weekly journal *"to defend the cause of the people." "One must not die before doing one's part to relieve human suffering . . ."* Of course, he is ridiculed with gross ironies. Worthy apostles who have never troubled themselves about the misfortunes of others, wherever they may be, and who would protest violently if a reform ever threatened their own interests in Hainaut, reproach him for being moved by the plight of the Caribs or the Kaffirs, instead of devoting himself entirely to local affairs. *"Our souls are sufficiently vast to encompass the world of all unfortunates, black and white; our minds are sufficiently keen to find ways of bringing them aid,"* protests the young idealist thirsting for action. The same need to be of service has induced Rémo to become one of the founders of the League of Peace, a small, isolated, somewhat absurd group that is trying, in this year 1869, to keep Europe from sliding down the treacherous slope toward war. Neither Cavour's wily Piedmont, nor France, trapped in its own politics of prestige, nor Prussia, with its Bismarckian aggressiveness, is willing to listen to this handful of scatterbrained fools. Spending a portion of his paternal inheritance on his cause, Rémo pays for the translation and printing of thousands of pacifist manifestos, which he distributes in the course of his travels. Gone with the wind, needless to say. The Liberal Empire subsequently brought a ray of hope, and

the triumphal election of his friend the republican Bancel, who had been one of the December Second exiles, inspired a brief blaze of joy. Coming so soon afterward, the catastrophe of 1870 was all the more tragic, and the nightmare of two hundred thousand corpses strewn on the battlefields was all the more hideous.

The young man is ashamed to see those Belgians who recently decried Prussian brutality, if not exactly fly to the aid of victory, at least defend the victor's motives. During the winter of the Terrible Year, the death of Bancel, exhausted at an early age by *"his life of opposition and protest,"* deprives Rémo of one of his few human supports. Then, in May 1871, comes the execution of Gustave Flourens, the young biologist, already famous, who was dismissed at the age of twenty-seven from his professorship at the Collège de France for alleged atheism and insults to imperial authority. It was with Gustave that Rémo traveled from Bucharest to Constantinople, where the tempestuous young Frenchman left him to volunteer his services to the Cretan insurgency. With a touch of envy, Octave imagines what passionate conversations the two travel companions must have had along the way. Named a general of the ramparts, Gustave was cut down by Versailles royalists on the threshold of an inn at Chatous as he was trying to cover the retreat of federalist troops. Rémo suffers all the more since he cannot imagine how this man, with whom he was briefly united in a common hope, will ever be rehabilitated in people's memories. None of the members of his family understands or even tolerates this subversive anguish: *"Between you and them,"* Octave murmurs sadly, *"the tie was broken. They thought you were a rebel when you were merely nobly outraged, ruthless when you refused to deviate from the narrow path of justice."* And Rémo himself, anticipating his brother's belated findings: *"Like flies settling in*

clouds on a wounded body, harsh judgments rain down upon me."
Nevertheless he carries on, thinks of founding a review that
would take over from the failed journal, composes memorial
essays on his dead friends for publication in provincial newspapers. Discreet witness of this solitary struggle (which reminds
one of the battle that Ibsen's Peer Gynt waged against the Troll
King at about this time), Octave sums up his young brother's
situation as if in a whisper: *"It would be better to die than to see
one's efforts fail."*

Still, in this last year of his life Rémo has also turned to
occupations less likely to cause displeasure: philosophy and the
natural sciences he once studied at Jena. But here, too, danger
lurks. His researches into plant life are oriented toward the
scandalous theories of Darwin; the reader of Hegel and Schopenhauer is no longer the adolescent who prayed in the chapel
of Acoz and devoutly took Holy Communion at Saint-Germain-
l'Auxerrois. At an early age Octave and Madame Irénée, who
are widely read, felt the approach of the disquieting shade of
the Apostate, bent over his books. To lose one's faith is not
merely a spiritual catastrophe but also a social crime, a perverse
rebellion against the traditions instilled from the cradle. *"The
people who surrounded this sensitive soul torn by the noblest
passions—it is all their fault. It was wrong of them to parade their
wisdom before his eyes. They exasperated his nervous sensibilities
with their advice and their reproaches, when instead they ought to
have soothed him; they needlessly aggravated his suffering by pointing
out to him his errors; they made him feel his unhappiness even more
acutely by proclaiming their inflexible judgments."* *"If I have any
reproach to make to myself,"* continues Octave rather obscurely,
as usual accusing and excusing himself at the same time, *"it is
that I tried to reason with Rémo. I ought to have tried to lift his
spirits by appealing to his heart instead. He hoped to be able to rely*

on me in his struggles with society . . . He was deeply saddened
when he saw that I was abandoning him because his new theories
made me uneasy, it having always been against my nature to undertake
any action whose outcome is unclear to me."

Pledging himself utterly to conformity, the older brother
believes that to effect a change in Rémo it would suffice to *"bring*
him together with some devout individual whom he could both esteem
and cherish," feelings that Octave himself, humbly aware of his
own shortcomings, no longer hopes to inspire in his ardent
younger brother. Their mother, certainly, could not inspire
these emotions in him either. With little inclination to philos-
ophize, or perhaps lacking the courage for it, Octave does not
clearly perceive how deeply this drama of ideas penetrates Rémo;
he sees scarcely more than a sort of visceral rending, which
more tender familial care might have been able to counter in
some way. The young man's materialist theories and radical
utopias remain, for the right-thinking mother and the prudent
older brother, symptoms of an illness they have no idea how
to cure. In subsequent years, how often Octave and Madame
Irénée went over the same incidents again and again in their
minds! How often they asked themselves what they should have
done to save Rémo and lead him back to sound principles! From
time to time, it is true, the *"radiant soul"* gave Octave glimpses
of dazzling lights from another horizon. *"He had perceived a new*
link in the chain that, in the infinite unity, connects all creatures
together." (*"Quis est deus? Mens universi,"* murmurs David de
Dinant six hundred years earlier as he is consumed by the
flames.) And the elder brother, anticipating the worst, receives
the sometimes visionary confidences of his younger sibling: *"It*
is when I cease to feel my personality, it is—in a word—when I
cease to be, that I am truly satisfied. But those moments of joy are
like brilliant flashes of light; they make the darkness of my daily

existence even more apparent." Such impersonal mysticism remains an enigma for Octave, sustained, or rather lulled, by his romantic Catholicism. This, too, exasperates Rémo, who has moved on to other realms: "*You think you are raising yourself to heaven on the wings of beauty, when perhaps you have plunged into the deleterious mists of your idealism.*" The two brothers continue to write to each other; yet during the two brief sojourns that Rémo has made in the past year at the retreat he prepared for himself on one of the family estates, he has not come to visit. His intelligent, timid older brother has joined ranks with his disapproving family. In his battle with the terrible angels, Rémo is all alone. "*He had neither human nor divine aid.*"

Octave stops short, tangled once again in his struggles of conscience: yes, this is indeed the way he tries to present the situation in his book . . . He erects for his brother a small stele of white marble . . . Rémo's tomb . . . But doesn't hypocrisy —which Rémo believed he had to combat until his dying day —already blur the memorial inscription? From the very first page, that formula "*a fatal accident . . .*" And farther on, "*he didn't know the gun was loaded . . .*" Surely this perceptive, widely read man is not unaware that, in days gone by, any disastrous event—and not only a random gunshot—could be nobly designated by the word "accident." Madame Irénée, despite the essays she has written on certain women of the Grand Siècle, does not examine the matter too closely, and considers that her Octave is conforming to what has become an article of faith in the family: Rémo died while handling a revolver that he did not know was loaded and that he absentmindedly pointed at his own breast. And certainly the phrase "*he didn't know the gun was loaded*" reiterates, this time explicitly, the pious lie. But is it credible that a young man smitten with Wagner, having wound up the delicate, expensive musical toy he brought back from

Germany, would have gone immediately into the next room to do a bit of straightening up? The grotesque phrase that Octave perhaps regrets having written but that he will not erase—"*The melodies transporting him to the realm of thought made him forget the terrible weapon he was handling . . .*"—was it not rather that this musically inclined brother had wanted to cross the ultimate frontier accompanied by "*those strange, sad melodies*"? This Rémo who supports himself against the mirror and watches himself die, this young man of letters, a classicist to the end, who greets a neighbor (whom the frightened servants have fetched) with the mournful Virgilian exclamation "*En morior!*" uttered with his dying breath—does he display the symptoms of stupor and horror of a man who has been struck down unexpectedly and who still hopes for material and spiritual succor? . . . Certainly not . . . And yet Rémo had just informed his family that he was coming to spend several days with them . . . Is suicide compatible with this plan, which indicates that his views were drawing closer to theirs and perhaps even changing altogether? Something deep inside Octave whispers that it may have been precisely the prospect of the usual reproaches and arguments that hastened the act toward which everything in Rémo converged, and that "*the yearning to repent*" which he attributes to the dying man "*cast into the abyss*" is likewise an unfounded hypothesis.

Rémo left not a single word of farewell, but every one of those ardent conversations between brother and brother, every line of the young man's letters had proclaimed his disgust with life: "*How little you know me, Cosimo . . . All the baggage of my life is lost if you, the confidant of my labors, do not appreciate its worth. You accuse me of materialism. Is it because I live only through the life of the mind? You also accuse me of misanthropy. Is it because I recognized the truth of that biblical phrase 'whited sepulchers' each* time I found myself amid the happy people of this world? A moment ago, I was about to ask you for advice and support. As I think back on the past, my pain revives, and now it is I who am trying to persuade you to accept my ideas in preference to your own. In doing this, I expose my soul in all its nakedness; you could bandage its wounds or pierce it anew with arrows . . . I am resigned. How many times, after wandering about all day with my head full of thoughts, have I returned to my room without finding the least consolation there. But I have no regrets! If I could live my youth over again, I would spend it as I have already done: I do not think it a reproachable life. Doubtless I am worth something only in proportion to the suffering that has been meted out to me. It is difficult, I admit, to keep always in one's mind 'the somber serenity of the constellations.' It is cruel to die misunderstood."

This flaming trajectory that plunges into the night—doesn't Octave deprive it of all its beauty by denying Rémo his ultimate resolution and by substituting for it a mere act of clumsiness, a death such as one might read about in the newspaper? Hasn't he committed a cruel and definitive betrayal? Doesn't he at the same time harm his own work, which will lose all the meaning he wanted to give it? He has chosen so carefully the quotations, the anecdotes, the formulas appropriate for showing this progression toward the realm of shadow: "*Rémo had misunderstood life, thinking it had demanded too much of him*"; "*it would be better to die than to see one's efforts fail . . .*" But precisely: he has said everything for those who have ears to listen. In his social milieu, the word "suicide" is an obscenity. Long accustomed to litotes and rhetorical caveats, the writer in him sets his mind at ease and imagines that the two or three adjustments which decency requires him to make are small things compared with that long elegy for a heroic soul . . . Besides, what right does he have to contradict a mother in mourning, who could not bear the idea that her son, the object of such concern, should have died in a state of mortal sin? He thinks back to the funeral vigil in the chapel of Acoz and all it meant to him: the body lying covered with flowers and illuminated by candles, surrounded by a group of Soeurs Noires at prayer, while *"the village, immersed in a silence full of rumors, devoted itself to explicating the tragic event, which everyone interpreted in his own way."* This somber happiness, this stunning rehabilitation of the prodigal child of the mind, would have been impossible had the family not denied that the death was self-inflicted. Octave's temperament makes him reluctant to oppose public opinion; even less is he inclined to disturb the pious and touching fictions of his family. Besides, no matter where a person goes or what he does, won't he always come up against truths that he must refrain from speaking about or, at the very least, only hint at cautiously and in a low voice, and that it would be criminal not to know how to keep to himself? Octave puts his mind at ease. His uncle Louis Troye, that judicious man, would not have done otherwise.

Night has fallen and weariness has overcome him, but finding himself once again on his own land, amid his own trees, soothes this male dryad. Nothing means so much to him as the plush softness of moss and the sinuous grace of roots. The château of Acoz, surrounded by the family's holdings, was bought and made habitable by Octave's mother only twenty years ago, but these rich woodlands, broken here and there by marshy fields, have been familiar to Octave from his boyhood. Here he played his childish games and, as a young man, lost himself in melancholy reveries. His subsequent travels to Italy were a golden dream, but his heart always remained here. *"How poor the southern soil seems to me! . . . I love the denseness, the moist air, and the cool shadows of a lush forest; the smooth paths beneath their leafy bronzed canopy, the queerly shaped mushrooms, the brook that winds past the roots, the crows bickering in the treetops, the impatient woodpecker hammering at a wormy stump, and all the vague cries that break the stillness."* It was here that, as an adolescent, filled with a passion whose object he neither named nor described, he carved in the bark of a tree the initials of his beloved. It was here that he took refuge with his books to pursue his studies alone when he could no longer bear the city, where he had been sent to school. Here he watched his brother grow up and taught him the names of the shrubs and trees. Rémo was eleven and he himself twenty-two when their father died, leaving him with mixed memories. For Benjamin Pirmez, *"hunting filled the void in an idle existence. He kept a pack of hounds, and from time to time newborn litters would be destroyed. On such occasions poor Rémo would be thrown into feverish agitation, for he wished to snatch those tiny doomed creatures from death. He would spirit them away without anyone's knowing, give them names, hide them in burrows that he dug deep in the woods and lined with hay. How he grieved when they were found! His cries were heartrending, his tears unquenchable. In secret, he would write of the cruel fate of his little wards, describing their appearance and the traits with which his childish fancy had endowed them. One day I discovered these accounts under some furniture, and was touched by their innocence. They were titled: 'On the Wretched Fate of the Little Dogs I Loved.' "*

Octave knows his classics too well not to see himself, so handsome at that age, as a young Hermes bearing the infant Dionysos in his arms. When the passage of time and Rémo's precocity had virtually eliminated the difference in age between them, they continued to come to these woods, to read ardently together their favorite poets and philosophers. In the course of these readings, they found the nicknames that they bestowed on each other and that seemed to express their true natures better than their given names did. Here Fernand became forever Rémo; he was also known as Argyros and Slavoï. Octave was dubbed Cosimo, Zaboï, and most often Héribert. One day in a clearing they unearthed bronze swords, helmets, and rusty lances, mingled with anonymous bones; they reinterred the relics in that ancient burial ground, which perhaps contained their own ancestors. Sometimes, by the hill where in feudal times a witch had been burned at the stake, Rémo would rail against fanaticism, denying that the ignorance of that era was sufficient excuse for such crimes, since every age has its enlightened, compassionate souls who deplore cruelty. He would compare the ruthlessness of religious zealots with that of the Jacobin fanatics of 1793. Octave always tried to stem these outbursts, in which Madame Irénée would have seen merely impudence and intellectual arrogance.

Later—only a little over three years ago—during a spell of windy weather that made *"the pale multitude of leaves"* rain down around Octave, it was here that a boy from the village brought him the shocking message: *"Come quickly. Something terrible has happened."* Octave ran to the stables, saddled a horse, and galloped at breakneck speed to the nearest station, at Châtelineau, where for three mortal hours he waited for a train, guessing everything even then and fearing not that Rémo would be dead but that he would be disfigured. Several days afterward, by the flickering light of torches, a funeral procession wended its way along these paths . . . But these memories, though destined, he thinks, to be with him even in death, are already fading beneath the regularity of his morning rambles with the dogs and his nocturnal walks along paths so familiar that he can find his way on the blackest of nights. Here, on sunny days or in light mist, fate once again lets him wander with young José, son of a neighboring landowner, to whom he enjoys playing elder brother. Here, most of all, he can be alone.

The gusts that buffet the traveler on the open road die down amid the trees, where the air is almost oppressively still. But the branches overhead snap and creak like metal. The treetops bow down before the wind, which sweeps from the east across the entire continent and which, at the very edge of Europe, a few hundred miles farther on, whips up the sand and the waves. On such nights, Benjamin Pirmez, as Octave now recalls, would say with a sort of pitying dread, "*At this very moment, there are ships foundering at sea.*" Then he would fall into a long silence. But death does not come only at sea. Octave, who has perhaps inherited from his father the gift of empathy, reflects that Louis Troye, sweating in his bed, doubtless lingered several more hours in his death agony. Here and there, other unfortunates, dying in less comfortable circumstances, toss and turn under their thin blankets in the hovels of Châtelineau or Gerpinnes. An opening in the foliage reveals a distant reddish glow: that of the blast furnaces which someday may devour these trees. Octave, aware that he is only a frail passerby in the life of the forest, fears that when he is no longer around to act in its defense, this fertile soil carpeted with billions of creatures we call grass and moss may perhaps be eroded and covered with slag. Unlike animals and people, the verdant gods so firmly rooted in the life-giving humus do not have the ability to resist or to flee: they are helpless against the ax and saw. Octave seems to see in the shadows around him a host of condemned.

Never one to let himself be taken in by the seasons' fanfares and splendors, he is keenly aware that autumn, when the barren trees leave wildlife exposed, is the season of sudden death and winter the season of hunger. He thinks of furry creatures cowering as the hawk dives upon them, of mice gnawing at tough roots. Who can say that his absence for even a day has not attracted predators to this place? Beneath these piles of dead leaves that will crackle at the first frost, an animal may lie dying in the jaws of a trap; and here, knotted to a stump, is a snare . . . The gamekeeper has no doubt gone to play at *boules* in the village. A distant gunshot at this time of year would hardly arouse comment . . . What would he do if he met up with a prowler dragging a bleeding doe stealthily through the darkness? He remembers suddenly that, contrary to habit, he is not armed. The anguish he feels is less a physical fear than a sort of mystical horror of violence, so strong that it overcomes his inherited affinity for the hunt, which he rarely gives in to these days; less the hatred of landowner for poacher than that of priest for defiler of the temple. He lets his horse, who knows the way as well as he, trot toward the warm stables.

At a bend in the path the château becomes visible, black against black, its windows dark as if the inhabitants have hurriedly deserted it. Only a yellowish light from the servants' hall glimmers on the water in the moat. The hounds begin baying, with that note of joy that announces their master's return. As Octave steps forward he receives full in the chest, like an ocean wave, a welcoming bound from his snow-white Saint Bernard. The other dogs, clamoring, press close as well. He quiets them with a word, fearing that they will disturb his mother. Yes, Madame is resting; she hasn't left her room all day. She asks that Monsieur wait until tomorrow morning to tell of his visit to La Pasture. Monsieur Emile dined upstairs with his lady, who by the way is feeling much better. Octave takes his meal alone at one end of the great table, his dogs lying at his feet.

He is not sorry to keep to himself for a few hours the myriad impressions of the day; he knows that when he shares them with his mother and brother, they will be reduced to a trifling account of a dutiful visit with his ailing uncle and to news from his Aunt Zoé concerning the dying man's last religious devotions. How is it that everything interesting and exciting to us, everything that nourishes the flood or the flame of our minds, is almost inevitably suppressed when we speak with our relations? In the opinion of her family and of her spiritual adviser, Madame Irénée has been an admirable mother. Those in her social set consider her exceptionally cultured. After all, hasn't she written, among other things, a distinguished essay on Mademoiselle de Montpensier, in the style of those women's writings of the day which Sainte-Beuve, when he mentions them, invariably says are the product of a subtle pen? Isn't she gathering descriptions of exemplary deaths of famous men, to be grouped (with a few accounts of impenitent souls, for contrast and a bit of a shudder) into a highly edifying volume? Doesn't she keep a diary of her own spiritual life, which she shows Octave so that he can prune here and there an awkward turn of phrase? Madame Irénée counts as her allies God, tradition, principles, and the exquisite science of what is and is not done; she has in large measure set forth the image of Octave to which he conforms. Mother and son have great respect for each other. She is proud of this writer who has retreated somewhat into a penumbral melancholy and whose affecting, meditative books express only fine sentiments. Rémo, who left the nest at an early age, moved ever farther away from her; it was doubtless because he failed to receive her maternal guidance consistently, Octave realizes, that Rémo came to a bad end. His own wanderings were less audacious, and nowadays he keeps his travels brief, so as not to leave his chronically ill mother—who is to survive him by eleven years—alone for too long. As for Emile, the second of the three brothers, that worldly *"big hummingbird"* who lives almost exclusively in Brussels or on his estate at Hanzinelle, Octave is quite fond of him.

He goes upstairs to his room. Even before the lamp he carries can illuminate it, he sees it by the ruddy light of the fire, which warms the October night air. Octave sits by the hearth. One by one, he throws onto the fire the pinecones he

has gathered in a large basket during one of his solitary prom-
enades in the woods, and watches the soaring, dancing flames.
This square of bricks and marble belongs to the element fire,
and Octave, avid reader of *The Mirror of Perfection*, recalls Saint
Francis, who out of respect for the flames refused to allow the
burning logs to be separated. Chilly drafts come in through the
tall windows, though they are closed and the red curtains are
drawn. Another window, giving onto the courtyard, looks out
on the chapel; Octave has often told himself that, as he lies
dying, he will be able to hear Mass from his bed. But chapels
are not open to heaven alone. Troubling presences counter those
of the angels: for a moment, Swedenborg overshadows Saint
Francis of Assisi. Octave glances out at the well of darkness
pierced by only a single light; then, almost superstitiously, he
draws the curtain over the window, restoring to the room its
human intimacy. As did Rémo not long ago in Liège, he leans
for a moment on the mantelpiece and gazes at himself in the
mirror—at that almost too handsome face, which shows few
signs of age.

He is forty-three years old and, unlike Louis Troye, is not
built of the stuff from which old men are made. The brief time
remaining to him makes him even more aware of the inanity of
his existence, which seems hardly worth such efforts. But
enough brooding! His book on Rémo will be only the beginning:
the sole task he will have accomplished during his life, a life
he condemns as self-centered, will be the editing of the deceased's manuscripts. His brother waits in the tomb for the
fulfillment of this service to him. Octave should set about it
this very evening. But the debate that raged earlier within him
revives with even greater force: *"No! Rémo confided his thoughts
to me, and I will not divulge all his sorrows; only if his efforts had
been crowned with success could they have been revealed."* The few

extracts contained in his book will no doubt suffice . . . Besides, how well does he really know this Rémo, whom he has never ceased to mourn? Methodically, he reckons up the days, the weeks, the months they spent together. In the twenty-eight years his brother lived, their shared life in the valley of Acoz amounted to a mere two years; their travels together occupied six months at the most . . . Well, what of it? Memories should be measured by their intensity. Those golden afternoons when Argyros and Cosimo, Slavoï and Zaboï, Rémo and Héribert sat beneath the entwined branches of two ancient lindens, surrounded by their notes and their books, in their green-carpeted study . . . The sacred rusticity of Hesiod's *Works and Days*; the sun-drenched landscapes and bodies of Theocritus; Tibullus; Lucretius, whose mystical materialism Octave condemned but Rémo fervently admired; Buffon; Hugo's *Contemplations* . . . Memories swarm in his head like lazy bees around a cluster of flowers. And he recalls the evening they were reunited by chance in front of a posting house on the Genoa corniche . . . Although he was ill, Rémo insisted that his older brother take the only remaining place inside the coach, while he himself sat on top in the wind and the driving rain. *"I can forget nothing of that nighttime journey. We were able to share our impressions only briefly through the coach window, whenever we arrived at a posting house. Each new team of horses would take off at a gallop, forcing us once more to confront the bleak landscape. Although we were separated by a partition, it seemed to us that we remained together, so certain were we that our hearts were beating in unison."*

And yet, he must admit it, his cherished memories are fading; his unbearable pain and sorrow are now hardly more than an occasional ache. He no longer hears in the night, as he did in the first months after his brother's death, *"a clear, plaintive voice"* coming from the next room. Moreover, how much of the old sweet Rémo still remained in that bearded young rebel, whose hair was already thinning above his lofty forehead? Only the affectionate look had not changed . . . *"Now, for days at a time, the fond image of the departed never once appears before my eyes. Seldom do I look at the portraits of him that are hanging in his room; seldom do I reread his letters, and when I find myself alone I am no longer surprised. When I write, I no longer think of his approval; when I am unhappy, I no longer recall how ready he was to comfort me. I am traveling life's road alone . . . Shall I do nothing but weep? Could I not devote my life to this brother who has died before me and who seems without a sepulcher because he remains unknown to the world? Indeed, I could! But the dead have been purified of the faults that plague us and are loath to fetter the living . . . Yes, I love my hapless brother in all the living who are dear to me. I will love him in all of you, my ephemeral friends!"* Thus closes, at least for this evening, the tomb of this heroic young man.

Friendship, love, the quest for other beings . . . Love meant nothing to Rémo: *"A passion for another creature would perhaps heal the frightful wound that the icy rays of science have made in you,"* suggested the older brother to the younger. And Rémo, ardently, humbly: *"I hold the opinion—wrong, no doubt, but firmly rooted in me—that we ought not to love one single being exclusively. I see egoism and tyranny in such a passion: it makes us forget the feeling of human brotherhood."* But Octave, for his part, has been in love. *"Ambition for honors I hold in contempt; of family life, I have not tasted all the joys; my country has not given me the opportunity to fight on its behalf; and love I know only too well!"* *"Shall I say it? I was once a passionate admirer of beauty: it frightened me. A single glance was enough to freeze the blood in my heart."* If he turns sadly toward the loves of his youth, it is because they appear to him, at this distance, limpid. *"I used to love like a child who has never loved before . . . So many emotions expended amid those trees and lawns . . . Who gathered them up? The wind . . . Scythe away, chop away, you reapers and woodcutters, so that I may forget the innocence of a past that shames the science of my present."*

What forbidden fruit has he tasted—other than the fruit of intellectual knowledge, with which Rémo glutted himself? At the age of twenty-six, Octave, having returned from Italy, was already distressed to find that the memory of so many charming beings, admired in the course of his journey, increased the sum of his regrets. What has become of those memories today, now that he is past forty? *"A spirit of discovery, a demon of adventure, used to make me roam through unfamiliar regions. I went here and there, squandering myself on people and fleeting images, ever more bruised and never disheartened . . . Let us close our eyes, O my soul! Yes, let us be blind to what must escape us; it is necessary in order to enjoy a bit of peace in love . . . If we set out upon the well-traveled road, if we pass through cities and hamlets, a thousand mortal gazes attract our attention, penetrate our being, rouse us to feverish excitement . . . Many of these transparencies, it is true, fade from our incessantly beleaguered memory, but a few remain alive there and, after many years, stir once again in those disquieting depths. Perhaps it is because my emotion is accompanied by pity that I am attached to it. I wish that I could assure them a refuge beyond reach of the ever-changing days . . . What an ephemeral shelter my love is!"* Thus exalted, passion is no longer necessarily (or so, at least, he hopes) an obstacle to that *"angelic life inside the body"* which he strives toward and which he well knows he will never attain. But nevertheless, how many snares, how many places undermined, how many desires, *"verses born of our spiritual death!"* He reproaches his soul for not knowing how to grow old.

The fire has died down. Wrapped in his dressing gown to ward off the chill, the poet sits down at his desk to write to José, as he does almost daily. But the account of his visit to Louis Troye, which he would like to make noble and touching, takes on a bombastic tone despite his efforts: he remembers, unfortunately, those descriptions of exemplary deaths that Madame Irénée is gathering. Does José really want to read such a homily? Certainly the friendship of this young man, wellborn, well-bred, not at all uncultured, is a grace for which the poet gives thanks to heaven. In his friend's family crest appear the two purest symbols in the world: a cross and a swan. José is approximately the same age as Rémo. *"What does one need in order to taste hours of profound joy? The sight of a face filled with innocence, the mere view of a pastoral countryside"* . . . Their meetings in the woods are a chaste Greek idyll in the dull Christian province of Hainaut. Sometimes they evoke such emotion that Octave, anxious to preserve his calm (*"I was unable to sleep for three nights"*) and wishing to set aside time for his work, decides to make them less frequent for a while (*"Let us see each other often in our minds, and may our invisible guardian angels agree to protect us . . ."*). But what do they mean to José? He has his family, a young woman whom he married last year and whom the letters do not mention, and a new friend with whom perhaps he can *"release the overflow of his emotions."* Above all, he has *"lighthearted youth."*

Octave remembers, with a certain embarrassment, that he offered his friend the same bribe that poets have been offering since the beginning of time. *"I assure you that I shall make you live on in my writings just as I do."* It was thus, but in more lyrically persuasive terms, that Shakespeare and old Theognis promised immortality to their friends. Shakespeare had every right to do so. And even Theognis kept his arrogant promise, since a few well-educated men like Octave still read his works today . . . But what of him, what of this Belgian gentleman who is writing down his solitary meditations? *"I see so clearly what tiny specks we form on the globe! I understand so well what nonentities we are in the context of the centuries! I am engulfed in my nothingness. And if perchance you should see me in my black suit, say to yourself that I am keenly aware of how ridiculous it is for a soul to be decked out like that, having nothing better for wings than the tails of a dress coat."* Who will remember Octave a hundred or even fifty years from now?

And here he is now, lying in that bed in which he has many times imagined his future death agony, experimenting at being dead. Not the throes of the last struggle, which his mother thinks of with shudders, not the physical destruction and decay that horrified and fascinated him when he saw the frescoes of the Campo Santo in Pisa, not even being forgotten, which presupposes the existence of survivors capable of forgetting, but night, nothingness, absolute absence. He once confided his fear of death to his young brother. *"Why be afraid?"* Rémo responded haughtily, this Rémo who was nonetheless so compassionate. *"You are nothing. God alone exists."* But this God of Rémo's, Octave feels strongly, is no longer the God of village and childhood; this Being is undifferentiated like the vast ocean, a vague and shapeless mass, inert and violent, before which Octave feels only a sort of sacred stupor. Octave does not love this Being; he loves all beings. He recalls his outings by barque at Capri, when, on that dangerous sea, he entrusted himself to the skill of the boys who ran boats out of the Marina Grande. If the barque had sunk, the current would eventually have carried his body and those of the children back to one of the island's beaches. How the Italian mothers would have wept and prayed for their sons! . . . Would anyone have prayed for him? But it doesn't matter: the children would already have conducted his soul to the throne of God . . . One could accept being shipwrecked in such a way. But this presence of death inside the bedcurtains . . . Should he relight the lamp, open a book of philosophy or poetry, or the writings of some saint? . . . He knows them all by heart . . . Better to endure like the creatures of the woods, who in the dark of winter have no need of a house guarded by dogs, of a room with a piano and books . . . Find an idea, some image or other that is not contaminated by pain or doubt . . . If José comes tomorrow, as he promised, Octave will ignite a Bengal light in his honor at the edge of the woods, on the brink of the marsh . . . A Bengal light . . . A popular tune crosses his mind, which sleep is overcoming at last; a memory comes to him, and now he can no longer tell very clearly whether the outing he is recalling is real or the product of some dream . . . Gay music is coming from the courtyard of an inn, where boys and girls are dancing . . . How mournful, solitary, and deserted the countryside roundabout looks . . . Gray twilight . . . Here and there, in isolated houses whose windowpanes sometimes glow with the last slanting rays of the sun, sit the old people, who do not dance . . . It is cold; his dogs, chilled to the bone, dragging their tails, follow close upon his heels. An old beggar gathers whetstones by the edge of the road, to sharpen a scythe . . . Sharpen a scythe . . . *"And now you are finished, evening of dreams!"*

On Sunday the thirty-first of October, eight days after what has proved to be his last visit to Louis Troye, Octave, in the prosaic light of morning, once more sets out on the road to Marbaix-la-Tour. But there is no longer any need to wonder if the shutters of a certain window at La Pasture will be open or closed. Alerted by a letter from Arthur, Octave knows what to expect. He is received in the entry hall by what he terms *"the grieving family"*—that is, by Zoé in the company of her daughter Alix, Alix's husband, and their two children. Arthur himself is not mentioned in Octave's account; perhaps he has just left again or, on the contrary, has not yet arrived from Suarlée. Bouvard is keeping watch in the mortuary room. Octave thought he had seen Louis Troye come to the end of his ordeal. He was mistaken; the man lying there has aged ten years in a single week. In the presence of this wax melted by death, Octave falls to his knees; his tears flow. With the ingenuous faith that continually wells up in him from deep in his childhood, he gives thanks to heaven for having granted his uncle what seems to him a splendid life, honorably lived; he gives thanks, as well, for the affection that the deceased felt for him.

Returning to the drawing room, and filled as always with a desire to do what is best for his family, he finds a somber pleasure in chatting with his cousins Alix and Jean. Their little boy and girl are wearing black sashes and scarves. Octave, who has a talent for winning children's trust, enters into conversation with little Marc and is moved to see that the boy, still so young, seems already to realize the loss he has just sustained in his grandfather. Soon he says his goodbyes and returns to Acoz.

The burial takes place on the third of November. Madame Irénée, who is running a slight fever, is unable to attend: she has not been back to La Pasture since the visit she made there to console her sister and brother-in-law for Mathilde's death. But she sends Octave laden with all the chrysanthemums of Acoz. Emile and his wife have doubtless gone directly from Brussels to Thuin. All along the main road, Octave is touched to see an unusually large number of people: the entire region is flocking to the funeral of Governor Troye, making this day of mourning into a kind of official holiday. At the church, Octave becomes absorbed in contemplating the high catafalque on which are displayed, like the thin golden chrysalis of some gigantic insect, the uniform and medals of the deceased. The prince de C., who has succeeded Louis Troye in his post, reads the funeral elegy. He is dressed in the same uniform, glittering with the same trimmings and the same medals. The contrast moves Octave to somber reflections, which he will impart later to José. *Pulvis et umbra*.

This time, Octave hasn't bothered to take a census of the family members kneeling at the prie-dieux, but he is virtually certain that Arthur was present at the funeral service, along with those of his children who were of an age and condition to accompany him, and that he took part, after the ceremony, in the substantial luncheon which was customary and which was, in any case, necessitated by the long journey that most of the guests had made. After grace was said, the clergymen present recited a prayer for the sake of the dear departed; then tact and good taste required that the mourners assume a demeanor halfway between a far too visible and joyous relaxation—a human reaction to the solemnity of the funeral Mass and one that, moreover, the excellence of the food and drink promoted—and a far too doleful participation in the family's grief. The prince de C. was obliged to tell a few fond anecdotes about his predecessor, which were of too personal a nature to have been included in the address read at the church. Repressing her grief, which she will give full vent to later, Zoé discreetly murmurs orders to Bouvard, who, in view of the occasion, has agreed to wait at table. Emile, *"the big hummingbird,"* describes nostalgically to Arthur the splendors of the balls at the Tuileries, where recently, in black breeches and white stockings, he was presented along with his wife to the emperor and empress of France. These gentlemen agree that Paris will never again be as it was under the Republic. Octave promises to give little Marc one of the wild animals he has tamed. The wheels of life begin once more to turn.

The preceding pages are a montage. Out of a concern for authenticity, I have allowed Octave himself to speak as much as possible, through excerpts from his own books. Even where I have not used quotation marks, I have often summarized the poet's notes, which are too diffuse to be inserted as they are. The phrases I myself have invented are at most only a sort of basting together; still, I have endeavored to infuse them with something of his own rhythm. Of course, I recognize the flaws in a procedure that compresses into a single day feelings and sensations that were in reality spread over many years of his life. But clearly these feelings, these emotions, run too consistently through Octave's surviving writings not to have incessantly preoccupied this almost morbidly reflective man. One single detail was definitely invented: nothing indicates that on October 23, 1875, the poet rode his horse from Acoz to La Pasture. But he has other, longer journeys on horseback to his credit. If he made the trip that day in his carriage, as he did on the two subsequent occasions, his meditations along the way would not have been different.

I am aware of the strangeness of this almost necromantic enterprise. It is less the shade of Octave that I evoke at nearly a century's remove than Octave himself, who, on a certain twenty-third of October 1875, comes and goes accompanied unwittingly by a "grandniece" who will not be born until twenty years after his death, but who, on the day she made up her mind to haunt him retrospectively, was approximately as old as Madame Irénée was then. Such are the mirror-games of time.

It took me a while, I confess, to become interested in my pale "Uncle Octave." Of my first visit to Acoz, I retain only those memories that are instilled in us by adults after the fact and that blur all traces when we later try to return to our true childhood memories. My father had not kept in his library any of the works of this relative of Fernande's: their melancholy style and solemn rhetoric had probably annoyed him. In his mouth, the modicum of information about the poet that had been provided by my mother, who as a little girl had clearly loved her "Uncle Octave," was reduced to something quite negligible. What struck him the most in this story of two brothers were the litotes that had surrounded Rémo's death. They aroused his indignation. It appears they had the same effect on Fernande. This exasperation in the face of the proprieties of a certain time and social milieu was not peculiar to my rather rebellious mother and father. After a good many years, a parcel of handsomely bound books which my Uncle Théobald had bequeathed to me arrived at my door. One of them, a small volume with a morocco spine, contained two obscure essays on Octave Pirmez that had been published in 1897; I shall come back to the first of these essays. The second mentioned Rémo's "accidental" death. Théobald had crossed out the adjective and written an exclamation point in the margin.

During the course of my stay in Belgium in 1929, I paid a visit, at Acoz, to Baron and Baroness P. (the family had in the meantime acquired a title), the poet's grandnephew and grandniece. Their son and daughter-in-law, Hermann and Emilie—young, vigorous, handsome, very at ease in life—were helping them to do the honors of that old house. There were some children in the nursery; others, quite a crowd of them, followed us about. Once again I saw the drawing room with its sumptuous seventeenth-century tapestries of mythological scenes, where Octave used to read *The Life of Rancé* to his mother. A fairly insipid portrait of him by an academic painter of the day, Van Lérius, showed a face that with a bit of goodwill could have been described as angelic, had it not been for the thin mustache and the tiny artificial beauty spot on the lower lip, which served as reminders that here was the face of a dandy of the 1860s; the hand was of a whiteness worthy of a Van Dyck. I also paid a visit to the chapel. I did not see the room that Octave piously restored to the way it had looked when his brother left it, six years before his death, never to return. The survivor had gathered the portraits and manuscripts of the deceased, the engravings and sketches brought back from his travels, the harmonium that had followed him from residence to residence, and the telescope he had trained on the heavens on summer evenings. Creating an air of scholarly disorder, he had replaced on the worktable retrieved from Liège the last books that Rémo had been reading, set on the mantelpiece Rémo's music box, fixed it at the final notes of that evil melody, stopped the clock at the moment of departure . . . A strange museum . . . Doubtless he also put there, under glass, the condolences that Hugo and Michelet had sent to the family after the *"fatal accident,"* homage from masters to a young man who had admired their work. But a half century and a war sufficiently excuse much that has been altered or forgotten. If this ghost trap still existed, no one would mention it.

Besides, the day was not devoted to literature. The prince de L. came to dine and to participate in a pigeon shoot. This took place in a sort of pavilion in the middle of the grounds. If I remember correctly, and if I am not confusing him with some of the family's other neighbors, the prince, rather short, rather stocky, had that slightly countrified polish that is common to many princes. For the first and last time in my life, I observed this sporting ritual. The lovely birds, feathered in shades of moiré silk and slate, were taken out of a basket one by one and inserted by a gamekeeper into a box made of unfinished wood; the guest loaded his gun; the bird, thinking itself free, rose into the air with a great flutter of joy; the gunshot brought it back to earth immediately, dead, inert as a stone, or else throbbing, struggling for a long moment on the ground until the keeper skillfully dispatched it. Then the whole process began again.

The following day I was in Thuin at the home of Paul G., who was the son of the little Louise whom Octave had seen dressed in mourning in the drawing room at La Pasture and who was now married to a granddaughter of the *"big hummingbird."* Their house, hung with cretonne, had all the charm characteristic of an old provincial dwelling: it was, I believe, Louis Troye's birthplace. An album of family portraits was displayed on a small table; two or three pages of it were devoted to "Uncle Octave." Octave in the act of writing, illuminated by two candles, which he is said to have kept burning even in the daytime, closing the shutters on the outside world; Octave holding a black velvet mask up to his face and then exchanging it for another mask; Octave posing with a skull; Octave bearing an armful of flowers like the one he doubtless brought, on Pentecost eve, to the reliquary of Saint Rolende; Octave and his tame boar. These poetic photographs naturally set me musing. I asked Paul if his library contained any books by our "great-uncle." He could find only the first, *Leaves*, and offered it to me along with the anthology of exemplary deaths compiled by my Aunt Irénée.

I have displayed a certain bias against my great-great-aunt. Irénée Drion seems to me to have belonged to a group of perfect and abusive mothers who were very common in those days and who weighed like an incubus on the destiny of their sons. In 1929 I knew nothing about her, but the lack of critical thought apparent in her work and her edifying platitudes dismayed me. Nothing was left out, not even, if I remember correctly, the godless Voltaire devouring his own excrement. One really must get to know this type of book before one can understand the virulent anticlericalism of the radicals of our youth and even the pitiful Museum of Atheism in Leningrad, which succeeded it. Nevertheless, I was not completely without respect for my great-aunt's compilation. That lady in crinolines had tried to confront the ultimate reality: she had armed herself with examples for the great crossing over. But this preoccupation was less unusual in her day than in ours. Saintly people, who would have been taken aback by the slightest word deemed indecent, thought nothing of devoting their drawing-room conversation to the topic of death agonies, including the foulest and most hideous details. We have changed all that: our love lives are public; our deaths seem to be conjured out of sight. There is scarcely any difference between these two forms of prudishness.

The book by Irénée's son fell from my hands after the first few pages. Its contents, composed of *pensées*, a form that he was always fond of and that accorded badly with his lack of incisiveness, distressed me almost as much as his mother's pious commonplaces. After a childhood devoted nearly as ardently to the classics as that of "Uncle Octave" had been, I had just discovered, all at once, my contemporaries: *Remembrance of Things Past, Lafcadio's Adventures, The Duino Elegies, The Magic Mountain*. Compared to these treasures, which were entirely new to me, the works by the solitary of Acoz seemed singularly colorless. In all likelihood, if that evening Paul G. had lent me *Rémo: Recollections of a Brother*, the antiquated style would not have prevented me from being moved by that brief work, which, for a reader who knows how to read, literally bleeds on every page. If he had offered me the *Letters to José* and if I had chanced upon some rather poignant memories of adolescence confided by the aging Octave to his younger friend, I would doubtless have perceived that the distress felt by that boy abruptly introduced to the routines of secondary school and the brutality of his peers, those mediocre studies, that flight into music which was Octave's great refuge at the time, that impaired health which finally convinced the family to let the boy return to his cherished solitude—all this resembled point for point the story of a young Austrian aristocrat as I had recounted it one year earlier in *Alexis*. I would perhaps also have perceived other, more intimate resemblances between Octave and the student of Presbourg. Poverty, however, which was such a determining factor for Alexis, was not a concern for the young Belgian, whose mother had inherited the income from a coal mine. It was fortunate for me that these two volumes were not contained in

Paul G.'s library, or at least that he was unable to find them that evening. One mustn't burden oneself too early with the family ghosts.

I remained at that point for forty years. To be sure, I do not include, in my quest for Octave, a visit that I made to Acoz in 1956. That visit had nothing to do with the poet. His grandniece Emilie P., along with two of her children, received me. Her husband and eldest son had been executed at Dachau. These already old facts were new to me—I was learning of them long after the event. A widow accompanied by a son and a daughter of about twenty, living in an ancient house surrounded by an encroaching November twilight, assumes a rightful place in the domain of poetry. Octave and Rémo, who had read Euripides' *Suppliants* together—especially Rémo, whose pacifism had been confirmed by the laments of the Trojan women— would have thought of Andromache remembering her dead. I thought, too, of those pigeons killed in mid-flight. Only last year, having already worked for several months on this book, did I seriously resume my quest for the pale phantom. Two of Octave's five books, though for my purposes the least important ones, had come into my possession. Thanks to the generosity of a Belgian friend, I owned the uncut volumes of a posthumous edition published in 1900 "according to the wishes of the author, by the Perrin Academic Library, and by Jacques Godenne, editor, at Namur." They had been offered to my friend's father, in those days a student at the University of Louvain, by the current chatelaine of Acoz, to thank him for having helped through his examinations a young Pirmez who had inherited no vestige of Octave's love for literature. (To judge from the dates, it seems that he could not have been that Hermann who was destined to be cut down by German bullets.) Whether or not I succeed in conjuring up "Uncle Octave" outside the somewhat yellowed pages of those volumes, I hope to free him at least for a brief time from the polite indifference that surrounds, and to a certain extent protects, within the graveyards of our libraries, those distinguished writers whose works have never been widely read.

Octave Pirmez's style could serve to illustrate the often enormous distance between a man's cultural knowledge and his writings. Well-read to an extent never encountered nowadays and only rarely encountered even in his own day, Octave came from a social milieu that was, if not literary (Madame Irénée seems to have been an exception in this regard), at least music-loving, and endowed with that scientific keenness of mind which had been fairly common, a generation earlier, in the families of the eighteenth century. Benjamin Pirmez had sought respite from the baying of his hounds by giving small chamber-music concerts with his brother Henri, his brother Victor, and his sister Hyacinthe. Uncle Léonard had written a treatise on astronomy, perhaps bequeathing to Rémo his telescope and his fondness for stargazing; Aunt Hyacinthe had had the *Bhagavad Gita* read to Octave. The extensive Greco-Latin education of the two brothers seems at first glance an ordinary phenomenon for those days; in fact, it was always rare in French-speaking countries, outside the community of specialists and professors, in whom such knowledge usually took on a more narrowly philological and scholarly aspect. It is in Germany and above all in England that one sees young men reading Hesiod and Theocritus during their leisure hours, under a tree in some park. Octave's first book takes as its epigraph a passage in Greek from Marcus Aurelius, whose *Meditations* were always to remain a spiritual tonic for him, along with the *Confessions* of Saint Augustine and the *Imitation of Christ*. When it comes to Italian, he is still of the generation that has learned to appreciate Petrarch and already of the one that knows and admires Jacopone da Todi. Among the French masters, he returns continually to Montaigne and Saint-Simon. There are no guides more manly, or better suited to teach a young writer the art of writing. But it seems that the great classics are like certain particularly nourishing foods, which can scarcely be digested unless they are mixed with other, more easily assimilated foods that dilute and sweeten them. Octave's work abounds in flaccid commentaries *à la Télémaque* and in Chateaubriand-inspired reveries. As a young boy, he saw René as his god and his double, and those voluminous draperies conceal his true personality utterly. The fashion for imitating Rimbaud has likewise given us, in the twentieth century, a whole series of slovenly dressed Arthurs.

Just as his admiration for Plutarch's heroes was of no help to Octave in confronting suicide, and just as his extensive reading of classical poetry did not relieve him of a certain near-Victorian prudishness in the expression of love, familiarity with the literary masters of past centuries was unable to inoculate him against the influence of those three women known for their sentimentally Christian writings: Madame de Gasparin, Madame Swetchine, and Eugénie de Guérin, the last of whom stayed constantly by the side of her Maurice just as Irénée stayed close to her son. These ladies were frequently read out loud in the drawing room at Acoz, along with eloquent defenders of sound principles such as Montalembert, who was appreciated all the more since he had married a Mérode, and Monseigneur Dupanloup, *"the celebrated bishop of Orleans,"* as Octave called him, whom Proust reproached for having taught bad French to an entire generation of young noblemen. These worthy authors are responsible for that cramped, correct style—often weak and bland, and displaying an affected loftiness of mind—that makes so much of Octave Pirmez's writing, despite its obvious sincerity, fall flat. And certainly we no longer believe, as Gide did, that it is out of good sentiments that bad literature is made; we know that it can be produced just as well with bad ones and that falsehood reigns no less in hell than in heaven. The fact remains, however, that Octave's style, already slightly outdated when he was employing it, was not, contrary to what one might think, a result of his being both a provincial and a Belgian. This same flaccid and solemn French was considered distinguished in the proper, rather doctrinaire drawing rooms of Paris: in the salons of Madame Dambreuse and the marquise de Villeparisis, no one spoke or wrote in any other way.

If instead of coming back from Italy and Germany with his *Days of Solitude*, consisting of travel accounts contrasted with descriptions of his homeland, Octave Pirmez had composed for us, on the same subject, a series of paintings steeped in languor and romantic melancholy, we would have appreciated an occasional touch of Piranesi or a scene *à la* Salvator Rosa, and everywhere a bit of the poignant charm of a color lithograph or the disarming solemnity of a Prix de Rome. This is because the art lover of our day is less readily put off by an unfashionable painting than is the modern reader by an out-of-date book. And certainly, in the *Hours of Philosophy*, Octave's most ambitious work, the unbearable droning of commonplaces soon diverts our attention from the few pure, delicate flowers of a mind and especially of a sensibility that are less banal than one might have expected. Even in the touching book *Rémo*, an excess of phrases like "brotherly devotion," "studious boyhood," "painful duty," and "faithful affection" makes us stumble from the very first page, preventing us from seeing the extent to which Octave succeeded in his undertaking, which was to give at once both a faithful likeness of his brother and a tragic funeral elegy. A ruthlessly bold anthologist, who would treat Octave Pirmez as we in fact treat Virgil (of whom the most cultivated among us know scarcely more than a couple of dozen pages)—excerpting a phrase here, a line there, further on a bit of a chapter, or perhaps merely a few isolated words whose very brilliance derives from their fragmentary nature—would obtain a slender volume that, as the author himself might have hoped, could be slipped into some corner of a library, between Guérin and Sénancour. There, one would find an often admirable mind, purged of all that is inessential.

Handbooks of literature accord no more than a respectful mention to Octave Pirmez, who was, chronologically, the first Belgian essayist of the nineteenth century, a distinction that is itself worthy of note. It has been pointed out that to find a somewhat representative prose writer from the same region prior to him, one must go back beyond two revolutions to the prince de Ligne, to the utterly different world of eighteenth-century Europe. After him, something of his melancholy cadences and thoughtful reverie passes to Maurice Maeterlinck, along with certain of the same defects but also with abilities that the "solitary of Acoz" did not possess. "Wisdom and Destiny," Maeterlinck's finest essay, is, whether its author so intended or not, an extension of the *Hours of Philosophy*. Even when

Octave Pirmez at twenty. Lithograph by Louis-Joseph Ghemar

VOICI LE CALICE DU SALUT
Leiden Christi stärke mich
Body of Christ, be my salvation

R · I · P

Octave's *souvenir pieux*

it comes to creating thrilling poetic and mystical effects, the Flemish writer who reinvented *Sister Beatrice* is not so distant from the Walloon who was moved by the pious loves of Saint Rolende.

If, as specialists claim, philosophy consists in elaborating systems and clarifying concepts, Octave Pirmez is by no means a philosopher. Moreover, he himself, anticipating some of the widely accepted givens of our own day, perceived that metaphysics is above all a form of semantics. If, however, philosophy is in large part a slow process of breaking through the habitual notions we have about things, a patient internal progression toward a goal we know is infinitely far away, Octave has some right to the title of philosopher. Slight indications show that in the end he devised a method for himself. He enumerates, though he does not claim to possess, the basic elements of the contemplative life: gentleness, tranquillity, purity, strength . . . It is interesting to see him, a mystic who dare not speak his name, and lacking an adequate vocabulary, touch on such great themes as the origin of the soul, the unity of all beings, destiny (*"Our life is but a long diamond-shaped vista. The lines of this geometrical figure diverge up to the age of maturity, then narrow imperceptibly until the throes of death, which wait at the end and strangle us . . ."*), make timid efforts to explore the corridors of dream, strive to observe the germination of thought itself, to break out of time (*"The present does not exist. There is only the flow of the future into the past . . ."*), define as best he can the relation between latent ideas and external reality (*"Our mind is like a female being that conceives only at the moments it is impregnated by sensations"*), glimpse in the end a state not so very far from that of the sages of India who fascinated his young brother: *"His gaze, oblivious to nearby forms, fixed on a point in space . . . What a marvelous mirror this man is, in whom are reflected the ephemeral and the*

eternal, the changing and the immutable . . . Sitting utterly mo-
tionless, he is intoxicated by the primal life-blood; in appearance the
most dead, he is the most vital of all creatures, living a sublimated
life . . . The object he contemplates grows larger before his eyes,
expands beyond all measure, summarizes existence, and this im-
mensity that he is dreaming diminishes until it condenses into the
contemplated point. He has enlarged his heart until it engulfs the
world and possesses God."

What he seeks, perhaps without even knowing it, is a
mystical morphology. The adolescent who at sixteen, having
been taken by his parents for the first time to a beach on the
North Sea, walked out on the jetty with his eyes closed, blocking
out the view of the waves so as to better hear their various
sounds (just as at a concert one distinguishes the different
instruments of an orchestra, trying to determine which shapes
those roarings and clashings could ideally correspond to), had
something of the seer within him. On occasion he speaks, like
an Orphic or a Catharist, of *"souls, perhaps germinated elsewhere,*
imprisoned in the bizarre shapes of matter." Further on, he notes
that *"all our thoughts find expression in earthly shapes"* and med-
itates on the animal analogies that human physiognomy can give
rise to; his allusion to Lavater is that of a man who has thought
as well as dreamed in these areas. His walks through field and
forest, the company not only of his dogs but of fox cubs and a
tame boar, the pageant of the seasons, which are more inex-
tricably woven together than the city dweller imagines—spring
already felt in the heart of winter, winter slyly hidden beneath
summer—have little by little helped him progress through that
syntax of forms, those *"phrases from an eternal discourse."* In
defending the visionary genius of Hugo against philistine attacks, Octave is, naturally, pleading his own case: his long
description of an aquarium recalls those lines in the *Contem-*

plations where the hideousness of the animals in the abyss is felt to be the symbol and residue of human evil. Certain traits characteristic of the naturalist give weight to this sometimes facile writing. His musings on the ferocity of carnivorous plants, moreover, incline him toward the eternal Manichaean solution: *"Since nature is artful, scheming, calculating, shouldn't we see in it the spirit of evil? . . . It is through this thought that I descended this evening into an abyss of reflection where I forbid myself your company. Let it suffice that I have given you a glimpse of it."* His love for animals is in part intellectual, born of his penchant for observing forms of life different from ours, the contemplation of which allows us to escape the confines of human conditioning. *"Every animal seems a life imprisoned in a form. The captive soul comes up to gaze at the light through two small attic windows pierced by nature at the top of the prison."* This sympathy extends to the tellurian world of reptiles. Forced to keep to his room by a sprain (he had wanted to prove his agility to a child who was accompanying him—a form of coquetry he would engage in till the end of his life), he amused himself by playing with snakes. *"They were the same ones I used to prowl the woods for at Fontainebleau, together with an old snake catcher. I let them slither about on my table, coil themselves up like a fruit basket, and there raise their crafty heads, darting out their forked tongues like little black flames. I'm fascinated by all these movements, which bespeak such graceful vigilance. I watched as they entwined themselves around the furniture, forming ornaments that would have inspired a sculptor."*

It is curious to see the man who loved boars and snakes, who felt himself *"part of the great family of all living things,"* contend so rancorously against Darwinism and take umbrage at the idea that he might have descended from the primates. He accepts the notion of a ladder leading by degrees from the black night of the animal kingdom to what he assumes is the broad daylight of man, but the triumphant positivism of the Darwinists offends both his humanism and his Christianity. We too easily forget that evolutionary theory passed rapidly from the level of scientific hypothesis to that of the sorts of debates which pit Monsieur Homais against the curé Bournisien. On the latter plane, to view man as the descendant of animal species was, in effect, an antispiritualist position, tending to disparage mankind rather than stress the existence of a mystical chain of creatures, which the Darwinists of the Café du Commerce, and even those of the laboratories, cared very little about. Octave Pirmez could not have foreseen the work of Teilhard de Chardin or a time when the most advanced minds within the Church would ally themselves with evolutionism just as it was ceasing to be a monolithic dogma for scientists.

This man who is so impressed by the stately longevity of great works of nature frowns at the discoveries of geologists and paleontologists, because these contradict biblical chronology. But if so many fine minds (among whom, when all is said and done, he counts himself) have been content for generations, despite the evidence of common sense, with the meager six thousand years of the Judeo-Christian past, it is doubtless because those six thousand years, which correspond roughly to the span of human memory, seem to constitute for most of mankind the extreme limit of the dawning of consciousness. The thousands of centuries of geological drama have no meaning for Octave Pirmez, just as light-years mean nothing to the readers of today's newspapers, who imagine they are on the verge of landing on the star Alpha Centauri. The one hundred and twenty generations that, in Octave's view, separated him from Adam were already enough to plunge him into a yawning abyss. Here there was a dangerous corner of ignorance, or rather of obscurantism. The Octave who was so moved by the splendid clockwork of the heavens (he would sometimes remember that in the time it took him to walk from the window to his worktable, the earth had hurtled forward in its orbit more than a thousand leagues) did not realize that in the sixteenth century he would have opposed Copernicus, just as in the nineteenth century he was opposing Lamarck and Darwin.

The fiery Rémo likewise had tics and prejudices that were typical of his age. His positivism, which he arrived at by means of the most exhausting mental asceticism, had all the rigidity of a dogma. During his voyage to the mouth of the Danube, having met a band of gypsies one evening, he snatches his hand away from the old woman who tries to read his future, affronted as if he had received an obscene solicitation, and mutters something about *"superstitions that have taken such advantage of the credulity of cowardly minds."* It does not occur to him to wonder whether a slender thread of truth might not be intertwined with the professional commonplaces of the prophetess: the age of parapsychological research (a fine name that allows one to study yesterday's rejected doctrines without examining magical bric-à-brac) has not yet dawned. The admirable young man suffers above all from the flaw that for two centuries has characterized leftist thought: optimism. Like his idols Michelet and Hugo, he believes that man is good, not only in his mythical and primal form but even today, and in the street. He accepts, just as they are, the premises favored by the advanced minds of his day. What does it matter that industrial blight is consuming the woods and countryside of Acoz, so dear to his brother, if industry will put an end to poverty? He believes—and the belief drives him to despair—that it will take centuries to free the black peoples of Africa. On the other hand, American slavery seems to him to have been abolished once and for all by Lincoln; he does not even imagine that the humiliation of people of color could be perpetuated under other names and in other forms.

Closer to home, his pen endows the laboring man with all the picturesqueness of a color lithograph: "*Come with me,*" he says in Paris to his older brother; "*let's go into that shabby-looking tavern, a workingmen's haunt. See how trustingly they speak with one another, those companions, and how they clasp one another's rough, dirty hands. They are the very soul of humanity . . . Can you believe that those hardworking men could ever wish anyone evil?*"

"*Yes, alas, out of ignorance,*" Octave murmurs diffidently.

"*Well, that ignorance must be resisted . . . We must arm those generous souls with thoughtful minds . . . They must learn how to do without the support of the powerful and, fortified by education, find help within themselves.*"

This demagogic rhetoric is worth no more than Octave's doctrinaire eloquence. Rémo does not sense that some of the passion that draws him to the common people derives from the immense need for camaraderie on the part of an adolescent whose social relationships have been excessively limited and who idealizes the "lower classes" from afar. These workingmen, who are as conventional as Octave's Capri fishermen, are characters of legend, just like the warriors in Slavic ballads and Kolokotronis's followers—so admired by those two brothers—who died bidding one another farewell with kisses. Without knowing it, Octave and Rémo aspire to a world of heroic simplicity and virile energy that is different from the bourgeois milieu in which they grew up. And the young enthusiast is not wrong: ignorance is at the bottom of all our errors, and knowledge is their cure. But the ignorance at issue here is more formidable than ordinary illiteracy and is not the sort that primary school can eliminate overnight. Rémo has been torn, as if by pincers, by the dilemma he confronts—on the one hand the goodness of man, which he believes in, and on the other the imperfection of human societies—just as innumerable Christians have been torn as they confronted both the existence of evil and the omnipotence of God. Embittered by the present, he needs to believe in the imminence of the Golden Age: *"To hope that the day is approaching when, by the increasing spread of education, the triumphs of brute force and cunning will be rendered impossible—that is my joy."* This awkward effusion of faith takes place two or three years before Sadowa and Sedan, fifty years before the trenches of 1914 (the village of Acoz will be burned, and the curé and three inhabitants executed), and a bit less than three-quarters of a century before the concentration camps (Hermann and his son will fall victim to Nazi bullets), the bombing of Hiroshima, and the mass defoliation of forests. But the pupil of the philosophers has formulated the problem precisely: he would believe in the future happiness of humanity if he did not know mankind to be full of vices and virtues, *"if, denying free will, I were certain of the destiny of the Good."*

Octave Pirmez wrote somewhere that one passes from love of beauty to love of truth and from love of truth to love of justice, rather than the other way around. He was no doubt thinking of his brother, but he himself underwent a process of evolution that partly relieved him of the romantic aestheticism that makes him seem (too often, I must say, for a reader saturated with Proust) like a sort of counterpart to the languid Legrandin of Méséglise. Neither a fighter nor a reformer, he was a privileged member of a system whose hateful aspects he clearly saw, and it was already a great deal for him to have perceived the drama of the workers' and peasants' wretchedness, which so many of the people in his social milieu denied and which almost all closed their eyes to. It is said that toward the end of his life he was bankrupting himself with almsgiving, the only type of aid he was in a position to offer. Yet we would have to be better informed than we currently are to know the truth of this statement, which all too often a person's family or friends will make casually or else for reasons all their own. His reflections on the functioning of what is called justice are audacious, if one takes into account the orthodoxy of his milieu regarding the defense of the social order. *"In the monstrousness of the crime,"* he writes, a Dostoevskian without knowing it, *"one ought sometimes to find extenuating circumstances."* This evidently represented something different from, and more than, the effect of his few sessions as juror in the law court at Mons. *"Consider that one is oneself a mass of incomprehensible virtues and vices, so closely interconnected, by a secret law, that the virtues tend to degenerate into vices and the vices are transformed into virtues."* He has made this eminently Christian assertion about himself: *"Every man is covered with stains of night."* Already we are verging on the "Do not judge" of André Gide.

There was some merit in speaking of the precariousness of civilization itself, at a time when the elite were gorging themselves on material progress (as well as on the profits that it brought them) and lulling themselves with the illusion of moral progress. *"He who would embrace in a single glance all the peoples on the face of the earth would be appalled at the savagery of men. Civilization is achieved only at certain points, and as soon as it seems to have reached its apogee, a convulsion destroys it."* He, too, however, as did Rémo not long ago, tries at least to hope for *"an imperceptible increase in clarity."* But the reality of the present and of the immediate future contradicts these dreams.

Around 1880, he describes to José a walk that he has just taken up one of the Rhenish hills:

"The view plunges toward the fertile plains of the Rhine, which bristle here and there with mountains that in the old days were strongholds. I thought of the misfortunes of those times that made it necessary to build such redoubtable fortresses, nowadays appreciated only as ruins. But my sympathies lead me more readily toward the ruins of monasteries . . . Amid the crumbling towns, I see only the marks of hatred and violence.

"I was just at this point in my reflections when the rhythmic sound of galloping horses reached me in the courtyard. It was a squadron of Prussian hussars riding through the streets of the city with sabers drawn. Barbarism is not dead: it slumbers, awaiting only the hour of reveille. Passing once more across the plain before returning to my hotel, I found myself in the village of Muffendorf, consisting of a long, narrow street lined with earthen houses whose blackish timbers traced a patchwork in their façades. Nothing could be more wretched or more sordid, and it was surprising to see this in such a prosperous region."

Compassion—a more explicit word than pity, since it emphasizes the experience of suffering with those who suffer—is not, as is too widely believed, an emotion that is weak or characteristic of weak men, one that could be placed in opposition to the more virile passion of justice; far from according with a sentimental conception of life, this pity raised to a white heat inflicts its knifelike pain only on those who, strong or not, brave or not, intelligent or not (such qualities are beside the point), have been granted the horrible gift of looking the world full in the face and seeing it as it is. From the moment one has experienced this inverse ecstatic vision, one never again speaks of beauty except with certain reservations. As early as the *Days of Solitude*, a poignant detail appears here and there amid the romantic rhetoric. One would expect that this young man of twenty-six, a passionate reader of Theocritus and Virgil, meeting some shepherds of the Roman Campagna, would shape this encounter into an idyllic description from which every incongruous detail would be eliminated. *"In a clearing located on the edge of the fields and separated from them only by a hedge of viburnum, I saw two dying lambs dangling from the branches of an ash tree. The shepherd had just slit their throats with his knife, and while pale streams of blood rained down on the moss, the ewes bleated, huddling close together with lowered heads. Such was, for me, the pastoral beauty of the land of the Sabines."*

As Octave is leaving Italy, returning to France by the Alpine route, he meets a small, exhausted group of travelers making their way on foot through the frost and the snow, numb with cold, dressed in rags and battered hats. They are former soldiers of Garibaldi's who are leaving their country to seek, far away, a freighter that will take them to Argentina. *"One of them, pale from hardship, had climbed up the craggy slope, and there, in a delirium of wretchedness, he was singing in a guttural voice: 'Dansa, canta, poverello . . .' His companions responded with despairing laughter, which was drowned in the noise of the foaming creek."* A romantic scene, reminiscent of Doré; but it brings the Italian voyage to a close with an image other than one of cathedrals, vineyards, and sun-drenched ruins. During this same journey through the Alps, Octave thinks of the animals that are pulling the coach: *"We were being drawn along by fourteen brave and patient mules. What a strange sight they were, those poor creatures white with hoarfrost, jingling their bells in a frozen wasteland lit by the melancholy light of the stars . . . We had arrived at the hamlet of Grand'Croix. Henceforth at the mercy of a single horse, whose outsize shadow, cast up on the mountainside, accompanied us like a phantom of sorrow, we began to descend, our sleigh whistling and sighing on the ice."* Beneath the affectation of the style, which is characteristic of the period, pity and sorrow burn like the ice itself.

The chasm grew wider in the works that followed. And finally, stretching out and falling away like a drop of clear water, come several incantatory lines, a canticle of pity that is not so much written as stammered: *"Let the silkworm spin. Do not disturb the eggs of the nesting bird . . . Do not walk on the ice when it is brittle. Do not trample the young shoots. Do not whistle when the migrating cranes seek a quiet refuge. Do not carve your name in the tender tree bark when the spring sap is rising to the topmost branches. Do not jump into the boat that is already heavily laden. Let the snow cover the moss, which is sure to grow green again . . .* A few years before his death, the poet confided to José that his memory had been painfully scarred by the scenes of misery he had witnessed. This capacity to suffer for others, and thus to include in the category of one's fellow creatures not only man but the immense multitude of all living things, is sufficiently rare to be noted with respect.

The correspondence with José might be expected to advance us a bit further in our acquaintance with the poet, but those letters were sorted and revised by Octave himself, shortly before his death, for the purposes of a posthumous edition that he wished to leave behind him as a sort of bouquet of forget-me-nots composed for his friend. As they have come down to us, they consist of miscellaneous writings, more or less successful, but in which the language of everyday life is reduced to the minimum necessary. Amid so many reveries and meditations that are too often bookish in tone, one is in the end charmed to learn that Octave, traveling alone in Germany, drank a bottle of Rhenish wine to José's health and that this fortyish gentleman dreamed of throwing snowballs with his companion. Sometimes we are struck by a more sharply realistic detail: nostalgically evoking a splendid day spent with José deep in the woods at Acoz, Octave mentions that the dogs caught a hare and that the gamekeeper's little boys, elated at the prospect of an improvised meal, cooked what remained of the animal over some burning twigs. Hereditary pleasures won out over *"the angelic life"* that day.

On the subject of hunting, Octave vacillated throughout his life. At twenty, irritated by the presence of gentlemen invited to a shooting party, and in particular by that of Arthur de C. de M., who had arrived eight days before with his servants, his horses, and his carriages, the young man announces that he will take part in *"this tiresome business"* but without a gun. As an old man, suggesting to José that they go for a walk in the woods, he speaks, in contrast, of taking along his carbine, which he now keeps with him at all times, but he stipulates that the animals be left in peace and contents himself with picking a few flowers, even though this gesture *"might seem equally blameworthy to a wise Hindu."* He almost regrets *"bending the grass beneath his feet."* At other times, he becomes once more the scion of that Benjamin Pirmez who, casting about for something to write to his sons at school, informed them proudly that he had already caught his fifty-seventh hare that season. The companion of the snake killer, the solitary who went walking with his boar and his six half-wild dogs—the pointer, the griffon, the setter, the sheepdog, the snow-white Saint Bernard, and the greyhound Schnell (as we shall see, he rather liked to let Schnell molest strangers)—the man who broke the wingtips of his caged hawks and owls to prevent them from resuming their predatory habits was not always the gentle dreamer that legend has made of him.

Félicien Rops, who was one of his friends at school and whose engravings he collected, wrote somewhere that *"this abstracter of quintessences was at heart a gay and lively fellow"* but that, anxious to preserve for his readers *"the ideality of a mask,"* he revealed himself as such only to his close friends. What did

Rops mean by that? Should we imagine an Octave telling jokes to his cronies at dinner and accompanying them on their trysts with ladies of the evening? An Octave doing honor to the fine little restaurants of the Grand-Place (*"It is when he is at table that man best reveals whether he is the master or the slave of his brutal instincts"*)? An Octave plunging into high-spirited intrigues *à la* Faublas or, wreathed in cigar smoke in the privacy of Rops's atelier, commenting animatedly on the engraver's erotica? Rops did not sufficiently take into account the way in which timid and melancholic people are subject to sudden accesses of gaiety, whether they are reacting against themselves or whether they are trying, as is most often the case, to put others on the wrong track. And one must consider this latter possibility in connection with a man who came from a severely formal milieu such as the one in which Madame Irénée kept Octave. The lover of masks could at various times wear that of the jolly companion, the careless roué, or simply the worthy Belgian— false faces that were even more blatantly artificial than the black velvet mask he wore in his role as romantic young prince. His true face, whatever it was, lay beneath all that.

The somewhat acerbic remarks of the free-spoken engraver are nevertheless justified by a letter Octave wrote to Félicien Rops dated March 20, 1874. Félicien had taken it into his head to publish in a small Parisian newspaper a few of his own letters to Octave, decorated with sketches and with vignettes of little cupids. If one is to believe Octave, these missives were *"light and fanciful in tone,"* and the addressee was liable to be suspected of having answered in the same spirit.

"I know that you can do as you like when it comes to publishing the letters you have written to your friends, and I would be ill-advised to want to oppose this, since you have right—that is to say, might

*—on your side. I would simply like to submit the following to your
judgment and your heart:*

*"For twenty years I have been laboring patiently and tenaciously
to create a consistent body of work that is elevated in style and
essentially serious in nature, sacrificing all my impulses toward levity
so as to allow only the emotional and philosophical side of me to
survive, and, so to speak, arranging the folds of my shroud every
day, so that the breath of time might not disturb them.*

"It is in my gravity alone that I wish to appear before the world.

*". . . I have spent delightful hours with you, during which we
yielded to our natural expansiveness and to a thousand caprices of
the imagination . . . But ought this private life to be displayed in
some newspaper and introduced into cafés and taverns? . . . I beg
of you: replace my name with a pseudonym."*

Even taking into account the social conventions of his day,
this forty-two-year-old man who was so embarrassed by the
letters written in his youth, and even by their reflection on
another person, reminds us of those "whited sepulchers" whose
presence in that same milieu Rémo had bitterly denounced.
Octave, in agreement with the rest of the family, had smoothed
the folds of Rémo's shroud as best he could. By his own admission, he spent the rest of his life doing the same for himself.
Rops's work being what it is—sometimes striking and somber,
often distorted, lewd, and coarse—one can understand why any
publicity based on correspondence between the two men might
have alarmed the lover of idealism. In addition, he may have
feared that the reprinting would come to the attention of Madame Irénée, even though she assuredly was not a regular reader
of *La Vie Parisienne* or any other paper of the same ilk in which
Rops proposed to publish the letters. Wherever one goes, falsehood reigns. In the twentieth century, which is crude, garish,

and loud, it most frequently takes the form of imposture; in the nineteenth century, a more subdued age, it took the form of hypocrisy.

There exists a curious portrait of Octave Pirmez left to us by a contemporary. Paradoxically, it was written by a railway engineer, a man of science for whom literature was merely a hobby. In 1879, four years before the poet's death, the young James Vandrunen was commissioned to survey the future site of a junction of two railway lines that would in effect divide the estate of Acoz. No doubt concerned about the way in which the owner would react to this project, the young man paid him a visit. He found the master of the property in a rectangular courtyard resembling that of a zoo, ringed as it was with cages in which were snarling, growling, yelping, and howling a variety of those wild animals that Octave kept near him for the purpose, he said, *"of teaching him pride."* A pack of dogs descended upon the intruder, baring their teeth, and the mild-mannered poet said not a word to restrain the beasts. Young James kept them at bay with the aid of an iron spike supplied by a railwayman who was accompanying him. A bit shaken, he presented his petition, which Octave listened to absentmindedly, though he broke in to say that the affairs of Acoz were of no interest to him. James, disconcerted, passed once more through the gateway in the fence, which was adorned with the remains of an owl that had been nailed to the planks. The master of the house evidently respected the worthy old customs of his gardeners.

James returned some days later and found himself once again in the presence of the gentleman in the dark gray jacket, his felt hat cocked over one ear, his useless gun slung over his shoulder, and a book in his hand. This time he was well received, and Octave, speaking with the glibness of a man who wishes to distract himself, suggested to his young visitor that they make a tour of the grounds. Feeling uneasy, as an engineer might feel today in the face of someone contesting the usefulness of a highway, James listens to his host disparage the railroads and define the industry as *"a collection of noises and timetables"* whose sole aim is to make a profit. He achieves nothing today (the project will succeed at a later date), but he has, without quite knowing how, conquered his adversary. Often, as he is working at his surveying out in the open country, he spies the fellow coming toward him, clad in leggings, bent on persuading him to take another stroll, sometimes talking feverishly and unburdening to the young stranger his metaphysical doubts and fears, other times in silence, overcome by a fierce sullenness. Each man is curious about the other. As they walk, James observes, as if furtively, that delicate, childlike face *"bearing the traces of gentle weariness,"* that mouth *"with its slightly pained smile"* from which issues *"a reedy voice"*; notices in his conversation signs of impatience and fretful anger *"like those of a woman before an unyielding lock."* The solitary of Acoz, for his part, is almost avidly interested in his young companion; he stops, looks at him, asks questions that the other man considers irrelevant: *"No doubt you're a nervous person?"*

He was himself nervous, and his relationship with his brother betrayed the same febrility. Octave, naturally, had begun by considering himself the protector of this child who was not yet called Rémo. When he had invited young Fernand to come with him on his first journey and asked him where he wanted to go, the little boy had answered, *"Very far away!"* That time, he had taken him to Hanover. But Rémo had gone far in every domain, and farther than his elder brother. Even prior to his courses of instruction at Weimar and Jena, the student-turned-guardian-angel, having put aside his own work at the

University of Brussels, spent long weeks revising the manuscript of Octave's first literary effort, making Octave reduce by half the five hundred pages in which he had been floundering for years. As a result, Rémo had failed his own examinations. This boy of seventeen, out of a concern for impartiality rare at any age, had done nothing to soften the expression of ideas that he deplored in his brother. (*"Would you have acted the same way toward me?"* he later asked bitterly.) He is afraid only of seeing the irresolute poet fall prey to his own caprices. *"I advise you to reread entirely the notebook full of comments I wrote for you last winter,"* he will say later. *"Do you perhaps remember it? Please believe, fratello mio, that it is not out of some foolish pride that I evoke this memory. I wish our past to be useful to your future. I would consider myself adequately repaid for several years of youth that I sacrificed completely to your ideas."* In his letters from Greece, he reiterates the apprehension he feels on account of Octave's literary anxieties and uncertainties, showering his brother, who is eleven years older than he is, with almost maternal admonitions (*"Go horseback riding less often; don't go hunting"*). After Rémo's death, Octave will remember that whenever they went walking together along a steep mountain path or a precipitous riverbank, the young man would always take the side nearest the void, fearing that his companion might let his mind wander or might suffer a sudden attack of vertigo. He once described a frequently recurring dream in which he was threatened by some deadly peril and rescued by his young brother. *"But you're dead!"* the astonished dreamer would cry. *"Don't speak to me about myself,"* Rémo would answer characteristically. *"I don't know."*

It is always hazardous to explain the life of a man in terms of the single chapter of it he has recounted for us. Octave had lived twenty-five years before Rémo assumed precisely this place in his life. Some incident we know nothing about, some encounter in the course of his travels, or perhaps that adolescent passion he continually thinks back on may have marked and bruised him more than the fortunes of Rémo. One senses that this reader of Theocritus acquired a taste for adolescent beauty at an early age. When still quite young, on the banks of the Sambre, he had watched the village children as they fished; the grace of their movements and their half-naked bodies had made him forget that the boys were there only *"to lie in wait for prey"* and had filled him with *"the same emotions that the Parthenon frieze would later inspire."* At the age of twenty, more dandy than student, he had dreamed of finding a handsome driver for his tilbury—a lad with all the beauty of one of Pinturicchio's page boys or an ephebe of Praxiteles. At twenty-six he brought back from Italy his young groom Giovanni, who soon created difficulties for him; subsequently, his faithful groom Guillaume became the companion of his forest excursions. As an old man he took under his wing a little boy from the village and, we are told, made the error *"of becoming attached to certain children who did not always deserve it and of displaying a princely generosity toward them."* Octave, who had once been touched by the epitaph on the ancient tomb of a master and servant buried side by side, surely sensed the poetry inherent in such allegedly unequal attachments, but the least that can be said is that they were not animated by the breezes of the mind.

Those breezes blew violently, in contrast, on his friendship with the younger of his two brothers. It is true that after the *"fatal accident,"* he himself described, with an acuteness that for once was almost Proustian, the first stages in the process of forgetting. But this forgetting extended only to the bright regions of consciousness: layers of blackness continued to fill up the deeper hollows. Octave tells us that he loved his brother in his *"ephemeral friends."* It seems that he continued, especially, to need that affection founded on brotherly trust; to need those conversations in which two minds unite with and confront each other in a kind of virile marriage, bringing into their relations the world of ideas, the world of dreams, and, quite simply, the World; to need that ambiguous situation in which the protector is at the same time the protected. Even at a distance, even when viewed with misgivings, Rémo sustained Octave with his strength. José seems, afterward, to have served as a rather pale substitute for the departed, although one cannot overlook the sweet comfort that this friendship must have afforded a weary man. During the walks described above, James Vandrunen took the place of José.

The death of Octave Pirmez seems to have been as banal as a death can be. For months he had been suffering from tightness in his chest, pains in his back, edema in his legs. In February 1883 he summoned the village curé to hear his confession and asked pardon from the assembled servants for any impatience he might have shown them. His young nieces decided to make a novena for him. His health subsequently improved: at the end of April he was feeling well enough to pay and receive visits; one evening he lingered over the details of his instructions to his gardener. The next night his illnesses suddenly reappeared: *"I see no way out; this is the end. Farewell, Emile! Forgive me, Lord! Forgive me, Mother!"* He died the death of a well-behaved child, which in certain aspects of his character he always had been.

Madame Irénée, who recorded these details, deplores the loss that Belgium sustained in the person of this writer "who made use of his impressive gifts only for the glory of God." She points out that the titles of her Octave's works, with the exception of *Leaves* and *Letters to José*, were ones that she herself had chosen. This means she was responsible for three titles that could hardly have demanded much creative effort, but Irénée wanted above all to prove that she had been her son's adviser until the end. She did not anticipate surviving him very long, she said. But one is always mistaken about death. She outlived by many years not only Octave but also Emile, who died the following year, and Zoé, her younger sister. The last of the Drion girls was hardy. As late as 1894 my mother paid a brief and respectful visit to this great-aunt so burdened with mourning.

It seems unlikely that Octave's highly discreet death could give rise to legends. They did spring up, however, as they always do on the graves of poets. One of them, which found its way into a few written texts, is so hopelessly romantic that it makes us smile: Octave is supposed to have caught a chill while playing the violin, alone in the woods, on a beautiful moonlit night. This is nevertheless the only legend that is partly based on fact. Since the days when it had soothed his unhappiness in secondary school, music had remained one of his passions, just as it had been for his brother, and he liked to hear it mingled with the sounds and scents of the forest. One of his letters mentions a Mendelssohn sonata that he played every evening deep in the woods on his precious Guarnerius. He adds that he long ago put an end to this sort of pleasure. Madame Irénée, however, notes that she was concerned, several days before her son's death, to see him linger outdoors with his violin on a damp April evening. Also, it was known in the village that the humblest group of strolling musicians, the humblest organ-grinder, the humblest little Italian guitarist strumming his Neapolitan refrains on the highroad were warmly received at the château by the man who was still known as "the young master" and who delighted in listening to them as they played camouflaged behind the thickets. These caprices reminiscent of Beckford or Ludwig II had evidently made an impression.

Other reports, ones without any foundation whatsoever, concern an attack on the part of some vagabond or poacher. They were doubtless inspired by the nocturnal walks that the solitary took, invariably armed with his carbine; by what was known of his too ready hospitality and generosity; and especially by people's immense and almost panicky fear of the bandits who infested the entire countryside. Last, some spoke in hushed tones of an accident comparable to the one that had recently carried off Rémo, of a gun that Octave on his walks had not known was loaded. The pious falsehoods that had surrounded the death of the young brother would explain this proliferation of fanciful rumors. A bit of poetic imagination came into play here, since everyone agreed that the incident that eventually caused the poet's death occurred at night, in those woods he considered a sacred place and where he had carved here and there on the tree trunks the words that evidently were the leitmotiv of his forest reveries: NOX—LUX—PAX—AMOR.

It is not only the precise notes made by Madame Irénée and the letters of the ailing man himself but also Octave's own temperament that argues, if there were any need, against a suicide attempt. The subject preoccupied him, as was only natural. He felt that voluntary death was, for certain people—among whom he certainly included Rémo—an ardent affirmation of life, the result of a surfeit of energy that was foreign to his own nature. What is more, his Christianity rejected this gateway out. We would thus have said everything there is to say about the matter, if we did not know the facility with which any man, even one more steadfast than Octave, may commit acts that he disapproves of or that contradict his beliefs, or at least jostle them until they make him dizzy. The wish to die could have been one of his *"stains of night."* Characteristically, at the age of twenty he had regretted he was no longer twelve; at forty-four he said he had ceased lamenting the death of Maurice de Guérin, whose work he passionately admired: *"He did well to die; he would have been sixty-six today."* At fifty he vacillated, by his own admission, between fear of death and weariness of life. At least a part of him aspired to escape from time, *"that restless sea on which forms float."* Often, in cases like this, everything happens as if the weary man's body took it upon itself to make the decision that his spirit did not dare to make. For Octave, acquiescence takes place on the physiological level, or rather on the alchemical, where the human being witnesses as if from outside, and without fully comprehending, a process of dissolution that it has unwittingly provoked. No violent gesture, no melodramatic scene was necessary. *"This perfectly natural thing, metamorphosis."* Death triumphed without any need for a Guarnerius played by moonlight, a blow from some peasant, or an absentmindedly discharged gun.

His life, which at first glance seems to us almost scandalously easy, doubtless had cost him exhausting effort. To his family, to the provincial upper-middle-class milieu whose obtuseness he condemned in terms sometimes as bitter as his brother's, and last to the worthy principles he always adhered to, he had made concessions in minor things, and in major ones as well. On other points he had displayed the powerful force of inertia that is so characteristic of the weak. His parents, and later his widowed mother, must have dreamed that he would achieve great things in secondary school and college, but he was not cut out for such successes; then they must have pointed out to him the advantages of one of those fine careers that were traditional in the family (*"I will not manage our estates; I do not intend to settle down anywhere; I will hold fast to my mountaintop"*).

It had been the same with marriage. This dandy, who admitted that he was a mediocre dancer and that he didn't know how to converse with young ladies about trifles, was urged to note the example of his cousin Arthur, who, after seeming for years to be stubbornly averse to conjugal bliss, had married his cousin Mathilde, a charming young woman and a good match. Later, Emile's marriage to the daughter of a senator had been the crowning happiness for Madame Irénée ("This is the most wonderful day of my life") and led her to hope that Octave might follow this good example. She hoped in vain. Matters were complicated by the mores of the age, which were rigorous on this point: when Octave merely confesses to an old right-thinking friend that he is engaged in a liaison *"with a blonde,"* the worthy fellow spouts fire and flame and begs him to break with her or marry her immediately, a dilemma that perhaps did not arise. The complexities of the heart and senses were given no legitimacy at all in this very proper milieu.

The intellectual aberrations of his young brother, *"that unfortunate boy,"* had apparently given rise within the family to endless debates, whose traces are discernible in Octave's books when these are carefully read. On this point, Octave had vacillated sufficiently to incur the reproaches of the one who was to depart so abruptly. To readers of today, his book on Rémo seems marred by hollow rhetorical formulas and vitiated by untruths so clumsily expressed, insofar as his protagonist's final moments are concerned, that one feels he hoped his readers would see through it. The prohibitions and constraints that weighed on Octave must have been severe, for in 1952 the author of a conformist biography of the poet still managed to describe Fernand-Rémo vaguely as "pursuing some obscure chimera" and to ignore his liberalism, his pacifism, and his positivism while camouflaging the drama of his disagreements with his family. The same biographer disdainfully applies the word "novel" to the only work in which Octave, drawing on his brother's letters, ventured to look reality almost squarely in the face. Such methods are not surprising: all too often, biographers suppress or calmly deny what is essential. The fact that Octave first published his little book anonymously in an edition of ten copies and then, encouraged by a few favorable comments, in an edition of one hundred likewise anonymous copies shows to what extent he was walking through a minefield. This diffident work had required courage.

Octave Pirmez once spoke of *"those existences that consume themselves over a strange and unfulfillable desire. However abnormal a hope may be, she always has her lovers."* This quest for the impossible seemed to him destined for a tragic end, whether its goal was truth—and this course was evidently the one he ascribed to Rémo—or beauty, which seems to have been his own aim. Rémo's pilgrimage had quickly ended with the homecoming of the young Siegfried, borne by torchlight along the forest paths; his own concluded more slowly, in a *symphonie pathétique.* His personal sorrows, made even more burdensome by the intolerable weight of the world's pain, were alleviated to a certain extent only by his faith in his powers as a writer. He passed judgment on himself, and did so with penetrating severity. *"I hereby admit,"* he declared as early as 1867 in a letter to Bancel, *"that I haven't the slightest talent. I am slow-witted; my thoughts are labored, as if torn from my flesh; I am as tedious as a translation; and, in truth, the language spoken by my most intimate self is yet to be found."* These signs of discouragement increased rather than decreased as the years passed. He was not unaware that he belonged to that race of stammering geniuses mentioned by Sainte-Beuve. He had arrived at the very impasse he himself had described: at that moment when the prisoner strangles in one of the points of the diamond.

The newspapers in Brussels announced his death in respectful tones. "He was a writer of merit," says *L'Echo du Parlement* laconically. "He was one of our few writers" is the subtle comment of *La Gazette de Bruxelles*, displaying sobriety and discernment. In the local papers, which are more effusive, there are many references to "one of the noblest and most highly respected families of our district," to his "noble and venerable mother," to the "worthy curé" who presided at the funeral, to the "young and personable author" to whom "the elite of the nobility, the clergy, and the local citizenry" had paid tribute. We are also told that the male choir of the village sang at the music lover's funeral. Until the very end he remained the dutiful son, the eternal young gentleman, and the wealthy philanthropist whose loss was lamented by all the charitable societies in the country. Nevertheless, the eulogies were carefully screened by the family before being delivered. They feared that "poor Octave" would be grouped "with the deists, or even with the materialists."

He was laid to rest close to Rémo in the choir of an old ruined church that he, with Madame Irénée's help, had transformed into a mortuary chapel to prevent its demolition. Lightning set fire to the roof in 1921. The monument still exists, hemmed about by the village's newer buildings. It is no longer quite the romantic edifice that the two brothers, raising their eyes from their books, contemplated in the distance beyond the groves of Acoz, thinking that there they would find their eventual resting place.

I transcribe here Octave's *souvenir pieux*, just as, ten years before his death, the poet himself transcribed in his book *Rémo* the death notice of Chancellor Goethe, which had kindly been sent to his brother, then still a student, by an elderly lady of Weimar who had numbered among the great man's acquaintances. In this case, however, the aim is not to compare, as Octave did with regard to the author of *Faust*, glory with immortality. But these few lines show how rapidly time effaces the distinctive features of a man who has been laid to rest in the earth.

Blessed are those who die in the Lord.

In pious memory of Monsieur
OCTAVE-LOUIS-BENJAMIN PIRMEZ
departed this life at the château of Acoz
on May 1, 1883, at the age of 51,
having received the sacraments of the Church.

Whosoever therefore shall confess me before men, him will
I confess also before my Father which is in heaven.
(Matthew, x.32)

I know that my redeemer liveth, and that I shall be brought
to life again on the last day. (Job, xix.25)

He stretched out his hand to the poor; yea, he reached forth
his hands to the needy. (Proverbs, xxxi.20)

I ask only one thing: that you remember me in your prayers.
(Saint Augustine)

Gentle heart of Mary, be thou my refuge. (An indulgence of
100 days)

Merciful Jesus, grant him eternal rest. (An indulgence of 7
years and 7 quarantines)

If I am not mistaken, Octave, who toward the end of his life said that he could no longer find refuge except in prayer, nevertheless mentions Jesus only twice in his work. In *Rémo* he points out that the humanitarian dreams of his day could call the Gospel to witness in defense of their cause; elsewhere, more poignantly, he evokes the tears that Christ shed over Lazarus. This text by Saint John, surpassingly lovely, would have served far better than the handful of all-purpose quotations cited above. Evidently no one thought of it, or perhaps the respectable banality of these customary verses was deemed preferable. Neither was any reference made to Francis of Assisi, his favorite saint.

But the image chosen for this commonplace *In memoriam* is not lacking in charm. In that Sulpician style which in those days still bore faint traces of the grand manner of the seventeenth century, one glimpses a Saint John with flowing locks, clad in regal draperies, gathering in a chalice the blood that drips from the feet of Jesus, who is nailed to a cross of which only the base is visible. This engraving would have pleased the man who strove to do likewise with the blood of Rémo.

Nevertheless, Octave Pirmez had his apotheosis, albeit modest and ephemeral and from an unexpected source. Apparently he followed only from a distance, and as if from above, the Belgian literary movements of his day. He had given De Coster, who died in poverty and obscurity about fifteen years before him, some intelligent advice that accorded with the strange genius of Till Eulenspiegel's father; it is said that he also lent him some money. But *Till*, whose poetic qualities he unfairly denied, doubtless shocked him with its violent realism, and even more with the whiff of revolt that rises from its pages. The homage of the young Georges Rodenbach and the enthusiasm of the young Jules Destrée came too late: he was dying. He did not live to see the brilliant flowering of Belgian poetry, for which he had timidly prepared the way, and it is not certain that his slightly old-fashioned classicism and romanticism would have appreciated these Symbolists. The Naturalist novelists, who strove sometimes clamorously to win recognition in what was then one of the most philistine countries of Europe, must have often shocked the sensibilities of Acoz, if not his own in

226

particular. One can scarcely believe that the somewhat coarse sensualism of Camille Lemonnier, precursor of D. H. Lawrence by half a century, found great favor with this lover of phantoms. Nevertheless, the article on Rémo that Lemonnier published moved Octave profoundly: he felt that he, as well as his brother, had been understood. When the novelist was accused of obscenity and, because of his quarrels with the courts, was forced to decline some national literary prize, the students at the University of Brussels decided that, by way of compensation, they would give him a banquet. They invited Octave, who accepted. He died three weeks before the appointed date. On May 25, 1883, the banquet was held, and an immense bouquet of wildflowers marked the place of the absent poet. His muted message, which he himself considered so imperfect, had thus been understood and received by a few people. He would have been touched by this tribute from what he called *"lighthearted youth."*

Before allowing these two shades to make their way back across death's infernal river, I would like to ask them some questions about myself. But first, I wish to thank them. After a long series of direct and collateral ancestors about whom I know nothing, aside from their dates of birth and death, at last come two minds, two bodies, two voices who express themselves now ardently, now reticently—two beings who can be heard sighing, and sometimes crying out. When, with the aid of fragmentary family recollections, I depict Mathilde, my grandmother, or my grandfather Arthur, I round out their images by using as well, consciously or not, whatever I know about devout wives and respectable landowners of the nineteenth century. In contrast, what I have learned about Octave and Rémo from their scant writings overflows, so to speak, the boundaries of their selves and spills out upon their times.

In order to place these two men once again in their proper perspective, let us review the little troop of human beings—greater than they were, or certainly more illustrious—who likewise "held fast to their mountaintop" during that same part of the century. In 1868, when Rémo is engaged in his struggles, a prey to the horror of universal evil, Tolstoy, lodged at an inn in the miserable Russian hamlet of Azamas, experiences the night of anguish and insight that will unlock doors previously closed to him (or ones he has already opened slightly without being aware of it), making him something more than a man of genius. In September 1872, while Rémo is carefully planning his suicide in Liège, Rimbaud embarks for England with Verlaine and, after this interlude, makes his way toward Harar and his death in a Marseille hospital. Octave, if he had chanced some two years earlier to enter the Cabaret Vert in Charleroi, might have found himself sitting next to this wild-haired boy, who had come on foot from his hometown of Charleville with the draft of "Le Bateau Ivre" in his pocket. I am not about to sketch a scene for a novel: the fiery archangel, his attention at that moment focused on the enormous breasts of the barmaid bringing him his beer, would certainly not have taken this well-dressed gentleman for a pale seraphim, and in the eyes of the latter, the visionary would doubtless have been merely a villain. In 1873, if the sound of Verlaine's gunshot in Brussels had reached Octave's ears, that quarrel between two dubious poets would have seemed to him one of those news items too sordid to be mentioned at the lunch table.

In 1883, less than three months before the death of Rémo's brother, Wagner suffers a heart attack and collapses in a palace in Venice, taking with him the secret of *"those strange melodies"* that had beckoned to the *"radiant soul"* from beyond the threshold. Marx passes away in the same year, preceded seven years before by Bakunin. Ludwig of Bavaria, the solitary of Starnberg, still has three years to battle with his phantoms and with his own flesh ("No more kisses, Sire! No more kisses!") before his plunge into the waters of the lake. Rudolf of Hapsburg, reduced to political impotence by his rank of crown prince, wanders from hunting party to hunting party and from mistress to mistress, following the path that will take him, in January 1889, to Mayerling. His mother, Elizabeth, that beautiful shade, re-reads Heine in her garden on Corfu and, lashed to her mast, revels in the storms that rage on the Grecian seas. Florence Nightingale, after returning from Scutari with heart disease, has been living as an invalid in London for nearly half a century. Dunant, founder of the Red Cross, roams from country to country seeking support for his work, which is still viewed with indifference and suspicion; in 1887, poor and half insane, he will apply for a place in an old-men's home in Appenzell, where he will live on for many years. Nietzsche, at Sils Maria, repelled by the mediocrity of bourgeois Bismarckian Germany, begins in 1883 to wield the lightning and thunderbolts of the Superman. On Christmas Day, 1888, in Turin, worn out, defeated, nearly blind, he will throw himself on the neck of a whipped horse and definitively enter his long twilight. Ibsen, living in Rome, has just written his prophetic play *An Enemy of the People*, in which a man fights alone against the world's physical and moral corruption. Flaubert, prematurely aged, passed away in 1880, as much at a loss as his Bouvard and Pécuchet. ("It seems to me that I am crossing an endless wilderness with no idea of where I am headed . . . It is I who am simultaneously the desert, the traveler, and the camel.") In the year of Octave's death, Joseph Conrad shuttles between Liverpool and Australia. Not until 1887 will he make his way to Brussels to receive his commission as captain of a ship plying the Congo, and not until two years later will he return to that same city, broken in body and soul from having contemplated the "heart of darkness" of colonial exploitation. Rémo, who would have thought and suffered as he did, fortunately died too early to concern himself with this aspect of Africa's tragedy. As for Hugo, the octogenarian prophet who will die in 1885, he is still polishing alexandrines, still making love, thinking about God, pensively contemplating nude women. Tennyson will wait until 1892 before crossing the bar. Next to these names so laden with prestige, it seems absurd to mention Rémo—dead but seeming unburied (as his brother said), surrounded by the public's indifference—and pale Octave, perfunctorily recalled in handbooks of Belgian literature. The two brothers were nonetheless swept away in their turn by the winds gusting high above their era, which seems to us from a distance to be thick and inert, hanging like some enormous cliff over the edge of the abyss of the twentieth century.

These two "great-uncles" are not exactly close relatives of mine, being merely Mathilde's first cousins. Still, the consanguineous marriage of Arthur and Mathilde brings these two shades closer to me, since one-fourth of my blood comes from the same source as one-half of theirs. But such liquid measures prove little. The reader who is curious about these details will already have noticed similarities and differences between the two brothers (themselves so dissimilar) and their distant grandniece. The differences in historical era, destiny, and sex are less significant than one might think, the freedoms and constraints of a young man around 1860 being not unlike those of a young woman around 1930. Most of the analogies are cultural, but beyond a certain point culture represents a choice and brings us back, whether we like it or not, to a network of subtler affinities. Like the two brothers, I read Hesiod and Theocritus under the trees; I unwittingly retraced their travels in a world that was already more damaged and eroded than theirs but that today, at a distance of forty years, seems in contrast almost clean and stable. The similarities and differences stemming from the servitudes of social position and money are less easy to define. In 1930 the former mattered much less, at least to me, than it did to Irénée's sons a half century earlier. Money, *il gran nemico*, but sometimes also the great friend, counts simultaneously for both more and less.

In one respect, at any rate, I find Rémo a bit tiresome. From the time he was twenty, and despite naïve hopes he did not keep, *"the inexhaustible soul"* (as his brother called him) felt the contrast between life, which is intrinsically divine, and what man—or society, which is merely man in the plural—has made of it. The ocean of tears he borrows from the Buddhist sutras by way of Schopenhauer was one whose shores I myself walked along at an early age; my first books prove it to me, at the very places where my memories lose their sharpness. Yet it was not until I was about fifty that his bitterness permeated me body and soul. Unlike Rémo, I cannot boast of having loved only *"that virgin clad in sackcloth: pure thought."* Thought, and sometimes that which goes beyond it, nevertheless did occupy me at a very early age. I did not, like him, die of it at twenty-eight. When I was about twenty I believed, as Rémo had, that the Greek response to human questions was the best if not the only one. I realized later that there is no single Greek response but a series of responses which derive from the Greeks and among which one must choose. Plato's response is not Aristotle's; that of Heraclitus is not that of Empedocles. I noted also that the givens of the problem are too numerous for any single response, whatever it might be, to suffice for all. But Rémo's moment of Hellenic enthusiasm, located somewhere in time between his

Itinerary from Paris to Jerusalem and his *Prayer on the Acropolis*, brings me back to my own youth, and now that all illusions have been dispelled, I still think we were not entirely wrong: "*Amid those ruins,*" he said, "*I remembered the ancients' notion of the Elysian Fields: a place of happiness where one conversed with the souls of the wise . . . What a noble dream! I imagined men who were in no way hindered in their moral development and who in their youth were allowed the freedom to grow strong. They were not wrapped, from the cradle on, in tight swaddling clothes . . . Reading Plato, I was struck by the wholesome atmosphere in which his thought works . . . The finest impression I shall bring back from my journey is that of having felt the beauty of this Greek spirit, white and solid like the marble of Paros.*"

During a stop at the port of Delos, which had not yet been spoiled by organized tourism, the young traveler went wandering one evening through a grove of laurel trees, which almost surely has since been cut down in the course of later archaeological excavations. There he spied a statue dating from Hellenistic times. "*The moon rose slowly, looking like a silver medallion . . . The sea broke on the shore, and I heard nothing but the clamor of the waves.*" Rémo wishes to beautify things, which is equivalent to saying that he wishes to give an impression of the beauty he felt in that sacred place, but his cast of mind engages him, quite unlike Chateaubriand or Renan, in a waking dream or in one of those *Märchen* of the German Romantics, which he had perhaps grown fond of in Weimar. By the light of the moon, he thinks he sees the marble face assume an expression of ineffable suffering: he imagines that he recognizes the triple Hecate, whom Selene represents in celestial form. He assumes that the star received the soul of the goddess whose image lies at his feet and which a ray of moonlight has for an instant brought back to life. *"I am Hecate; I preside over my own expiation for having spilled the blood of so many innocent victims."*

Between the young man of 1864 and his eventual grand-niece, who will herself wander through this part of the world around 1930, thousands of pilgrims have passed by these same sites; others, crowds of them, have come there since. How many have given thought to the animals that were sacrificed daily on these marble altars adorned only with boughs? This shared preoccupation unites us. But the reign of Hecate has not yet ended, as Rémo seemed to believe it had. In the past century, billions of animals have been sacrificed to science, which has become a goddess and, from goddess, a bloodthirsty idol, as happens almost inevitably with deities. Slowly strangled, smothered, blinded, burned, cut open alive, they die in ways that make the sacrificer of antiquity seem innocent, as do our slaughterhouses, where the animals are strung up alive to facilitate the killers' repetitive work, making the mallet of the hecatombs and the victims garlanded with flowers seem comparatively decent. As for human sacrifices, which the Greeks relegated to the age of legends, they have been committed in our own day to some extent nearly everywhere—inflicted by thousands of men on millions of men, in the name of fatherland, race, or class. The ineffable sadness of that marble face has surely deepened.

With Octave, whose character is more vague, my relations are less easily defined. I described earlier his fervent desire to reveal only what he deemed best in himself: when I was twenty, I would have understood this. At that age, my ambition was to remain the anonymous author (or one known at most by a name and by two perhaps disputed dates) of five or six sonnets that might win the admiration of half a dozen people in any generation. It was not long before I gave up thinking this way. Literary creation is a torrent that carries everything along with it; in this stream our personal characteristics are, at the most, sediments. A writer's vanity or modesty counts for little in the presence of that great natural phenomenon for which it serves as a theater. Nevertheless, compared with the unhealthy exhibitionism of our own day, Octave's reserve, though likewise unhealthy, is appealing to me.

All attention now, I listen to his various reflections on history. At best, history is a source of examples for him, as it was for most of the worthy minds of ages past and as it is becoming again for us in times of adversity. Nevertheless, I hear resounding within him a more intimate note. As he sits among the tiers of the Colosseum, thinking of the young Christians who were said to have been martyred in this place, he is overcome with anguish at the thought that the sufferings of a multitude of young unknown victims, who are in a way summed up in the lovely form of Saint Sebastian, will always remain for him the object of a generalized pity; he will never know the slightest pang of those vanished agonies. It is a wave of melancholy not very different from that which grips him whenever he thinks of the unknowns, his contemporaries, whom he could have loved but whom he can never possibly meet amid the millions who inhabit the earth. The historian-poet and novelist that I have tried to become are continually struggling with this impossibility. Octave did not do so to the same extent, but I admire his gesture—his outstretched arms.

There is a touch of the miracle in every coincidence. Octave, visiting the Uffizi around 1865, notes along the way those paintings that have made the greatest impression on him. His taste is somewhat different from ours, aesthetics being a perpetual seesaw. He still admires the academicians, then at the peak of their glory—Domenichino, Guercino, Guido Reni—and with them the *"radiant realism"* of Caravaggio, all of whom the two or three subsequent generations would spurn and who in our own day are once more winning favor. He already likes Botticelli, whose paintings would cause people to swoon almost indiscreetly for fifty years. But the work that he describes in greatest detail and to which he devotes an entire page is one of those primitives that he still considers delightfully maladroit, *The Thebaid of Egypt*, attributed in those days to Laurati and since then to several others. It is the same painting whose photograph, half icon, half talisman, I took with me everywhere for twenty years. In a landscape that is desertlike and pure but enlivened here and there with a Tuscan grove and a chapel of quiet Florentine grace, mystical monks are taming gazelles, dancing with bears, harnessing tigers, ambling about on docile deer; they converse with the lions who will bury them in the sand at the end of their days; they live familiarly with hares, herons, angels. I am amazed, perhaps naïvely, that this image, which to me represents perfect life, represented angelic life to "Uncle Octave."

During the summer of 1879 or 1880, the poet, wearing his handsome suit of white rep and doubtless a straw hat purchased in Italy, is walking along the beach at Heyst. It was in this little fishing village on the coast of West Flanders that I set the episode in *The Abyss* in which Zeno, fleeing Bruges, which has become a deathtrap for him, attempts to find passage to England or Zeeland and gives up, disgusted by the baseness, the double-dealing, and the arrant foolishness of the people who offer to help him escape. At the time, poring over a road map of Flanders, I had looked for the places closest to Bruges that would have allowed the fugitive to embark without being closely observed and that this vigorous man of fifty-eight could have reached on foot. I also had to avoid names that sounded like advertisements for bargain vacations on the North Sea: Wenduyne, Blankenberge, Ostend. Heyst had an unmistakably Flemish ring to it without being associated with tourists, and at the same time was close enough to Bruges for my purposes. Of course, I did not yet know that Octave and his mother, disdaining the casinos and cocottes of the fashionable resorts, had chosen this out-of-the-way spot for a summer holiday eighty years earlier.

Between the sixteenth century and 1880, the place had no doubt changed very little. Nonetheless, the town fathers had built a seawall (a sine qua non of coastal resorts) and very probably a bandstand for concerts as well. Stylish villas did not yet mar the dunes. *"The beach is nearly deserted. Ten or twelve fishing boats come at night to cast their anchors on the sand, unloading the strangely shaped fish they have netted from the ocean's depths. In the morning the bathing huts are rolled down to the shore, and women emerge from them to swim in the sea. Young foreigners who a short while ago were strolling on the seawalls in their elegant dresses have come to do battle with the great foaming waves,"* and their fearful, childish movements make them dear to him, because their weakness is thus proved.

Leaving his mother ensconced in a sheltered armchair to absorb as much of the bracing sea air as is needed, and no more, he walks by himself toward the water, now at low tide. He wishes *"to hear the expanse quiver,"* as he puts it. He is sad. Anxious not to get his shoes wet, he carefully skirts the great gleaming pools left a few hours earlier by the receding water. He dislikes the sea—*la mer.* (Psychoanalysts will no doubt pounce on this remark; but only in French is it a play on words, mer, sea, being a homonym for *mère*, mother.) *"O poor village of Heyst—how bleak you are, and how pale your sea!"* He is looking forward to greeting José, who has sent word that he will be arriving in a few days, a human presence that will cheer him after all his gazing at the waves. *"Nature is champing at the bit. She is not satisfied with her lot; she aspires to break her invisible chains and to fill the observer's soul with great uneasiness. The sight of this immense slavery distracts him from the sufferings of his fellow men; social injustices and private griefs fade before his eyes. He could eventually conclude that might indeed makes right . . . The nobility that people ascribe to the sea escapes me. I see only violence, fever, a succession of attacks, falls, and retreats."* In that tumult of matter crashing against the breakwater, he senses the voracity of a multitude of creatures hideous to look upon.

Suddenly, in the bright light of midday, appears a shabbily dressed man who walks past him and the English ladies without seeing them. *Aqua permanens.* The vast expanse of water, so terrifying to Octave, is a purifying element to this stranger. For him the surf and its dispassionate violence, the infinity of sand grains encompassed in his every stride, and the pure curve of each seashell compose a mathematical, perfect world that compensates for the atrocious one in which he must live. He takes off his clothes; at this moment he is no longer a man of the sixteenth century but simply a man, a man thin and robust, already advanced in years, with his well-muscled arms and legs, his prominent ribs, his gray-haired sex. Soon he will die a harsh death in a Bruges prison, but these dunes and this border of waves are the abstract site of his true death, the place where he has eliminated all evasion and compromise from his thoughts. The lines that intersect between this naked man and this gentleman in the white suit are more complex than merely those of different time zones. Zeno precedes Octave at this point on the globe by three centuries, twelve years, and one month almost to the day, but I shall not create him until forty years later, and the episode of the swim off the beach at Heyst will not take shape in my mind until 1965. The only link between these two men—the invisible one, who does not yet exist but who carries with him his clothes and accoutrements of the sixteenth century, and the dandy of 1880, who in three years will be a phantom—is the fact that a little girl to whom Octave enjoys telling stories bears suspended within her, infinitely potential, a part of what I shall someday become. As for Rémo, he, too, is somewhere in this scene, a filament in the consciousness of his melancholy older brother. Eight years earlier he suffered a bloody death comparable to that of the man of 1568, albeit briefer, but the account of it will not become known to me until 1971. Time and dates ricochet, just as the sun's rays ricochet off the tidal pools and grains of sand. My relations with these three men are very simple. For Rémo I feel an ardent respect. "Uncle Octave" sometimes moves me and sometimes irritates me. But Zeno I love like a brother.

FERNANDE

$\mathbf{M}$athilde's death did not bring about great changes in the daily routine at Suarlée. Fräulein had years before assumed the roles of educator and steward: she continued to fulfill these functions according to the instructions that had come from Madame or that she herself had long ago suggested to Madame. It was in conformance with the tastes of the deceased that the young ladies were dressed and the carpets and wallpaper, when necessary, were replaced. For a time, this regent probably dreaded that Monsieur might remarry, an event that would have disrupted the family's ways and customs. He did nothing of the sort, as we know: compared to what such a change of regime would have meant, the Woman of Namur, whom no one ever saw, was a bearable compromise. It was only hard to accept that the best of the fruit, the finest of the spring vegetables, the choicest game of the season went to the person in question. Fräulein never forgave Monsieur de C. de M. for this permanent insult, felt at every meal, and she passed on to the children her indignation about the matter.

So long as I was content to evoke in a general way Fernande's childhood and adolescence and the life she shared with seven brothers and sisters, I imagined a group of children such as one might find in Tolstoy or Dickens: a gay band scattering their laughter through the drawing rooms and corridors of a great house, informal dances, parlor games, kisses exchanged on Christmas Eve with cousins and country neighbors, girls in rustling dresses sharing confidences about lovers or fiancés. But aside from the fact that Hainaut is neither Russia nor England, it does not seem as if the conditions of life at Suarlée really lent themselves to these graceful tableaux. I forgot that frequently there are enormous differences in age among offspring in large families, especially when several dead children come between living ones in the series. Fernande was two years old when her sister Isabelle, then about twenty, was married at Suarlée to her third cousin Georges de C. d'Y. It was a good, respectable match that had surely been cooked up at an early date, as they all were, with attention paid to the precise relation between the two parties' portfolios and landed wealth. Mathilde had perhaps approved it before her death. On the day of the wedding, Fernande doubtless made no more than a brief appearance in Fräulein's arms during the dessert course, so that the women could coo over her appropriately.

Georgine and Zoé, ten and nine years older, respectively, than the toddler Fernande, had more of an opportunity to play the role of little mother and big sister to her. But they completed their education in a convent, as Fernande herself would later. Zoé is a boarder with the Dames Anglaises of Passy, where she writes her father sensible little letters about the raw meat she eats to make herself strong and the difficulties that Paris presents to a young girl who rides horses, the manège on the Champs-Elysées being too expensive and the one at the Château d'Eau frequented by ladies who are not *comme il faut*. Octave

Grounds of the château of La Boverie at Suarlée. Fernande and
her older sister Zoé are at right, with Fräulein in the background.
The man at the left is unidentified

and Théobald are in secondary school. As for Gaston, by now
almost an adult, we have seen that he has been reduced to a
familiar domestic presence—accepted, one might say, without
any tenderness but apparently also without that blend of disgust,
vague repulsion, and slight fear which the mentally ill sometimes evoke in their brothers and sisters. Nevertheless, Fernande, who confided many things to her husband, never said a
word about her older brother's abnormality, which seems to
prove that the poor boy's existence was an embarrassment to
the family.

Fräulein wakes the little girls at six o'clock in winter and
at five in summer; Jeanne, who dresses more slowly, gets up a
few minutes earlier. They pass noiselessly by the door of Papa's
room. Jeanne goes down the stairs on her bottom, as she will

all her life, and the girls can never resist a few good-natured pleasantries, which they utter in whispers. Fräulein and a chambermaid take the invalid by the arm; if the weather is wet, the little cortege, sheltered by umbrellas, makes its way to the church in raincoats and shiny boots; thick overcoats, hoods, and slipper-socks worn as a precaution inside the boots are obligatory when it is snowy. In summer, the girls' bright dresses and Zoé's and Georgine's parasols enliven the scene. Little Fernande brings up the rear with her tiny steps, which will later cause her to be nicknamed "Low Gear" by her French brother-in-law Baudouin, a great bicycling enthusiast. Each time they leave the church, Fräulein stops respectfully before Madame's grave.

Breakfast, at which Monsieur is never present, is eaten, so to speak, in German. The same is true of lunch. A period of study, with some brief recreation, occupies the intervening hours. Twenty minutes of rest follows the midday meal. Fräulein pretends not to be dozing in an armchair in the small drawing room. The older girls take up their embroidery, an art for which little Jeanne early shows surprising aptitude; her tiny, restless hands, which are unable to hold either a cup or a spoon, manipulate the needle intelligently and calmly. Other pastimes are painting on porcelain and découpage. At two o'clock schoolwork resumes until six, interrupted by a walk and the ever-delightful pause for refreshments. At six o'clock, if it is vacation time, Fernande accompanies the older girls and boys as they clamber up the stairs to wash their faces and hands, using hot water from a little pitcher that the maid has placed at the foot of every washstand; each girl takes off her pinafore and ties a ribbon in her hair. Jeanne receives the same attentions on the ground floor, so as not to have to climb the stairs. On Fridays and Saturdays the bath is heated, and the girls plunge into the water in flannel shifts. Fräulein, who washes with ice-cold

Fernande's sister Jeanne

Fräulein, about 1895

water morning and evening, disdains this overly luxurious form of cleanliness.

Monsieur de C. de M. almost always presides at dinner. To the extent that there is any conversation, it is therefore conducted in French. But a monastic silence usually reigns: those at table partake silently of a copious series of dishes, all good, all plain and hearty. But as everyone knows, the first vegetables from the garden are missing, and the fruit presented is meager. The children are allowed to open their mouths only if Papa has asked them a question first, which he rarely takes the trouble to do. At the most, he will now and then inquire unexpectedly about the boys' studies or the young ladies' lessons, and his offspring, taken aback, will not always have the presence of mind to respond. But these mute repasts were apparently traditional at Suarlée. Great-aunt Irénée's journal indicates that fifty years earlier, the four Drion girls likewise kept silent at table.

After dinner Papa settles himself, in both summer and winter, by the fireplace in the drawing room. He tears the wrapper off his Brussels newspaper, and the silence during the ensuing half hour is even more profound than that which prevailed during the meal. Fräulein sits beneath a lamp embroidering on a tambour frame, and each time she uses her little scissors, she manages to replace them on the table next to her without a sound. The children sit ranged along the wall, their backs held very straight against the hard, contoured spindles of the chairs, their hands resting quietly on their knees. This period of immobility is considered to be an exercise in posture and decorum. Little Octave, however, has invented a wordless game to pass the time: they compete at making faces. They puff out their cheeks or suck them in; they screw up and widen and roll their eyes; they draw back their lips, ferociously baring their teeth; they stick out their tongues obscenely or dangle them limply like rags; they let their mouths go slack as if they were toothless old men or distort them hideously, so that their young faces look apoplectic. They wrinkle their brows; they wiggle their noses like rabbits. Fräulein, who sees everything, lowers her head over her tambour and feigns ignorance. According to the rules, one has to maintain the utmost seriousness while engaging in these contortions. A chuckle or even a soundless burst of laughter might be enough to make Monsieur de C. de M. raise his lorgnon from the perusal of his paper, and the thought of the disasters that would follow causes the children to shudder. Monsieur de C. de M. passes from news of the court and the city to the parliamentary debates, which he reads without skipping a line; he glances at the bulletins from abroad, savors every detail of the law-court proceedings, the stock-exchange reports, and the reviews of plays that he will not see. He refolds the paper methodically and places it in the kindling basket so that it can be used to light the next day's fire. The faces along the wall have once more become bland and innocent. The children rise and approach Papa one by one, to hug him and wish him good night.

During the summer there is a quarter hour's grace that is spent beneath the lime trees, and Fräulein, who takes herb tea every evening, brews in her cup the little blossoms that adorned their branches the previous year. The powerful life of the nocturnal world murmurs and stirs: rustlings of moonlight-frosted leaves, the cheeping of nesting birds frightened by a predator, a chorus of frogs in the dewy grass. Insects flutter against the large oil lamp and threaten to fall into the governess's tea. A horse kicks the side of its stall nearby; the coachman passes with his lantern, bidding everyone a good evening; a farmer slams the heavy door of the stable across the way, where Rosie has just had her calf. But the children of Suarlée are city dwellers at heart: they are in no way touched by the natural world that surrounds them. The cigar tip they see glowing on Monsieur Arthur's balcony receives more attention than the stars and planets that dot the sky. It's time to go in: Fräulein has declared that the air is too cool. Everyone takes a candle from the console table in the vestibule. Having played at making faces, the children now play with their shadows on the wall of the staircase. Jeanne goes up the stairs the same way she came down that morning. They lower their voices as they pass by Papa's door, since they already consider him to be asleep. In principle, at least, no one will forget to say his or her prayers before going to bed.

On December 31 the children are obliged by custom to write a New Year's letter to their father, doubtless recopied many times before attaining the desired degree of correctness. Chance has preserved for me the letters thus written by Fernande between the ages of nine and twelve. Here is one she wrote when she was eleven:

> *Dear Papa,*
>
> *Permit me on the occasion of the New Year to come and express to you once more—along with all my best wishes for a good year, perfect health, and long life—my great and profound gratitude. I pray, dear Papa, that in the year 1884 the Good Lord may shower you with his best blessings and grant us the happiness of keeping you, for many more long years, in good health and in the sincere affection of all your children and grandchildren, and most especially of your very respectful little daughter,*
>
> *Fernande*
>
> *Suarlée, January 1, 1884*

I do not know how Monsieur de C. de M. responded to these effusions. The New Year's Day gifts had no doubt been chosen in Namur by Fräulein. In any case, the children each received a piece of gold that they were entitled to keep until the evening and that was subsequently taken to the bank and deposited in an account, at compound interest, in each child's name—a gesture that was supposed to teach them economical habits and the value of money.

In our own day, such a family life seems grotesque or odious, or both. But it did not leave the children of Suarlée with especially unhappy memories. Thirty years later I listened to Octave, Théobald, Georgine, and Jeanne, all now grown old, speak of their childhood with discreet smiles and voices full of affection. The young, somewhat sickly shoots had succeeded in taking root and flourishing between the stones.

Jeanne's physical misfortune and Gaston's mental misfortune perhaps accounted in part for the almost complete absence of social life at Suarlée. Certain official ceremonies were, however, obligatory. Monsieur de C. de M. surely appears at the governor's receptions; and his daughters, now occupying the narrow space between boarding school and marriage, attend the balls of the provincial nobility. The girls spend a great deal of time preparing for these, and a great deal of time reliving them afterward. Now and then Mademoiselle Fräulein takes the young ladies to Namur, so that they can go shopping and pay a visit to the nuns in the Convent of the Soeurs Noires. The coachman helps Mademoiselle Jeanne get in and out of the carriage.

For family visits, they take the train. In the year 1880, railroads are proliferating like the highways of our own day, and seem as if they will grow and multiply forever; the train station is the symbol of modernity and progress. But even though the strict segregation into three classes and the availability of compartments for unaccompanied women assure that propriety is rigorously observed, traveling by rail subjects the young ladies of Suarlée to the jostlings of big-city stations such as those at Namur and Charleroi; Zoé and Georgine are stared at by salesmen, and as they mount the steps into the train they are liable to attract overly solicitous attentions from elderly gentlemen. In addition, Jeanne's infirmity does not make this type of travel easy. Fräulein prefers the proper old carriage for her girls or, if the journey is decidedly too long, a combination of conveyances: the coachman from Suarlée deposits his young mistresses at one station, and their hosts send a coachman to pick them up at another, thus sparing them complicated "connections." In the carriage they feel at home and can eat a light meal; Fräulein makes her pupils recite their lessons or entertains them yet again with selections from her large stock of amusing moral anecdotes, which will exasperate me a generation later.

There is the story of the old, slightly senile grandfather whose son and daughter-in-law make him take his meals alone and whose food is served in a wooden bowl that will not break if he drops it. One day, the son notices that his own little boy is hollowing out an abandoned bit of timber with his pocketknife. "What are you doing?" "I'm making a wooden bowl for you to use when you're old." Another tells the story of a little boy walking home with his father, who has just bought three kilos of cherries at the village market. The boy does not want to carry the basket, which he finds very heavy. So the father carries it himself, eating cherries as he walks and spitting out the pits. Every five minutes, as an act of kindness, he also throws away an entire cherry, which the boy must retrieve from the dust. That's what one gets for being unwilling to help. And finally, addressed particularly to the two young ladies who are already betrothed, there is the terrifying story of the girl who wants her hands to be very white on her wedding day. On the eve of the marriage, she clasps them behind her neck and sleeps on them all night. Early the next morning she is found dead. To lift the pall that this anecdote has cast over their spirits, Fräulein offers one of her innocent pleasantries, always the same ones, and all of a rare foolishness. By temperament and on principle, she continually teases the girls, such banter in those days being considered an infallible method for shaping character. From time to time, a word to the coachman stops the carriage, and whichever young lady it is who feels a need slips discreetly into the bushes.

Visits to Marchienne are rather rare. Though lacking any document on the subject, I nonetheless find it difficult to believe that Monsieur de C. de M. feels no regret at seeing this estate, whose name he bears, pass to the children of a second marriage. It is true that many years have elapsed since that disappointment, if indeed it was one. In this family in which offspring who die young are haloed by legend, people still refrain from mentioning Arthur's half sister, Octavie de Paul de Barchifontaine, who died in childbirth at twenty-six. Likewise, nothing is known of his half brother Félix, who lives in Paris. But Emile-Paul, who lives at Marchienne, is a familiar figure, along with his young Irish wife. Their children Emile and Lily, and later Arnold, play with those at Suarlée, but such get-togethers are few and far between. No one would ever admit, though, even for a minute, that the families did not feel the greatest affection for each other.

La Pasture is a paradise whose doors are always open. The good Zoé, very lonely since the death of her husband, welcomes her grandchildren warmly. She tends to dwell a bit on the subject of her beloved Louis; each time they visit she asks them to admire the portrait of him in full uniform, not forgetting the companion portrait that depicts her, with a little handkerchief between her fingers, wearing a wide-skirted dress of dark silk brightened by a lace collar and lace cuffs. The elderly lady shows the children the slightly yellowed originals of these adornments. She plies her visitors with culinary treats: nowhere are the desserts more decorative and more exquisite than at La Pasture. The boating parties on the pond with kind Cousin Louise and handsome Cousin Marc are memorable occasions, which Octave and Théobald spoil a bit, whenever they are there, by threatening to capsize the skiff. Zoé will die in her seventies in 1888, and her *souvenir pieux* will liken her to the holy women of Scripture. Her daughter, Aunt Alix, will follow soon after, but the widower, Uncle Jean, senator and burgomaster of Thuin, will carry on the worthy traditions of Louis Troye. A photograph recently sent to me shows him as he was around 1895, his hair completely white, strolling through the grounds of La Pasture with Fernande, who had come from Brussels with her brother Octave and Fräulein. The latter is wearing her black dress with the jet buttons and her air of a German duenna. Fernande, very pretty and very coquettish, takes shelter from the sun beneath a large parasol. Octave's thin, bearded face is not yet the mask that it will later become: it betrays that indefinable feeling of unease that will eventually lead him to the asylum at Geel.

But let us return to the years at Suarlée. Until 1883, Acoz remains the place that Fernande likes best to visit. As soon as they arrive, the young ladies take a seat in the handsome drawing room hung with tapestries; Jeanne, settled in an easy chair, moves no further, and is treated like a grownup because of her condition. The mistress of the house shows a preference for her goddaughter Zoé, who owes one of her given names to her: that of Irénée, which, albeit masculine, must have been taken for a woman's name because of its ending, even though in the

Roman calendar it designated a bishop of Lyons who was martyred under Marcus Aurelius. The conversation centers on marriages. Madame Irénée assesses at their precise value the
projected unions of the two young ladies, and since their future
husbands are neither noble nor titled, she places all the more
stress on the fact that they come from excellent families. By
virtue of their Troye and Drion blood, Irénée and her late
husband, as well as their granddaughters, are themselves members of that same bourgeois aristocracy. But with this pious
woman, conversations soon tend toward religion. There is much
discussion of good Christian deaths, her specialty. A nun in a
neighboring convent has just died in the odor of sanctity: her
body was displayed in the chapel for eight days without the
slightest sign of putrefaction. In a different convent another
nun, something of a recluse, sweats blood. Such miracles are
not bruited about too much, for fear of provoking sneers from
godless souls and radicals. Fräulein and the young ladies listen
respectfully. Fernande is bored.

Fortunately, "Uncle Octave" himself comes to take the
little girl by the hand and leads her away to see his wild animals
and his hounds. She trots beside him as they pass the flower
beds. She is still too young, thank goodness, for false timidity
and coquettishness. She is not even pretty—nothing but a frail
and slender shoot. Her blurry features are still unsure of their
final form, but Octave thinks he recognizes the narrow, curved
profile that he loved in his young brother and of which he is
not unaware when he looks at his own face with the aid of two
mirrors. Moreover, she bears the feminine form of the name
that Rémo had had before he was forever rechristened Rémo.
A bit more than thirty years ago (already!), he likewise took
Fernand to examine the seedlings beneath the glass cold frames.

The child used to call him his "dear nurseryman." Why must this inconsequential detail bring back unbearable memories of something he believed was finished and accepted, if not forgotten? The little girl prattles away. She is afraid of the big dogs and the wild animals, but she likes flowers; she remembers their names. From time to time, her little hand reaches out and awkwardly gathers, or rather uproots, a stem or a cluster. Her somewhat solemn uncle protests: "Think of the mutilated plant, of its hardworking roots, of the sap that flows from its wound . . ." Fernande raises her head, perplexed, sensing that she is being scolded, and lets fall the dying flower she has been clutching in her damp fist. He sighs. Has she understood? Is she among that small number of people who can be instructed and formed? Will she remember his admonition years from now when she goes to evening parties, wearing in her hair or at her bosom what Victor Hugo calls a bouquet of death agonies?

If he is in the mood, he tells her stories. Only one has come down to me: that of the Merovingian anchorite Saint Rolende, the glory of local folklore. Every year on the Monday following Pentecost, a procession wends its way over some thirty kilometers, carrying through the fields the saint's reliquary and that of a pious hermit, her contemporary. The great courtyard of Acoz is traditionally the site of one of the cortege's temporary altars; Fernande doubtless helped to strew flowers on some of those occasions. With her child's fresh eyes that marvel at everything and are surprised at nothing, she will have watched the strange parade: the drum major and the male choirs from the villages, preceding the clergy; the marchers in fanciful uniforms which they have made themselves and whose variety is a visible reminder of the different armies that have swept over this corner of the earth; and the charming disarray of the choirboys. She will have smelled that odor of incense and crushed

roses, blended with the stronger one of light wine and a perspiring crowd. "Uncle Octave," who feels honored to be able
to carry the shrine partway along its journey, doubtless appreciates these pagan elements, which are likewise sacred and even
more ancient than the pious virgin of Gerpinnes, who lives on
in this solemn rite. The sturdiest men and women from the
villages have been chosen to lead the ranks, this selection traditionally taking place at the inn with the aid of brimming
tankards; the peasants are delighted that the procession will
cross their fields and in this way enhance the fertility of the
soil. When the fervor and excitement are at their height, the
boys who are leaping around the reliquary almost like fauns,
much as they do around the bonfire on the festival of Saint
John, rush off in pursuit of the girls, mimicking an episode from
the legend of Saint Rolende. The revelers call out lighthearted
jests at the expense of the saint and her pious friend the hermit,
and local tradition maintains that the two shrines, whenever
they meet, hasten toward each other of their own accord.

   The story of Rolende's life, as Octave told it, bears no
resemblance to that novelistic bit of eighteenth-century apoc-
ryphal hagiography *The Fugitive Princess, or The Life of Saint
Rolende* or to the solemn prose of the brochures distributed in
church. A poet has clearly left his mark on it. I make no claim
to imitate here the style of the teller, which will doubtless differ
from that of the writer. At least the account incorporates whatever was retained, during her last visits to Acoz in Octave's
lifetime, by the eleven-year-old girl who was listening.

   *Didier, King of the Lombards, had a daughter named Rolende
who was as beautiful as the day. He had promised her in marriage
to the youngest of his liegemen, Oger, who was known to be a prince
from beyond the seas and a true son of the King of Scotland. Didier*

and Oger were pagans who worshipped trees, springs, and the giant upright stones that can be seen on the moors.

But Rolende had converted to Christianity and was secretly devoted to God. Realizing that her vows would not be respected by either her father or her intended, she resolved to flee. As light as a leaf borne by the wind, she crossed the passes and valleys of the Alps, and then began to make her way through the Vosges. Oger, alerted by a traitorous servant, took off in pursuit. It would have been easy for him to catch up with her and seize her by her flowing hair. But he loved her: he could not bear to see her reduced to desperation, like some wretched animal cornered by a beast of prey. So he remained a certain distance behind her.

When the exhausted Rolende paused to sleep, he paused as well, hidden behind a rock or a clump of trees. When she stopped at the door of a farmhouse to ask for bread and milk, he came after her and begged for the same food.

Only once did he meet her. One morning when she had not arisen from her bed of leaves, he ventured to draw near and heard her moaning from an attack of fever. He looked after her for several days. As soon as she was better, he disappeared before she could recognize him and allowed her to continue on her way.

At last they came to the Ardennes forest. Rolende's steps grew slower. In a valley between the Sambre and the Meuse he saw her suddenly kneel down to pray, then rise and go into the woods to gather some boughs, which she wove together to make a hut. He did likewise on the opposite slope of the valley.

For several years they lived this way, eating wild berries and food that the villagers offered them. He prayed from afar, just as he saw her praying.

A day came when the peasants found Rolende dead in her rustic chapel. They decided to bury her in a heavy pagan sarcophagus, which they brought to the hermitage in an ox-drawn cart.

Fernande

Oger watched the funeral from a distance. He lived several more years of the life Rolende had taught him to live. At last, one evening, he died. The villagers, who were proud of their two hermits, conceived the idea of uniting them in the same tomb. They brought Oger on a litter to Rolende's chapel. And as they raised the lid of the great sarcophagus, the saint's skeleton opened wide its arms to receive the best beloved.

What frustrated love, or on the contrary what ardently gratified love, or what combination of the two was Octave drawing on to have transformed the legend in this way? I went back and consulted the little hagiographic tracts: they make much of the glorious genealogy of the saint, recorded in what might be called the Almanach de Gotha of the seventh century; Rolende's parents likewise take up the pursuit of their daughter and subsequently embrace religion; the faithful prince doubles confusingly as a servant, equally faithful, who accompanies the princess along with a servant girl. Octave includes no mention of any of this, or of a visit that Rolende is supposed to have made to the Eleven Thousand Virgins. On the other hand, he has highlighted the theme of a Christian Daphne pursued by a pagan Apollo; and he has above all invented the poignant gesture of her death—or perhaps he heard this marvelous detail, which the sacristans would have found too profane, from the lips of an old woman of the village. As it stands, his account takes its place among the legends of tender passion and of reunion in death—flowers, perhaps from an ancient Celtic world, that shed their petals from Ireland to Portugal and from Brittany to the Rhineland. One wonders if Fernande, having become a Wagnerian, might not have recalled the saintly lovers of Gerpinnes as she listened to Isolde's *Liebestod* at Bayreuth. It seems that such a story, learned in childhood, must surely leave its mark forever on a feminine sensibility. It did not always prevent Fernande from lapsing into the formulas of sentimental romance. But something of it remained, like gossamer on a summer's morning.

Octave is remembered as dying a Christian death on the night of May 1, 1883—a magical night, traditionally devoted to fairies, witches, and the spirits of the woods. On the preceding April 2, Zoé had been married at Suarlée. To Fernande, the news concerning the death of her "uncle" perhaps mattered less than the postcards sent by the newlyweds in the course of their honeymoon trip. Early that autumn Monsieur de C. de M. received a letter from Zoé, now settled in the little château of A., located between Ghent and Brussels; it was an affectionate note in which she thanked him for having married her to Hubert, such a worthy fellow, so polite and well-bred. These adjectives make one wonder: after four months of conjugal intimacy, Zoé speaks of her husband just as she would have spoken of some amiable stranger she had noticed at a ball in her youth. But "upset by all that" (and it seems quite likely that this turn of phrase refers both to the marriage and to her frequent sessions at the dentist's), Zoé joyfully announced that she was planning to visit dear old Suarlée, accompanied by Hubert, who was coming along for the hunt. While waiting, she summoned her two young sisters and took them to a dressmaker in Brussels. The little nymph Fernande and Jeanne the Invalid had the pleasure of trying on dresses in the good seamstress's mirrored salon. But these novelties were, for Fernande, only a prelude. That autumn she experienced the most important event that can take place in a young woman's life prior to marriage: she entered boarding school.

I shall not burden my readers with a description of the boarding school run by the Sisters of the Sacred Heart in Brussels during those years. I have no idea what the place looked like or what kind of life people led there; my depictions would at the most be derived from novels of the time, or approximately of the time, in which a few pages are devoted to such institutions. The most substantial evidence I have about this period in Fernande's life is a sheaf of notes and trimestral reports, accompanied by a copy of the school regulations, carefully written out by hand on lined paper. (*Blot: one demerit. Notebook not open to the lesson: one demerit. Pen tray lacking the necessary objects: one demerit. Three errors: recopy the exercise. Three hesitations: lesson not learned. Inattention: one demerit. Responding without being asked: one demerit.*) The reports are pink (*very good*) or blue (*good*); the yellow ones (*fair*) and the green ones (*poor*) obviously were not saved. Anyway, until 1886 the records give the impression of a model student. Fernande was first in her class in religion, French, composition, history, mythology, geography, cosmography, penmanship, reading, arithmetic, drawing, gymnastics, and hygiene. She was second in literature, elocution, and natural science. Later, things deteriorated.

I often heard Fräulein discuss the reasons for the precipitous decline that followed these triumphs. She believed it to be the result of an infatuation, which is tantamount to saying a love affair. A certain Baroness de T. from Holland, although a Protestant, had entrusted her daughter Monique to the Sisters of the Sacred Heart so that her education and her French might receive a final polishing. In fact, Mademoiselle de T.'s French was of that exquisite type which is sometimes handed down in old foreign families and could only have suffered from consorting with various Belgian accents. However that may be, the arrival of Monique de T. (the given name and the initial have been changed) caused numerous ripples in the little world of the convent. The young baroness, as she would have been called in those days in Belgium, was extremely pretty, endowed with the almost Creole beauty that one sometimes sees in Holland and that takes one's breath away. From the very first moment, Fernande loved those dark eyes, that golden face, those heavy black tresses pinned up so simply. Morality also played a part in this enchantment. Compared with those young ladies who strove to produce an effect of keen vivacity in the Parisian style, Monique radiated an air of grave gentleness. Fernande, for whom religion consisted mainly of a series of lighted candles, flower-laden altars, pious images, and scapulars, was surely surprised by the controlled fervor that animated her friend: the young Lutheran truly loved God at an age when Fernande had scarcely thought about Him. Moreover, she was less prone to qualms of conscience than the other girls, who were accustomed to making confession and to keeping a strict account of their minor sins. Fernande surrendered to the charm of an ardent nature combined with a calm demeanor. If Fräulein is to be believed, the decline in the trimestral grades of a hitherto exemplary student was due to one of those heroic sacrifices such as are made only in adolescence: in order to cede first place to the foreigner, Fernande became self-effacing, did her work poorly, stammered on purpose. Such abnegation, almost sublime if one considers it in its time and place, is not impossible, but we must also take into account the degree to which love monopolizes a person's attention (*Inattention: one demerit*), as well as the feeling that, next to love, everything else is worthless, even the gilt-edged prizes of the Convent of the Sacred Heart.

I know that I am liable to be accused of omission or innuendo if I fail to mention the role that sensuality may have played in that love. But the question in itself is pointless: all our passions are sensual. At the very most, we may wonder to what extent that sensuality was translated into action. In those days and in the social milieu we are concerned with here, the complete ignorance of carnal pleasure which schoolmistresses strove to preserve in their young charges makes it relatively unlikely that desire would ever be fulfilled in such a way between two students of the Sisters of the Sacred Heart. Ignorance, certainly, is not an insurmountable obstacle: in most cases, it is only superficial. Physical intimacy between two persons of the same sex is too much a part of the behavior of the species to have been excluded from even the most straitlaced boarding schools of the past. It was surely not limited to the knowing little girls of Colette or to the hybrid, rather artificial young women of Proust.

But this carefully guarded innocence was reinforced in those days (paradoxically so, if one thinks about it) by a prudishness that was inculcated from an early age and that makes it seem as if all the mothers, maids, and governesses in those pious families, and later the vigilant nuns, suffered unwittingly from a sort of sexual obsession. Their fear and horror of the flesh are expressed in hundreds of minor prohibitions that are accepted as self-evident. A young lady never sets eyes on her own body; to remove one's chemise in the presence of a friend or relative would be as shocking as the most deliberate carnal intimacies; to clasp a girl friend around the waist would be indecent, like exchanging glances with a handsome young man in the course of a stroll. Sensuality is not presented as culpable; it is vaguely felt to be unclean and, in any case, incompatible with good breeding. It is not inconceivable, however, that two passionate adolescents—overstepping, consciously or not, those strong arguments concerning feminine nature—might have discovered sensual pleasure, or at least a presage of it, in a kiss, in the suggestion of a caress, less plausibly in the complete union of bodies. It is not impossible, but it is doubtful, perhaps improbable, and one might as well wonder to what extent the breeze could bring about a union of two flowers.

In any case, the trimestral report for April 1887 testifies to Fernande's academic decline. The student who until recently was so brilliant is now twenty-second in religious instruction and arithmetic, fourteenth in epistolary style, thirteenth in geography. In grammar, where formerly she was fifth, she nevertheless wins, as if by chance, two first places in the course of the trimester. Her readings out loud are unintelligible—which is surprising, considering that they will later charm her husband, a demanding critic. When it comes to needlework, Fernande outdoes herself: she is forty-third out of a class of forty-four. She has made some progress in neatness and in economy, and her teachers admit she has applied herself, a fact that contradicts Fräulein's hypothesis. Her demeanor in class is somewhat improved, but her personal appearance is quite careless and she makes no effort to correct it. She continues to like the natural sciences, perhaps recalling the names of the flowers that "Uncle Octave" taught her. Her English is "not taken seriously enough." As the report indicates, "her character is still unformed."

Was a more confidential report, alluding to Fernande's crisis, sent to Suarlée at the same time? This is possible, given that educational institutions, like governments, prefer to conduct their business by means of secret documents. In any case, Monsieur de C. de M. summoned his daughter home, perhaps deeming it useless to keep her in a school where she was not learning anything. Such excessive devotion to a Protestant girl was, moreover, considered undesirable. Besides, Monsieur de C. de M. was growing old, apparently already weakened by the long illness that would get the better of him three years later. His life at Suarlée, where he was now confining himself to an ever greater extent, was not particularly cheerful, with Fräulein on the one hand and Gaston the Simple and Jeanne the Invalid on the other. He may well have wished to have near him once more a person brimming with youth, keen of mind and sound in body.

I once saw a portrait of Fernande painted around that time, doubtless by Zoé, who had a taste for the fine arts and who enabled me to discover the color of the subject's eyes. They were green, as those of cats often are. Fernande was depicted in profile with her lids slightly lowered, giving her a somewhat secretive expression. She was wearing an emerald-green dress, which the artist had thought to match with her eyes, and an enormous hat adorned with loops of plaid ribbon, which she also sported in a silhouette executed at about that same time. She could not have been older than fifteen.

Another portrait, taken by a photographer in Namur, commemorates a visit that Isabelle and her children made to Suarlée two years later. Fernande and Jeanne stand on either side of a pedestal on which is perched a little girl wearing a white dress adorned with eyelet embroidery. A slightly older girl, sickly in appearance, leans against Jeanne's skirts. No crystal ball is needed to foresee the fate of each of these four people: it is inscribed there. Jeanne, firm and frail, has the intelligent, slightly cold gaze that I shall later come to know. Not yet twenty, she looks scarcely different from what she will be at forty. The little girl in the embroidered dress, my future Cousin Louise, her nose prettily uptilted, seems very happy with her elevated position. This strong little body and self-confident little soul have what it takes to endure the trials of nearly three-quarters of a century: she reigns over her aunts just as she will reign over her wounded, her sick, her nurses, and her stretcher-bearers throughout two world wars. Mathilde, the wan-looking child, rigged out in a hideous sailor suit and a beret that ill becomes her, gives the impression of being a total mistake: she will take leave of the world at an early stage.

Fernande is more mysterious. Having definitely attained the status of a grown-up, she wears numerous thick petticoats. In her lady's toilette, she appears quite round, perhaps owing to the cooking at the boarding school she has just left, but even more to the blossoming of adolescence, to a new abundance of flesh and blood. Her breasts swell the outline of her high-necked bodice. She must have combed her hair before posing for the photographer, but even so she has missed a small lock, which dangles untidily ("Fernande's personal appearance is quite careless") and which will dismay her later. The eyes this time look directly at the viewer. The elongated lids rise imperceptibly toward the temples, a trait that is rather common in the region and that is found frequently, as well, in old paintings of what is today known as Belgium. Behind this young lady in her voluminous skirts, I glimpse the plucky girls in striped breeches who followed their men into Macedonia or up the Capitoline slopes and those who were sold at auction after Caesar's campaigns. I even go back several more centuries to the women "of the tribes dwelling deep in huts," allegedly from the region of the Upper Danube, who used to draw water in their buckets of gray clay. I think, too, of Blanche of Namur, who went to

Norway with her ladies-in-waiting to marry King Magnus
Eriksson, nicknamed Smek ("the Fondler"), and lived an uninhibited life at an uninhibited court, though she and her
pleasure-loving young husband were insulted by the austere
Saint Brigitte. Fernande knows nothing of all this: her studies
in history do not extend that far. Neither does she know that
she has passed the midpoint of her life: fourteen years remain
to her. Despite her ladylike finery, nothing sets her apart from
the young women of the village or the little factory girls of
Charleroi, with whom she refuses to associate. She is, like them,
merely warm, soft flesh. As the Sisters of the Sacred Heart
have pointed out, her character is not yet formed.

The episode that follows is so ugly that I hesitate to write it down, all the more so as Fernande's is the only account of it I have. One evening in September 1887—that is, during the autumn the girl remained home at Suarlée instead of returning on the appointed day to her boarding school in Brussels—Fräulein, Fernande, and Jeanne heard a violent quarrel break out in Monsieur Arthur's study. Inarticulate exclamations and the sound of blows came through the closed doors. A few moments later, Gaston came out of the study and went upstairs to his room without a word. He died eight days later of a raging fever.

Described in this way, the incident appears not only odious but absurd. Rarely will a father of fifty-six attack with all his strength a son of twenty-nine, and such brutality becomes even more incredible when the son is simpleminded. What misdeed could Gaston the Imbecile have committed? A doctor has reminded me, however, that the mentally retarded are often violent, that Arthur could legitimately have tried to control his son, and that anyone can rapidly inflict an unlucky blow causing serious injury, fever, and death. It would be easy to reject this entire story as the invention of a slightly hysterical girl, or at least reduce it to reproaches shouted by an exasperated father at a feebleminded son, toward whom he adopts, despite himself, the tone that some people use when speaking with the deaf; or perhaps reduce it to a slap, an awkward blow of a fist, and the crash of a chair being overturned. As for the fever, this family apparently lived in a chronic state of uncertain diagnoses: it could have been one of the cases of typhoid fever that were rife in those early weeks of autumn, and the quarrel merely a co-incidence, or Fernande may have moved the date of its occur-rence unduly close to that of Gaston's death, to make a more dramatic situation. But even if fabricated in every detail, Fer-nande's account would still have the merit of showing us how a young girl invents tales about her own father, or, rather, against him.

Out of a kind of familial shame, Fernande, as we have seen, never told her husband about Gaston the Simple's infirm-ity. In relating the incident, she said that her unfortunate brother was twelve or thirteen, which actually brought him closer to his true mental age. It is strange that Michel did not notice there was a factual impossibility in the story as it was presented: since Mathilde had survived Fernande's birth by only a year, Fernande could not have had a brother who was two or three years younger than she was. But the precise date of his late mother-in-law's death was doubtless the least of Michel's concerns.

I have devoted a good deal of time to describing Fernande. Perhaps the moment has come to describe my grandfather as well during those years. In one photograph taken a bit earlier, when he was about forty, the former dandy is stout and some-

Fernande at fifteen

Arthur de C. de M., about 1885

what flaccid; in another, Monsieur de C. de M. looks about fifty and has recovered his style. His abundant hair, already receding from his forehead, has evidently been the object of a hairdresser's attentions. A thick imperial covers his lower lip and chin, making it impossible to assess the lines of his mouth. The eyes behind their pince-nez are sly and a bit roguish. It is the portrait of a gentleman who can easily be imagined telling a good story as he puffs on a cigar, negotiating shrewdly with a farmer or a notary, or hefting the young partridge he has just shot. I could even imagine him breaking plates in a private dining room, if what I know of him did not make me think that his life, at least after his marriage, admitted of few private dining rooms and few opportunities to break plates. I cannot say I heard the cry of blood when I looked at that photo; in short, it is not the image of a man who would rain blows on someone weak or impaired.

Let us look somewhat more closely at this indistinct Arthur, since it is the last chance we shall have to concern ourselves with him. After losing his mother when he was eight days old and his father at thirteen, he was raised by his stepmother (née de Pitteurs de Budingen) along with her own children. He was educated in Brussels at the same religious institution as his cousin Octave, and it seems that he also took the same course in poetry, a coincidence I find touching. It would be interesting to know, in addition, what the professors at the Collège Saint-Michel offered their students in the way of poetry during the academic year 1848–49: Lamartine and Hugo or Lefranc de Pompignan and the Abbé Delille? In Liège, where he studied law, Arthur seems to have been above all a young man of fashion, but he lacked the aesthetic ambitions and the cravat pin in the form of an ivory skull that his cousin Pirmez sported in Brussels around the same time. At the age of twenty-three, which is a bit too early for someone described as resisting wedlock, he came to a premature end, so to speak, by marrying his first cousin. I am surprised that he renounced Marchienne so blithely, in a country and in an age in which families maneuvered to evade the Napoleonic Code and remain loyal to the principle of primogeniture. But we do not know what arrangements had been made with his stepbrothers: Arthur, wealthy from the dowries of both his mother and his wife, had certainly not been dispossessed.

Around the time of his marriage, he wrote a letter to his cousin Octave, then traveling abroad, in which he gives a possible explanation for the fact that he preferred idyllic Suarlée, and the provincial tranquillity of the region around Namur, to the industry-ravaged Hainaut: "*I understand more than ever,*" he assures the poet, "*why you are so reluctant to sequester yourself here with us . . . It's a dreary place: mud and muck up to the knees, people who think of nothing but physical objects, who speak of kilos, hectoliters, meters, decimeters, or of expropriations, transactions, excavations, extractions, who spout numbers, calculations, and accountings, and who have neither the time nor the inclination to be friendly . . .*" This letter shows that my grandfather, as early as 1854 or 1855, was not insensible to the disfigurement of the world, but it ends on an approving note: those who have profited from the industrial invasion that will transform Marchienne into a black landscape are, Octave's correspondent concludes, "*honest and estimable men.*" Who would blame him? In those days, no one challenged the dogma of progress, and a person would have been thought sentimental if he had deplored the mutilation of a landscape. Those who would understand that to destroy the beauty of the world is also to destroy its health had not yet been born. The fact remains, however, that compared with Marchienne, whose environs bristled with smokestacks, Suarlée would have seemed a peaceful refuge to Arthur.

In any case, he lived there thirty-four years, seventeen of these as a widower. Born to idleness, he does not seem even to have attempted one of those careers which were traditional in the family and in which his father-in-law Troye could have aided him. If he does not, like Octave, *"hold fast to his mountaintop,"* he at least holds fast to his peaceful way of life. It is true that he administers his large fortune quite effectively, which is tantamount to saying that he compels himself to be his own manager throughout his entire life. Among his papers there still exist sheafs of documents containing detailed reports on the finances of the families into which he married his daughters. This sedentary man who envied his cousin Octave his sojourns in Italy seems scarcely to have set foot off his own estate. This man who evidently had no love for children gave his wife ten, of whom two died in infancy and two were impaired, the latter perhaps being an eternal affliction to him. Only Zoé's affectionate little letters prove that, in his relations with his family, he was not always the grim tyrant who so frightened Fernande. He is not known to have had any particular interests or tastes: hunting seems to have been primarily a matter of ostentation with him. Despite the handsome bookplate with the seven silver lozenges on a sky-blue ground, what I saw of the remains of his library consisted largely of devotional works belonging to Mathilde and respectable German novels ordered by Fräulein. The Woman of Namur is the only liberty he seems to have taken—which, of course, does not mean that he didn't take others. If, in a moment of uncontrollable anger, Arthur did indeed strike his imbecile son, this frightful incident is the only one in his life that inspires any emotion in me whatsoever, and that emotion is, in essence, pity.

The disease that was ravaging him forced him little by little to discontinue his visits to Namur and his tours of the farms: henceforth he managed his affairs from his study. It has perhaps not been sufficiently noted that the harshest effect of any illness is the victim's gradual loss of liberty. Monsieur de C. de M. soon found himself confined to the interior of the house or to the terrace. Then came a day when he could no longer go up and down the stairs: his remaining choice was between taking his meals and reading his paper in his bed or in his armchair, which was pushed close to the window. One day, even this choice was taken from him: he stayed in bed.

I have no reason to think that Arthur was of a meditative cast of mind. Nevertheless, like everyone else, he must have occasionally pondered his life. You give your consent when your wife engages a governess for the children, a German girl with a face like a ripe apple, and there she is presiding at births and deaths for twenty-five years, reigning over the house, admitting the curé and the doctor and retiring discreetly on tiptoe, but without ever oiling the hinges of the door to prevent them from creaking. Even though he has reminded her about this twenty times. And it is this foolish woman who will close his own eyes: it might as well be her as someone else. Fifine (let's call her Fifine) has given him pleasant moments, but amid the torments of his sickbed he thinks back on these with as much pleasure as a man suffering from nausea recalls a boating party: a day comes when he no longer understands why he once found this little woman in dishabille attractive. In any case, he has managed things well: the bequest *inter vivos* that he has had the foresight to make her will not wrong his children, since it comes from a modest sum that he made on the stock exchange. As for the Good Lord and one's last moments, all will take place according to the rules, and there's no use worrying about something that happens to everyone.

274

Fernande

Monsieur de C. de M. died in 1890, on the day after New Year's. No one knows if Jeanne and Fernande had, as usual, slipped their respectful little letters under his door. His *souvenir pieux*, adorned with an image of the Man of Sorrows, alludes to the lengthy sufferings that purify the soul. In other respects, it might easily be mistaken for Gaston's *souvenir pieux*, ordered from the stationer-engraver two and a half years earlier. Gaston's beseeches the Lord not to deliver up the soul of the deceased to the Enemy, a request that might seem superfluous in the case of a man whom God had neglected to endow with reason. Arthur's *souvenir pieux* asks us to pray that the dead might be forgiven their sins. After the funeral and probably the same evening, another ceremony, almost as solemn, took place at Suarlée: the reading of the will.

That document contained no surprises. Monsieur de C. de M. left his fortune, divided in equal parts, to his seven surviving children. It was large enough, even fragmented in this way, to assure his heirs a very comfortable life. With the exception of a portfolio of reliable (or supposedly reliable) stocks, his wealth consisted entirely of landed property, which everyone considered the only really safe investment. It would be twenty-five years before war and inflation would undermine this confidence. Neither Théobald, who had just completed a more or less serious course of study leading to an engineering degree, nor Octave, who had not been trained for any sort of profession, would have been capable of managing these assets for themselves and their sisters, as Monsieur Arthur had done. The income from the farms would henceforth be deposited on fixed dates in his heirs' accounts by estate managers and rent collectors. There was of course some risk here, but these agents had recently worked for Monsieur Arthur and under his supervision; they were, from father to son, devoted to the family. The children of the deceased congratulated themselves on the convenience of such an arrangement. None of them noticed that they were making a transition: from the rank of great landowners to that of people living on unearned income. At the same time, the weak and not always friendly bonds that had joined Monsieur Arthur to his peasants had been definitively broken.

Suarlée was sold, not only because its upkeep would have been too great an expense for whoever might have accepted it as his or her share, but also because no one wanted to live there. The married daughters had their estates elsewhere; Théobald, who had firmly decided to put his diploma away in a drawer once and for all, thought only of the comfortable, peaceful bachelor's life he was going to lead in Brussels; Octave was planning to travel. Jeanne, knowing well that her infirmity was incurable, had decided to move to the capital, where she would buy a comfortable, modest house that Fräulein would manage for her and that would be her home for the rest of her days. This house would also be a home for Fernande until such time as she married, for it was to be hoped that her future husband would have his own château or manor house.

Still, Monsieur Arthur's children were reluctant to put the old house into the hands of an estate agent. They sold it to a distant cousin, Baron de D., who did with it what we have already seen. The furnishings, whose value they exaggerated, were as carefully divided up as the estate lands had been. The married sisters each received the pieces that had furnished their own bedrooms, as well as those from a little drawing room and a smoking room. Octave and Théobald had plenty to furnish their bachelor apartments. The shares that fell to Jeanne and Fernande virtually stuffed the house that Jeanne had bought in Brussels. Every death of a paterfamilias, no matter how poor the family, is always the end of an era: after a mere three months, almost nothing remained of a household and a way of life that for thirty-four years had seemed unalterable and that Monsieur Arthur had doubtless imagined would in some fashion or other live on after him.

Prior to the departure of the two young ladies and their governess (the two brothers had already left Suarlée), Fräulein and Fernande took a last tour of the grounds. For Fernande, completely occupied with her dreams of the future, there was certainly nothing sentimental about this walk. It was otherwise with Fräulein. Once again she saw standing before the wrought-iron gate a tall man, slightly stout for his age, with a scar on his cheek—allegedly from a saber cut received in a duel, but in those days German students often had themselves slashed like that, to be fashionable. In truth, the visitor was neither a former student nor a duelist. He was a traveling representative for a manufacturer of farm equipment based in Düsseldorf, and each year he came to see if Monsieur de C. de M. needed anything. For Fräulein, who had been born in some little village near Cologne, the annual visit of this salesman from Germany was an event. They were permitted to take their dinner together in the little room where refreshments were offered to the farmers when they came to renew their leases. Madame Mathilde having approved the governess's engagement, Fräulein entrusted all her savings to her intended, so that he could furnish an apartment for them in Düsseldorf. The suitor decamped, as one might guess, and was never seen again. Inquiries made at the firm by Monsieur Arthur, through the Belgian consul, revealed that the fellow was still selling farm machinery but had been reassigned, perhaps at his own request, to another field of operations. He had married and was now traveling in Pomerania.

The servants at Suarlée gloated over this disappointment, which they succeeded in nosing out somehow or other. Fräulein, who ate at table with the master and mistress, was not well liked. The children knew nothing of the matter; Mademoiselle Jeanne would not learn of it until many years later. Only Madame Mathilde knew that instead of being outraged, Fräulein prayed for "that poor man" whom she had led into temptation by entrusting him with her meager fortune. The foolish woman had her saintly side.

This is not the first time that Suarlée, whose name apparently means "house of the chieftain" in Frankish, has seen a worthy family take leave of the estate and crumble away, as worthy families do. If, as we are assured happens on Christmas night, flames flare up wherever treasures are buried, this peaceful countryside would be glowing with other lights than those of the village lamps or the chandelier that dimly illuminates the empty drawing room of the little château now up for sale. The museum in Namur contains some fine Late Empire coins and Belgo-Roman jewelry that were found at Suarlée. Their owners doubtless hid them the day before an invasion, with the customary precautions: they would carefully tamp down the soil so that no one could tell it had been recently dug up; they would strew rubbish and dead leaves over it. Or they might hide the precious objects in a hollow in the wall and carefully replace the paneling or wallpaper. This is what Irénée and Zoé Drion did during the glorious days of 1830, when they were frightened by the local unrest and fled Suarlée to take refuge with Amélie Pirmez; they soon remembered, with shouts of youthful laughter, that the clock they had hidden along with their jewels was still running, and that its ticking and chiming were sure to give away the hiding place. But the patriots did not indulge in any looting that time. A quarter of a century later, in Flanders, the descendants of Arthur and Mathilde will do likewise, and they will not always come back to retrieve their valuables; or if they do return, they may not find them. The Belgo-Romans of Suarlée did not find all of theirs either.

But domestic life always continues more or less the same, with its trivial, deeply ingrained routines. At a site nearby, excavators have unearthed some little stone dogs, very fat, with foolish-looking faces and bells around their necks, faithful portraits of that species of mother's little darling that yapped around the chair of some mistress of the house in Nero's time. It so happens that Mademoiselle Jeanne has a dog of precisely this kind, which she feeds tidbits to at the dinner table. Always sensible, she decides not to bring him to Brussels: he would be an inconvenience at the pension where they are to spend several days before moving into their new home. The dog will be left with the gardener.

The morning of the departure, the young ladies doubtless go to pray one last time in the empty chapel. The German woman surely devotes a thought and an *Ave* to Madame. Fernande's own thoughts are far away: she is dreaming of the gaslights of Brussels.

As soon as she was settled in her house, located on a quiet street near what was then the aristocratic avenue Louise, Jeanne sat down in an armchair on the veranda and henceforth scarcely left it except to walk to the Carmelite church every morning to attend Mass. She thus accomplished at one and the same time an act of piety and a healthful exercise. The people of the neighborhood became used to watching her pass by, with her halting movements, supported on one side by a maid wearing an apron (to indicate clearly her status as a maid) and on the other by a lady in an old-fashioned black dress. After Mass came another exercise, consisting of one hour of variations on the piano, executed coldly and correctly by Jeanne, who doubtless took pleasure in feeling her fingers obey her as they moved over the keys. Embroidering chasubles and altar cloths had become an art that occupied the rest of her time; she subsequently donated these articles to various churches.

She took for herself the master bedroom, draped in scarlet, whose furnishings had formerly belonged to Arthur and Mathilde; Fernande took the green room; in the blue room, which became hers, Fräulein rehung the photograph of Germany's royal family. A chambermaid and a cook who had been brought from Suarlée occupied the garret and the damp rooms in the cellar and set about once more polishing the silver, waxing the furniture, frying, roasting, boiling, and braising.

Plates that the young ladies had painted adorned the wall of the veranda; the rectangular garden contained a few trees. Twelve Henri II chairs and two buffets dating from about 1856 crowded a medium-sized dining room. Enthroned between the two buffets was an overscaled copy of *The Broken Pitcher*, which Arthur and Mathilde, during their honeymoon trip to Paris, had purchased at the Louvre from an artist working on the spot. No one, not even Arthur, had given a thought to the charmingly salacious connotations of that blushing maiden, her breasts barely concealed by a carelessly draped scarf, her broken pitcher held close to her side. People would never have suspected that a reproduction purchased at the Louvre could have so many indecent implications. The charming pitcher-bearer would reign over this interior for thirty-five years.

The only indication that there had been some decline in social status, the members of the household felt, was the lack of a horse and carriage. But Jeanne never went visiting, and whenever Fernande made an appearance in society, they summoned a livery carriage for her.

The fairy-tale world of society quickly disappointed Fernande, perhaps because her own successes in it were far from brilliant. The two sisters had only a small number of connections in Brussels. Doubtless a few cousins who may or may not have been titled and a few dowagers who were family friends took care to invite, or to urge invitations for, the young lady. Her friends from boarding school, all wellborn, were, so to speak, a willing means of access: Fernande often had their brothers as dance partners. The capital, which Fernande was unfamiliar with, having seen little of it as a boarding-school student, is divided into two parts. The bustling "lower city" is noisy, crowded with shops and with bodegas where businessmen sip port; the large dray horses stumble on its greasy cobbles. The "upper city," which Fernande hardly ever leaves, has handsome tree-lined avenues where footmen walk dogs and maids walk little children, and each morning in its peaceful streets one can see the raised haunches of servant girls as they scour the door-steps. But these neighborhoods so lacking in lyricism are magically transformed at night in the eyes of a young girl "who goes out in society"; the well-to-do residences with their rough stone façades become, for a few hours, fabulous palaces from which emanate snatches of music and the sparkle of chandeliers and to which Fernande does not always have access. She is invited only to large receptions or small dinners—rarely to both in the same houses. Out in the country, the de C. de M. family had naturally held a position of the first rank. Here, this ancient but largely forgotten name has almost no value in the marriage market. In those days it had not yet acquired the additional glossy veneer that it would derive, in the course of the upcoming generation, from the brilliant diplomatic career of Cousin Emile. Jeanne did not receive visitors: the age and situation of the orphans would in any case have prevented this. Fernande must have envied her friends who gave parties at which butlers in white gloves passed trays of petit fours and who organized dance classes in their homes.

Her tidy fortune was not the "pile" that professional wife hunters were seeking, and they could not hope that a father, grandfather, uncle, or brother of the girl would help launch them in politics, high society, the Congo, or administrative circles. Mademoiselle de C. de M.'s beauty was not sufficient to make men fall instantly in love with her—such thunderbolts, moreover, never striking in good families, where a marriage based on love and lacking more solid support would have been considered indecent. Fernande's brothers had seen that she was invited to the balls of the *Concert Noble*, of which they were members. She danced a good deal on these occasions, if I can believe her *carnets de bal*. But around one in the morning a small, exclusive group—the golden youth of Brussels—would make a noisy entrance, determined to have fun and to dance the cotillion only with one another. Fernande and her brothers, along with other representatives of the more sober high-class circles, would feel vaguely insulted, as if they had been scorned or in any event pushed aside.

Naturally, she had her little triumphs as well as her little setbacks. A photograph inscribed in her large angular hand to Marguerite Carton de Wiart, one of her closest friends from her Sacred Heart days, preserves the memory of a *tableau vivant* or an operetta staged by a group of amateurs. Fernande gracefully wears an authentic Neapolitan peasant's costume. Obviously that fine embroidery, those delicate tucks, that openwork, and that diaphanous apron have never belonged to the tinselly stock of a costumer. Perhaps they were brought back from Italy by one of the two Octaves, the brother rather than the "uncle." A single lapse of taste: instead of the mules that one would expect, peeking out from under Fernande's long skirt are the gleaming high boots that were fashionable in 1893. Sure of being applauded, she seems to be taking a curtain call; the slightly languid gaze is eager to please. Bearing as little resemblance to a Neapolitan peasant as can possibly be imagined, incongruously posed by the photographer amid the greenery of

La Cruche cassée (*The Broken Pitcher*), by Jean-Baptiste Greuze
(1725–1805)

Fernande costumed as a Neapolitan peasant, 1893

a winter garden, she reminds me of Ibsen's Nora learning to dance the tarentella in a drawing room in Christiania.

People are beginning to reproach her for being eccentric. The slight bit of learning she has acquired, which she seeks to augment by reading everything that comes to hand, including dangerous novels with yellow covers, frightens the mothers: a young lady who has read *Thaïs, Madame Chrysanthemum,* and *Cruel Enigma* is no longer completely marriageable. Too often, she recounts historical anecdotes that have fascinated her and that refer to personages her dance partners have never heard of—the duc de Brancas, for example, or Maria Walewska. She has begged an old priest she knows to teach her Latin; she succeeds in construing a few lines of Virgil and, proud of her progress, tells people about it. She even admits to having purchased a Greek grammar. With no one supporting or even approving these projects of hers, they come rapidly to an end, but Fernande has unjustly acquired a reputation for being a young lady with ideas, which she really isn't.

Jeanne's house had become a pied-à-terre for her married sisters living in the country. They limited their stay to the interval between trains, and timed their visits to coincide with sales at the linen shops or the sermon of a famous preacher. Zoé, especially, made frequent trips to Brussels to consult her doctor.

Sometimes, as if reluctantly, she would invite Fernande to spend several days at A. Hubert's family, long established in that tranquil Flemish region, owed its renown to an eighteenth-century sculptor whose Baroque angels and virgins adorned a number of altars and pulpits throughout the Austrian Low Countries. The little château was a pleasant place; the village and its fine old church were located some distance away. At five in the morning in summer and at six in winter, the melancholy Zoé left the house to attend early Mass. Every morning, turning back toward the hall with her hand on the doorknob, she would speak from a distance to the chambermaid who was supposed to be "doing the drawing room" and would give orders for the various little tasks to be accomplished before her return.

She was not unaware that Cécile (the maid's name was Cécile) was at that moment slipping into the handsome bedroom on the second floor, the hour of Mass being, for Hubert, the hour of bliss. But the pathetic comedy was repeated every day to mislead the cook and the kitchen maid, who were nonetheless privy to the whole affair, and little Laurence, asleep in her nursery, who at the age of eight or nine knew everything. And with great dignity, a bit wearily, clothed, hatted, and gloved as in the city, Zoé—the living emblem of resignation—would leave for Mass.

Still, things had not deteriorated until after the death of their second child, the son they had so longed for, who had been taken from them in infancy. The angelic Zoé submitted humbly to the will of heaven; the simple Hubert spewed curses, pounded his fist on the table, and declared that the Good Lord did not exist, and his wife's terrified protests served only to inflame him further. I do not know if it was around this time that Cécile's winsome face came between them; in any case, if, as the scene described above indicates, that pretty girl ever was one of the household servants at A., she did not long remain in that subordinate position and soon had her own house in the village. The complaisant father of this acknowledged mistress was a brewer whose small firm was going bankrupt and who was set on his feet again by this morganatic son-in-law. He was a radical, perhaps a Freemason, and for these reasons was despised by good families. This milieu had an influence on Hubert, already furious at the parish curé, who tried to interfere in his household affairs. One fine day, readers of the district's progressive newspaper learned that Monsieur Hubert D., well-known man of property, had accepted the presidency of the anticlerical club, and this news was accompanied by a savage attack against the cloth. Zoé doubtless did all she could to bring

Hubert back to God, if not to her, and these efforts caused the break between them.

There were, however, a few embers of conjugal love remaining. In 1890 the estate of Monsieur de C. de M. was divided at Suarlée, and Zoé received her share both of the paternal wealth and of Louis Troye's legacy, which had until then been jointly held. Hubert immediately sold the lands located in Hainaut in order to buy others, close to A., a decision that doubtless showed good judgment and that increased his prestige. He also bought, with his wife's money, a restaurant on the village square, and there installed Cécile's nieces. Two sons were born to the legitimate wife during those years of euphoria inspired by easy wealth, but the second of those two pregnancies left her with an ailment for which the gynecologist in Brussels could find no remedy. This time, their conjugal relations came to an end. Perhaps she did not regret this, except for the fact that after she was definitively set aside, the way was left open for what the curé, in the confessional, would have called impurity—that is to say, Cécile.

She becomes more devout than ever. She takes Communion every day, and to spare herself two journeys on an empty stomach she henceforth eats breakfast at the little Catholic café across from the church. Even though she speaks only the most broken Flemish, she sometimes engages in conversation with Hubert's tenant farmers and promises to help them obtain a reduction in rent or a delay in payment that Hubert himself would not consent to, his brand-new radicalism having failed to turn him into a philanthropist. He grants her these concessions fairly often, and even displays a princely generosity when it comes to his charitable contributions. In the afternoon or evening, if there are vespers or a benediction, Zoé returns to the village and also busies herself with teaching little girls their catechism. Hubert spends most of his time at Cécile's house, or at the nieces' restaurant, where he gives a breakfast on the days he and his friends go hunting. He can be seen there drinking beer with the opinionated locals and doubtless making biting remarks about the curé.

It is unlikely that Zoé would have confided all her troubles to Fernande's still virginal ears. But the girl had eyes. Indifference reigned in the little château. Zoé, disheartened, no longer gave orders to the servants, who for the most part did not understand French anyway. Hubert sometimes gave orders in her stead, then gave up. He was courteous toward his young sister-in-law, who doubtless sensed a poor confused man in this monster. Laurence was a sharp-featured little girl, deceptively precocious, who thumped away at the piano in the drawing room. The two boys were still at the age when all children are cherubs. Zoé entrusted them to a maid, her cough sometimes making it inadvisable for her to care for them.

It may be that the sight of this household, and of some others, inspired Fernande with disgust for what would have been the traditional solution for her—namely, marriage to the son of a longtime neighbor from the country or to a member of one of Namur's best families, discreetly chosen through the mediation of a mother superior, a parish priest, or an elder woman of the family such as Madame Irénée. But these wise arrangements, which had been employed for generations, were no longer entirely suitable for a young lady of 1893, whose situation permitted her a certain degree of independence. Fernande wanted something different, without quite knowing what.

The only course remaining was to fall in love with a man who was not interested in her or, for the moment, in marriage. That is what she did. Baron H. (the initial has been changed) belonged to a new aristocracy of wealth; his father and his grandfather had achieved success, for themselves and for their associates, in a certain number of financial ventures, and had been rewarded with a title. The young baron (his given name escapes me) was in no way inferior to his forebears: he was said to be prodigiously clever. But he was also a dilettante, a collector, and a passionate lover of music. He played the organ well, and prided himself on being one of Widor's best students. His wealth allowed him to acquire a superb instrument and to build a music room for it in one of the wings of his mansion. I imagine that room as resembling many others of its kind in those days: half like a chapel, half like a love den, with leaded windows and with Turkish carpets covering the divans. Perhaps he even burned incense there.

Fernande, who was musical, though she herself could not claim more than a bit of skill at the piano, plunged delightedly into that hothouse atmosphere. *Melody, melody, the language that genius invented for love* . . . This definition, which is valid only for a certain type of romantic sensibility, precisely suited Fernande's emotions, at least for one season. Bach and César Franck were transformed, for her, into sweet ripplings of sound. Baron H. was kind enough to show her his collection of beautifully bound books and his illuminated manuscripts: she knew nothing about such things, but the comments she made were nevertheless not as foolish as the ones he had heard from other girls and young women of the world. For the first time since her childhood days with "Uncle Octave," Fernande finds herself in the company of a refined, discerning man, one of those who are beginning to be called aesthetes and whom she herself describes as having an artistic nature. To tell the truth, he does not have the handsome face of her angelic uncle: when people point out that the baron looks insignificant, they have said all there is to say about his appearance. I would like to be able to assume that Fernande, rejecting all the prejudices of her family, fell in love, perhaps unwittingly, with a member of the race that has given the world an abundance of bankers, prophets, connoisseurs of music, and collectors; but I know nothing of Baron H.'s forebears.

In the social order, their relations went no further than a few waltzes (the baron was a good dancer but did not like to dance); once or twice, when invited to a supper, she found herself sitting across from him at one of the customary little tables. Fernande would sooner have died than declare her love, in those days an unforgivable crime for a woman, but her silences and her eloquent yearning looks spoke for her. The young baron, immersed both in business affairs and in the arts, saw nothing or appeared to see nothing. Either he was not paying attention or he was being cautious. Many years later he married an ugly, completely untalented woman whom he is said to have methodically surrounded, during her confinements, with reproductions of classical statues and Donatello's bas-reliefs and who bore him beautiful children. But for two winters Fernande had lived on this love, or, as Fräulein would have said, on this infatuation. At the end of the evening, as she replaces in her drawers and closets the feathers and furs that she is no more ashamed to wear than any other woman of her day, she nevertheless realizes that once again she has been merely marking time or dancing in place. Her life is an empty measure. At the same time, the immense longing that fills her heart transforms her in her own eyes, makes her like the heroine of a novel whose pale cheeks and sad eyes she admires when she looks in her mirror.

This failure perhaps increased Fernande's taste for traveling: besides, as we have seen, such an inclination was not rare in her family. To travel alone would have been unthinkable for a self-respecting young lady; to travel with the escort of a chambermaid or lady companion was already quite daring. But Fernande had attained her majority; she had her own means of support. Neither Théobald (out of indifference) nor Jeanne (out of wisdom) raised any objections: the family had its good side. Nevertheless, neither the brother nor the elder sister would have agreed to let Fernande stay in Paris, where only a married woman accompanied by her husband would not have been completely out of place. Italy, which for people in the north always evokes images of vague sensual pleasures, would not have been approved either. But Germany was entirely safe, and Fräulein, who longed to see her homeland once more, heartily praised its virtuous people and pure morals. On several occasions Jeanne let her sister borrow her indispensable governess, whom she would replace temporarily with a woman recommended by the nuns. Fernande thus spent several summers and autumns traveling on the Rhine or the Neckar, admiring old castles, con-templating the Madonna of Dresden or, in Munich, the ancient statues of the Glyptothek (which Fräulein, however, considered indecent), and above all growing languid or intoxicated as she listened to the endless stream of music that flowed, so to speak, out of Germany—from its operas, its concerts, its bandstands, and its restaurant orchestras.

They stayed in pensions recommended in their guidebook, which were considered more suitable than hotels. There they made the acquaintance of educated people. The pensions were full of budding writers, eternal students, and foreigners in search of culture. Hedda Gabler glances at the masterpieces in the Pinakothek and browses in the shops, while Jörgen Tesman makes notes on the domestic industry of the Middle Ages; Tonio Kröger and Gustav von Aschenbach pause for several days on their way to Italy, or else on their way back, and speak dreamily of nighttime in Naples and dusk in Venice; Oswald Alving, returning to Norway and concerned about his dizzy spells, stops in Frankfurt or in Munich to consult a good doctor. Obsessive travel, for a youthful heart, is almost always the corollary of obsessive love: around the bend of every landscape, upon the plinth of every statue, Fernande eagerly anticipates the ap-pearance of one of those exquisite beings so frequently found in novels and poetry books. The somewhat insipid style of these daydreams does not prevent them from embodying something essential: the need for love, which Fernande envelops in clouds of literature, and the need for sexual satisfaction, which she does not acknowledge.

Pale idylls must have begun to take shape in the pension whenever a book was borrowed or returned, whenever the ami-able Herr X politely offered to accompany Mademoiselle on a stroll through the park, or simply whenever some unknown young man was spied reading at the next table, never to reappear the following day. But the feminine element prevails. There are the proper English and American misses, virtually indistinguishable from one another except for their accents, who have come to improve their solfeggio or their technique on the piano. There are also more robust women, deliberately ill dressed, sporting cravats and sometimes wearing glasses, aggressively indifferent to their own plainness or beauty. These women are busy copying paintings in museums, sketching nude models, studying the dramatic arts, or sometimes distributing socialist tracts. Once or twice a lovely, disheveled girl, who has left her respectable family far behind somewhere in Scandinavia or Poland, invites Fernande to her room to share a cake laced with kirsch. But extreme feminism, the assertion that everything in the ethics of love is in need of revision, frightens the young lady from Suarlée; she withdraws her hand, which the young anarchist has been stroking affectionately.

She is alone here, just as she was in the house in the Ixelles quarter. She begins to perceive that unless there is some elective affinity (always rare), human beings draw close to one another and form long-lasting ties only when social milieu, education, ideas, or mutual interests unite them and when their thoughts are expressed in the same idiom. Fernande does not speak the language of these passing acquaintances, who are more liberated than she is. Unlike them, she does not have any raison d'être. She does not seek to improve her skills in music; she will never be a poet or an art critic; she is incapable of painting even a clumsy watercolor. Social injustice, which distresses the Russian girl in the starched collar who lives on the same floor, is, in her own world, merely a commonplace evoking images of striking workers, and she does not understand that a woman might have political opinions. But where does she belong, and what is she to do? Devoting oneself to good works, which Jeanne advises as a way to keep busy during the winter, seems to her to be the business of authoritarian women of the military type, who sew baby clothes and lecture unwed mothers. The convent, which on her deathbed will seem to her the best solution for her daughter, holds no attraction for her at this time: the austerity of the contemplative orders appalls her; the idea of having to care for the sick inspires her with a disgust that she knows she can never overcome; the habit of the Sisters of the Sacred Heart does not appeal to her either. None of these things will ever bring fulfillment to her life. Marriage is the sole way out, if only so that she will not have to retain the inferior status of a young woman with no house of her own. But Oswald Alving and Tonio Kröger are making no offers, and the only practical solutions are those that can be found dressed in tails in the drawing rooms of Brussels.

Nevertheless, she did have her German idyll. One fine September she stayed with Fräulein in a little hotel on the edge of the Black Forest. She went out by herself for a long walk. Fräulein, who suffered from migraines and who moreover continued to put faith in Germanic virtue, accompanied her less and less frequently on such outings. There were few other people to be seen that day; the students who wandered through the woods singing—sometimes bawling—the lieder of Schubert had returned to their universities. Mademoiselle de C. de M. made her way along one of those paths on which it is impossible to get lost, so plainly is every fork marked with blue or red signs. At last she sat down in a clearing, on a grassy knoll. No doubt she had a book with her as usual. Soon a young woodsman in knee breeches sat down beside her. He was handsome, with the blond beauty of a Siegfried. He spoke to her; clearly he was not entirely a peasant. They exchange the customary banalities:

she mentions the country she comes from and explains that she likes Germany very much. Little by little they draw near each other: this handsome, artless boy has charmed her.

She receives a kiss, then gives one in return, then agrees to accept a caress. Their boldness does not extend very far, but Fernande has at least rested her head on a man's shoulder; she has felt the warmth and movement of his hands; she has abandoned herself to that violent sweetness that throws one's entire being into confusion. Henceforth she knows that her body is something other than a machine for sleeping, walking, and eating, and also something other than a flesh-and-blood mannequin to be covered with a dress. The soft sylvan wildness transports her to a world where there is no longer a place for the false twinges of shame that paralyze her at the pension. Fräulein mentioned yet again that the fresh air was doing Mademoiselle a world of good.

She was too scrupulous not to confide this tame adventure to Monsieur de C. in later years. Michel had very broadminded views on the freedom of unmarried women: a confidence of this type was called for only if the encounter produced a child, who would have to be provided for and who might someday be a cause of blackmail. Fernande's confession, which he thought foolish, irritated him. Apart from prostitutes and a few madwomen who did not concern him, Michel, as I have said, liked to imagine all women as creatures innocent of any carnal impulse, who yielded only out of affection to the man capable of seducing them and who felt in his arms no other joy than that of sublime love. Though his own experience had continually warred against this notion, he held on to it all his life, concealed in the depths where we store those opinions that are dear to us but that the facts contradict. It reappeared from time to time until the end of his days. Unless, going to the other extreme, he took all women for Messalinas, which would likewise present difficulties. On this occasion, Fernande seemed to him a simpleminded woman who had imagined she saw the light of love in the eye of a German lout, instead of seeing what Michel called crude desire, whenever it was not he himself who was feeling it. That she might have felt pure sensual delight would not only have been disgraceful for her—it would have been inexplicable. But women, thought Monsieur de C., are beyond comprehension.

The days that followed were rainy: Fernande never again saw her Siegfried. At the onset of winter, she returned with no great pleasure to the social round. Baron H., noticed several times at evening parties, was now scarcely more than a lovely faded dream. A feeling of déjà vu lent a gray cast to everything. She was disgusted by the very real coarseness of some of her dance partners: that rough laugh that bursts out all the more noisily the longer it takes for the joke to be understood, those conversations between two gentlemen, overheard at the buffet table, dealing with nothing but stock-market tips, hunting stories, or women. Her *carnet de bal* from that winter shows me that she counted among her dance partners at least two young men who later made honorable careers in politics or letters, but it is unlikely that people would have spoken of literature between contradances, and if anyone had discussed the fall of the minister, Fernande probably would not have listened. It was doubtless at this time that she took as her motto a thought that she had gleaned from some book or other: "To know things well is to free oneself of them." She later passed on her fondness for it to Monsieur de C., who allowed it to pervade his thinking. I have often taken exception to it. To know things well is, on the contrary, almost always to discover in them unexpected contours and richnesses; it is to correct the flat, conventional,

298

and summary image that we form of objects we have never examined closely. In its most profound sense, however, the phrase touches on certain basic truths. Yet in order to make them truly our own, we must be satisfied in body and soul. Fernande was far from satisfied.

Time passed, no one knew quite how. On the twenty-third of February 1900, under a gray winter sky and with a heavy heart, she celebrated her twenty-eighth birthday.

In the same week, or nearly so, she received a letter from an old family friend, Baroness V., which requested an immediate response. (Once again the initial is fictitious, since I have forgotten the name of this lady, whom I can rightfully call the author of my days.) This dowager, who felt the greatest affection for Fernande, was inviting her to spend the Easter holidays in Ostend, where she owned a villa pleasantly located in a secluded spot on the dunes. Baroness V., who scorned the fashionable Season, hardly ever went there, and received visitors only in the spring and fall. She informed Fernande that this time her guests would include, in addition to acquaintances whom Mademoiselle de C. de M. already knew, a well-bred Frenchman of about forty, who carried himself handsomely and whom her young friend was sure to find excellent company. Monsieur de C. had lost his wife the preceding autumn; he had a fifteen-year-old son who was looked after primarily by the maternal grandparents; instead of traveling, as he usually did, he had spent the winter at his town house in Lille. In the hills of Flanders, not far from the Belgian border, he owned an estate that on clear days afforded a lovely view of the North Sea—a view that the baroness greatly admired. It was to be hoped that a week spent with a few pleasant people, at the home of an old friend, would help this recent widower recover a bit of his old gaiety and confidence in life. Fernande accepted the kind dowager's invitation, as she had on several occasions in the past. She did what every woman does in such cases: she bought one or two new dresses and had several others refashioned.

When she entered the baroness's drawing room on the evening of her arrival, she spied amid a group of people a tall man who stood very straight, held his head high, and spoke with great vivacity. He did not in the least look sad. Monsieur de C. spoke brilliantly, as a number of people did in those days and as scarcely anyone does today, when it seems as if human beings are communicating less and less. He did not monopolize the conversation: he was, in contrast, one of those people who lend their interlocutors more fire, intelligence, and spirit than they actually possess. His closely cropped hair and his long drooping mustache made this northern Frenchman look deceptively like a Hungarian magnate. His deep-set eyes, so intensely blue that they gave him a touch of the sorcerer, gleamed beneath his bushy brows. Fernande, who was not very observant, doubtless did not notice on that first evening his high, finely shaped ears, which Monsieur de C. prided himself on being able to wiggle whenever he pleased. Seated next to him at the dinner table, she probably admired his large hands, those of a horseman or a blacksmith, without noticing that the middle finger of his left hand was missing its first joint. All these details, which I find it convenient to give here, might easily have imparted to Baroness V.'s guest a strange, almost intimidating aspect, had not his qualities as gentleman and man of the world so clearly predominated. Toward Mademoiselle de C. (who had been described to him in a letter analogous to the one Fernande had received concerning him), he showed all the requisite attentions. When someone suggested after dinner that it would be nice to hear some music, Fernande excused herself, reminding her hostess that she could neither sing nor play the piano very well. Monsieur de C., who was no admirer of such social talents, was pleased at this.

The baroness, a benevolent matchmaker as so many women of her age and class instinctively are, lets them spend a good deal of time alone together. Most of the other guests have already departed. In the morning, Fernande and Michel take a walk along the beach, still deserted in this chilly month of April. Hampered by her long skirts and by the veil she wears to protect herself from the sand, Fernande yields to the force of the wind. Michel must slow his pace, a symbol of future concessions. He hires a horse. She is in no sense a horsewoman and, in fact, scarcely knows how to ride; he tells himself that this is something she will learn in good time. She watches him from the veranda as he performs caracoles in the dunes. The great beauty of this coastline, even defiled as it already is in Fernande's day, consists in the fact that as soon as the visitor turns his back on the ugly rows of villas on the embankment, his gaze is filled with that fluid immensity, nameless and ageless, that gray sand and pale water ceaselessly swept by the wind. From the distance at which she is watching them, Fernande can no longer make out the details of the man's clothing or the trappings of his mount: they are merely a horse and rider, as if in the dawn of time. At low tide Michel heads toward the water; the animal wades in over its hocks, to cool itself. The horseman contemplating the open sea is at this moment a thousand miles from Fernande. On rainy days, chatting by the fire is the best way to pass the time. He notices that she has an admirable way of telling stories, quite like a poet. Thank goodness she has no accent, which this Frenchman would have found intolerable.

His mind wanders: two or three years before, during another holiday at Ostend, he had suggested to Berthe, his first wife, that they take a walk on the dunes. She had suffered a dizzy spell. (Women were all alike, laced up so absurdly in their corsets.) They were passing by the gate of a villa; a servant was arranging the rattan chairs on the porch. Monsieur de C. asked if Berthe might be allowed to sit down. The baroness, who at that moment appeared, invited the two strangers to stay awhile; a friendship was born, more between Michel and the elderly lady than between her and Berthe, whom she considered somewhat dry and cold. Is it necessary to begin all over again just because he suggested an autumn walk on the beach two or three years ago? The description of Fernande that the baroness sent him is not inaccurate. Beautiful hair badly coiffed. Imploring eyes, and not only because she wishes to please him: she looks with the same vague tenderness at the city street-sweeper and the woman who runs the newsstand. For a woman of her class, she is well read. Her age is appropriate. Monsieur de C. believes that if a forty-year-old man marries a girl of twenty, all his country neighbors will inevitably pinch her bottom. (I let Michel keep his own choice of words; otherwise I wouldn't recognize him.) For the same reason, it's fortunate she's not a raving beauty. She's a thoroughbred, in any case, and this is a point that matters to him—despite his continual assertions that breeding is nothing, a name is nothing, social status is nothing, money is nothing (though he spends it with great zeal), and in general everything is nothing.

He expects that his mother will make bittersweet remarks; but kindness is not one of Madame Noémi's qualities, as everyone well knows. He has worries about money, or would have if

he were capable of them, and already foresees the extra expense
that Fernande will cause him; but spending money on a woman
is part of the pleasure he expects from her. Besides, Mademoiselle de C. de M. luckily has her own little personal fortune,
which she can fall back on if ever there should be some sort of
rupture between them. The winter spent with his mother was
gloomy; traveling alone is not always fun either. Moreover, she
is a woman, and he is a man who likes women. Adulterous love
affairs take time; prostitutes are out of the question; chambermaids are not to his taste. Clearly, he could marry one of
Berthe's sisters; but this, too, is out of the question. He glances
appreciatively at Fernande's soft, somewhat languid form.

But when he begins to make overtures, Mademoiselle de
C. de M. hesitates. Not that the baroness has misled her: he
is quite suitable. The amiable matchmaker has nevertheless
been vague about certain minor details, of which she herself is
perhaps ignorant. This "fortyish" Frenchman is, to be exact,
forty-six years old. The sudden death of his first wife shook
him; it did not break his heart, as the baroness's letter might
lead one to believe. The town house in Lille actually belongs
to the stout and wealthy Noémi, who likewise holds sway over
Mont-Noir and its lovely view, which she will not relinquish
until the moment of death. Michel is at home only in various
Grand Hotels. The baroness has said nothing concerning the
past of this presumptive fiancé, but the story of his haphazard
life, more characteristic of the eighteenth century than the
nineteenth, would doubtless have been exciting rather than
worrisome to Fernande. Without knowing why, and without
using this phrase, which is not in her vocabulary, she feels
herself in the presence of a human being of the noblest order.
But this impetuous and free-living Frenchman does not inspire
her with those tremblings of delight that to her mind constitute

love. It is not her fault if she prefers the angelic type, the
aesthetic type, or the Siegfried type to the cavalry-officer type.
Michel, who is not accustomed to feminine resistance, is disconcerted and annoyed. Finally he hits upon the proposal that
wins the day:

"You say you would like to spend the summer in Germany.
What pleasure it would give me to discover with you that land
I know so little about . . . We shall take with us the Fräulein
you've spoken of so often . . . We must observe the proprieties,
so long as they are not too much of an inconvenience."

This offer took Fernande's breath away and utterly
charmed her. Returning to Jeanne's house, she announced to
her family the news of this engagement trip. They were shocked.
The most scandalous thing of all in this affair was Monsieur
de C.'s nationality. Nearly ten years later, I heard Cousin
Louise, filled with patriotism and sadness, cry in unforgettable
tones, "What a pity, all the same, that Fernande's daughter
should be French!" Things had not yet reached that point.
Nevertheless, Théobald made a few comments, on principle.
Jeanne made none, knowing that Fernande would do as she
pleased anyway. Fräulein went upstairs grumbling, to pack the
trunks.

Those trunks were the first mishap of the trip. In a moment of absentmindedness, Fräulein booked them to Cologne on a freight train. They arrived the day before the three travelers left that city. The delay gave Michel an opportunity to offer Fernande a certain number of trinkets that she temporarily lacked and that he chose for her in shops specializing in English leather goods and Parisian novelties. Fräulein took advantage of a pause in Düsseldorf to pay a visit to the offices of the farm-equipment company that her former fiancé had represented. She was told that Herr N. had died in Pomerania; she had a Mass said for the scoundrel's soul and performed this pious ritual every year until she died. Michel and Fernande, who had gone to tour the little rococo château at Benrath and to dream of gala entertainments, knew nothing of the austere governess's grief. Nearly twenty years later, one of Jeanne's former chambermaids, in whom the elderly German woman had confided, laughingly told me the story.

Michel and Fernande immersed themselves in the Germans' good-natured friendliness. Both of them liked the village festivals, where handsome boys waltzed with pretty girls, and, at the English Garden in Munich, the groups of placid middle-class people sipping their beer by the Chinese Tower. The Passion Play at Oberammergau delighted them. Michel persuaded Fernande to give up staying at cozy but uncomfortable pensions. From the window of her hotel room, Fräulein, whose attitude toward Monsieur de C. has changed from peevish mistrust to boundless admiration (he treats her courteously, and even gallantly), waves her handkerchief when she sees the carriage rattle by with these unusual fiancés, whom she does not want to burden with her presence and who are setting off to sightsee in the city and its environs. A victim of recurring migraines, she asks Monsieur and Mademoiselle to go to the pharmacy for her and purchase special remedies with forbidding names and Moliéresque effects. She thus unwittingly provides the indispensable element of humor for their romantic comedy.

Both of them share an admiration for Ludwig II of Bavaria: they find his châteaux delightfully situated, but it is fortunate that the guide who takes them from room to room does not understand the Frenchman's comments on the Louis XIV consoles and the Louis XV chairs from the Faubourg Saint-Antoine with which the poetic king furnished some of his residences. Fernande kindly points out that these lapses of taste are rather charming. They take a turn on Lake Starnberg in an old gilded steamer which was formerly a royal vessel, looking together for the spot on the shore where the Lohengrin suspected of madness once strolled with his alienist and led that stout fellow in spectacles and umbrella to a watery death. Certain of Michel's scornful opinions, however, have begun to influence Fernande: she no longer regards swashbuckling military officers with the respect that Fräulein instilled in her.

At Innsbruck, toward the end of the summer, she felt a

bitter wind, brought from France by Monsieur de C.'s son, who at sixteen was still called "little Michel." His father had unwisely invited him to spend two weeks in the Tyrol with his future stepmother, between the dull vacation at his maternal grandparents' house and his return to a school somewhere in Lille, Arras, or Paris (Monsieur de C. was no longer sure of the city, the unruly boy having changed his address so often). Neither Michel nor Berthe had ever taken much interest in their son. Almost a year earlier, the adolescent had angered Monsieur de C. by refusing to enter the dying woman's room: to hear his father tell it, he would have spent those several agonizing days at the fair, playing the penny machines. Monsieur de C. had not seen, beneath that surly indifference, the effects of a bitter and frustrated childhood, aggravated by the drama of a mute conjugal conflict that was perhaps more painful to the young boy than to his parents themselves and finally reinforced by the horror of that week of deathbed suffering. He did not realize, moreover, that in the eyes of an adolescent, even if he had had little love for his mother, a widower of forty-seven who dances attendance on her replacement could seem odious or vaguely obscene. Fernande will make the situation worse with her vain efforts at maternal solicitude.

Fifty years later my half brother wrote a brief description of those days, the memory of which had soured within him during the intervening years. In his account, the rage of the adolescent is mingled with the prejudices of the mature man. This amateur genealogist who spent his leisure hours diligently noting the dates of births, marriages, and deaths, including those of Fernande, claims in his memoir that his future stepmother was thirty-five, an age she was destined never to attain.

Fernande

As we have seen, she was twenty-eight. Adolescents almost always tend to assume that adults are older than they actually are; it is not surprising that the boy should have made this mistake, but it is symptomatic that he repeated it fifty years later, despite the dates that he himself had recorded elsewhere. He makes fun of the fiancée's pinched-in waist and the curves that his father found so attractive, without realizing that he is judging a woman of the Belle Epoque according to an aesthetic standard that expects all women to look like stringbeans. The photographs of the Fernande of those years show what one would expect: the discreet sinuous lines of a silhouette by Helleu. Still, I wonder whether the stepson has not unconsciously superimposed, on this first image of his future stepmother, the one preserved for us in a photograph dating from several months before my birth, apparently the last one taken prior to those likenesses refined by death. Here Fernande appears suddenly stout, laced into a shapeless traveling outfit. It is thus that Madame Noémi and my half brother would have seen her depart from Mont-Noir, never to return.

His reproach concerning her acne was perhaps more justified. The ailment was frequent in those days, as is proved by the advertisements for pharmaceutical specialties in contemporary newspapers. The hostile gaze of the schoolboy could have detected it beneath the rice powder. That Monsieur de C., so pitiless toward the most minor physical flaws in his women, never referred to it at least shows that those blemishes did not disfigure Fernande. The reproach of affectation was perhaps not without some basis in an age when this was rife. In any case, that lady who readily quoted her favorite poets while gazing at landscapes of her own choosing could not but appear affected to a boy who was a dunce in school. My half brother adds, with unconcealed satisfaction, that he soon learned the unfortunate stranger was quite wellborn. It is to be hoped that this remark was made retrospectively, and that a sixteen-year-old had not yet acquired such immense respect for good families.

The sullen boy having returned to his school and its worthy priests, Michel and Fernande could peacefully enjoy the late-summer days amid the lakes near Salzburg. There was a hint of autumn in the air. Something was coming to an end: their future travels would never completely recapture the impulsive freedom of that long prenuptial trip. Early one morning as the mist was slowly evaporating in the sunshine, they went walking deep in the gloomy park of Hellbrunn. Rounding a turn in the path, they came upon a pedestal that had no statue. Fernande drew Michel's attention to the vapor emanating from the moist earth—to the remarkable way in which it was condensing, rising from the pedestal like smoke from a sacrifice, then rising still higher, changing, taking on a vague resemblance to the white form of a goddess or a ghostly nymph. Michel had had a passion for poetry all his life; he had found it above all in books. This was perhaps the first time he had seen a well-educated young woman, through a graceful play of the imagination, bring this poetry to life around her in all its freshness. He felt as if he were in fairyland.

But fairies are changeable creatures, and sometimes quite mad. When Michel, after his return to Mont-Noir, came to Brussels for two days to issue the banns, he found Fernande in tears, bemoaning her waning life, her broken heart, her dismal future. As a heavenly body perturbs another when it passes in its vicinity, Baron H., spied at some evening party, had perhaps caused this crisis without being aware of it. Fernande declared that if she married, it would only be in deep mourning. Monsieur de C. did not become upset over such a trifle:

"What, my dear? . . . Black chantilly lace? . . . You'll look ravishing."

Fernande gave up the idea.

But a few days later, having once again returned to France and having attended the Mass commemorating the anniversary of his first wife's death, Michel, on what was probably an overcast morning in late October, received a letter from Fernande that he afterward carefully preserved. It bore witness to all the young woman's finest qualities.

> *My dear Michel,*
>
> *I would like you to receive a note from me tomorrow. The day will be a sad one for you. You will be so alone.*
>
> *See now: how stupid social conventions are! . . . It was utterly impossible for me to come with you, and yet what could be simpler than for two people to hold each other close and help each other when they are in love . . . Beginning with these last days of October, forget all that is past, dear Michel. You know what good Monsieur Feuillée says about the notion of time: that the past is truly past for us only when it has been forgotten.*
>
> *Also, have confidence in the promise of the future, and in me. I think that this dull, gray month of October is merely a cloud coming between two periods of sunshine, that of our charming trip to Germany and that of our life to come. Here, surrounded by family, we again fall prey to the worries and cares of existence, to rumors, to that fearful and cramped state of mind that afflicts everyone. Over there, traveling beneath a clearer sky, we shall recover our joyful*

*lightheartedness—that all-embracing tenderness and intimacy,
free from disturbance and vexation, which we found so
pleasant.*

*It makes me very happy to think that only three weeks
remain . . . And during these two days I shall say not
"Don't be sad" but "Don't be too sad." I look forward to
seeing you in the evening when you come on Tuesday.*

*Give our little Michel a hug for me. Best regards to all
. . . I love you very much.*

Fernande

The "good Monsieur Feuillée" must have been Alfred
Feuillée, a philosopher with a fair-sized readership in those
days, and the reference proves yet again that Fernande did not
scorn serious books. The "best regards to all" seems to be a way
of vaguely alluding to, without actually naming, Madame
Noémi, whom she already detested. The reference to "little
Michel" shows that the innocent Fernande still entertained
illusions about the degree of affection she might someday inspire
in her stepson.

Michel needed this talisman to help him confront not so
much the celebration of the Mass marking the anniversary of
his first wife's death as the celebration of his marriage, a trying
experience for a man of forty-seven who has already passed once
through those Caudine Forks. Two days before the wedding, a
solemn rite took place at Jeanne's house: the dividing up of the
silver, which had been bequeathed jointly to the two sisters. A
great quantity of it was spread out on the dining-room table,
mingled with tissue paper. Fräulein bustled about, counting
and recounting the place settings. A detailed list gave the description, value, and weight of each piece. It so happened that
the latter two bits of information were lacking for a large pair

of sugar tongs shaped to look like bear paws entwined in the coils of a snake—a dreadful object that Michel would gladly have sold for a pittance. At that late hour of the afternoon, the jewelry shops were closed. Théobald donned his hat, overcoat, and boots and paid a visit to a goldsmith he knew, who was glad to come down to his shop to weigh and appraise the item. Michel thought these scrupulous people were acting like petits bourgeois. When it had come time for him and his beloved sister Marie to divide up the jewelry and knickknacks bequeathed to them by their father, the brother and sister had amused themselves by drawing lots for each piece, and he had cheated so that Marie would win the ones she liked best. Those vaguely symbolic bear paws spoiled the wedding for him.

The morning of November 8 at last dawned—foggy and cold, I imagine, as November mornings in Brussels usually are. The weather would favor neither tender emotions nor light-colored dresses. The parish church was commonplace and ugly. Michel had invited very few people. His mother and son had come from Lille, the former already fretting about offspring who would eventually decrease "little Michel's" portion of the inheritance. Draped in gray taffeta or watered silk, she presented to the world the majestic remnants of a beautiful woman whose own marriage had taken place about the same time as that of Eugénie de Montijo and Napoleon III. Michel's sister Marie de P. had come, probably from Pas de Calais, with her husband, a courtly, gloomy fellow who combined a Jansenist austerity with old-fashioned royalist elegance. The excellent and rough-mannered Baudouin, Berthe's brother, had come out of loyalty to Michel. The charming matchmaker Baroness V. doubtless occupied a prie-dieu. But the numerous members of Fernande's clan were quite enough to fill the nave. She would have to break away from all those people.

A surprise was in store for Michel. At the last moment, Fernande introduced him to her maid of honor, the lovely Dutchwoman Monique, who had come the day before from The Hague and who was returning home that same evening. Wearing a pink velvet dress and a large felt rose in her dark hair, Monique dazzled and charmed Michel. If only Baroness V., the previous Easter, had invited to Ostend that golden face with its large eyes . . . But it was too late, and on top of everything Mademoiselle de T. was engaged. Moreover, Fernande looked quite charming in white lace. He thought her even more so in her severe traveling outfit, ready to accompany him to some distant place, far away from all complexities.

In 1927 or 1928—that is, a year or two before his death—my father pulled from a drawer a dozen pages of manuscript, wider than they were long, like the paper which Proust used for his rough drafts but which I don't believe is sold anymore. These made up the first chapter of a novel, begun around 1904, which he had not developed any further. With the exception of a translation and some poems, it was the only literary work he ever undertook. A man of the world, whom he called Georges de——, doubtless about thirty, leaves for Switzerland with the young lady he has just married that very morning at Versailles. In the course of the story, Michel inadvertently altered their destination, making them spend the night in Cologne. The young woman is distressed at being separated from her mother for the first time; the husband, who, not without a feeling of relief, has just broken with a mistress, now thinks of that woman with sadness and affection. The innocent freshness of his very young traveling companion is touching to

Georges: he thinks of the coming evening, when, in a moment, he will cause her to lose that fragile quality and will make her into a woman like all the rest. The somewhat constrained politeness and shyly affectionate gestures of these two people, recently united for life and finding themselves alone together for the first time in their private compartment, are skillfully rendered, as is the slightly embarrassing process of choosing a room with one bed in a Cologne hotel. Georges, leaving his wife to make her preparations for the night, engages in idle conversation with the waiter in the smoking room. Half an hour later, avoiding the elevator for fear of being subjected to the scrutiny of the attendant, he climbs the stairs and enters the room, which is now bathed in the dim light of a bedside lamp. Slowly and methodically he takes off his clothes and then, with a mixture of impatience and disappointment, goes through the motions too often made elsewhere with casual mistresses, all the while wishing for something different but not knowing what.

I was quite taken with the true-to-life tone of this story, which had no literary pretensions. Those were the days when I was writing my first novel, *Alexis*. From time to time I would read a few pages of it to Michel, a good listener who was capable of entering immediately into that character's inner life, so different from his own. It was, I believe, my description of Alexis's marriage that reminded him of the story he had drafted years before.

Some of my work had already been published in periodicals—a story here, an essay or poem there. He suggested that I publish his tale under my own name. This offer, unusual if one thinks about it, was typical of the sort of free and easy intimacy that prevailed between us. I refused, for the simple reason that I was not the author of those pages. He insisted:

316

"You will make them your own by revising them to suit you. They have no title, and it will doubtless be necessary to flesh them out a bit. I would like to see them published after all these years, but at my age I am not about to submit a manuscript to some editorial committee."

The playful scheme tempted me. Michel found nothing incongruous about attributing to my pen this story of a honeymoon trip circa 1900, any more than he was surprised to see me writing Alexis's intimate thoughts. This man, who continually repeated that nothing human should be alien to us, viewed age and sex as merely secondary contingencies in the matter of literary creation. Problems that at a later date would leave my critics perplexed were not problems for him.

I no longer remember which of us decided to call that little tale "The First Evening," and I still don't know if I like the title or not. In any case, it was I who pointed out to Michel that that initial chapter of an unfinished novel, thus transformed into a short story, left the reader hanging, so to speak. We cast about for an incident that would tie up the loose ends. One of us thought of having the hotel porter bring a telegram to Georges just as he is about to go upstairs; it informs him that the mistress he is thinking of half regretfully has committed suicide. The detail was not farfetched; I did not notice that it gave a banal ending to the narrative, whose greatest virtue was to be as open-ended as possible. This time we set the wedding night in Montreux, since we were not far from that town at the time we were engaged in this tinkering. My way of "fleshing out" the tale was to make Georges an intellectual with a constant tendency to immerse himself in profound reflections on any subject that came along—a trait that, contrary to what I thought, did not improve him. Touched up in this way, the story was sent off to a journal, which rejected it after the usual delay, then to another, which accepted it; but by that time, my father was dead. The piece was published a year later and received a modest literary prize, an outcome that would have amused Michel but also would have pleased him.

I have sometimes wondered what elements of lived reality were contained in "The First Evening." It seems that Monsieur de C. exercised the privilege of the genuine novelist, which is to invent while relying only here and there on his own experience. Neither the Berthe of days gone by, headstrong and bold, nor Fernande, more complex and an orphan besides, bore the slightest resemblance to that young bride who felt such love for her mother. Moreover, the second honeymoon trip, the only one that concerns us here, was far from being an occasion on which two people who scarcely knew each other were united for the first time in the swaying, jolting intimacy of a private railway compartment. And it is doubtful that Michel had had to renounce a titular mistress in order to marry Fernande: on the contrary, it seems to have been the loneliness of that winter in Lille that persuaded him to try this new venture. The traces of personal experience are to be found, rather, in the tone of tender and disillusioned sensuality, in the confused notion that such is life and that it could conceivably be better some other way. *Mutatis mutandis*, we can imagine Monsieur de C. in some Grand Hotel on the French or Italian Riviera, a resort with few patrons in those early days of November, as he spends a long half hour in the smoking room or on the slightly damp terrace that overlooks the sea and where, out of a desire to economize, the management has thus far lighted only a few of the large white porcelain globes that in those days adorned the terraces of good hotels. Like the character in his story, he would take the stairs in preference to the elevator. Making his way up the red carpet that is held in place by copper rods and that leads to what the Italians call the *piano nobile*, he ascends to his room at a pace neither too rapid nor too slow, turning things over in his mind and wondering how they will all work out.

That honeymoon trip, together with the lengthy prenuptial travels, lasted nearly a thousand days. Michel and Fernande, more like idlers than genuine sightseers, never weary of repeating a kind of seasonal circuit that brings them back to their favorite places and hotels. Their route includes Switzerland and the Riviera, the Italian lakes and the Venetian lagoons, Austria, with a brief visit to the spas of Bohemia, then across to Germany, which remains a homeland for Fräulein's pupil. They make only quick trips to Paris, to go shopping or to attend some fashionable play. Spain—about which Monsieur de C.'s knowledge, for the moment, goes no further than the Andalusian women of Barcelona celebrated by Musset—does not appeal to them: if they holiday at San Sebastián, it is because Fernande wanted to make the journey to Lourdes, thus turning their attention toward the Pyrenees. Hungary and the Ukraine, which Michel visited with Berthe, are now inappropriate for his itinerary; the same is true of England, which for him remains the province of another woman, loved to distraction. Neither is there any question of taking Fernande, a poor sailor, to the islands off Holland or Denmark, whose coasts he had navigated in days gone by. Michel and Fernande dream from time to time of a voyage in a dahabieh, which they will never make but which has left its trace in some of Michel's poetry, evoking nostalgic references to pink ibises and silver sands.

What they are searching for above all is the good life. Famous places and monuments matter to them, certainly, but not so much as mild climates in winter and bracing ones in summer, and that picturesqueness which Europe still has in abundance in 1900. Moreover, for them as for so many of their contemporaries, the hotel is a magical place, blending elements of the fabled Oriental caravanserai, the feudal castle, and the princely palace. In the restaurant, they enjoy the professional obsequiousness of the headwaiter and the wine steward, and the domesticated wildness of gypsy music. After a day spent wandering through the pleasantly sordid streets of an old Italian town, after mingling with the crowd at the flower festival in Nice and with the Oktoberfest revelers in Dachau (that charming little Bavarian village so beloved of painters), they return to their hotel as to a privileged place, almost extraterritorial, where luxury and tranquillity can be had for a price and where they bask in the attentions of the concierge and the manager. Barnabooth, Proust's Marcel, and the characters of Thomas Mann, Arnold Bennett, and Henry James do not think or feel any differently.

Nonetheless, neither Michel nor Fernande completely belongs to this parti-colored world, which they frequent along with everyone else on the roster of foreigners. Certainly, Michel does not find it disagreeable to kiss the hand of the grand duchess, who occupies the suite on the second floor and who has been quite gracious to Fernande; it is exciting to emerge from one of the Sacher's private dining rooms and encounter the archduke just coming out of another, three sheets in the wind and two demimondaines in his arms. The picturesquely wealthy Yankees who trail across the lobby after their guides make entertaining companions, and Sarah Bernhardt, dining with her impresario, adds to the charm of a Grand Hotel. But Sarah Bernhardt is, when all is said and done, interesting only on the stage; Americans are people whom one does not care to know; and Monsieur de C. is fond of repeating the irreverent adage "Russian princes and Italian marquis make poor company." Even the relationships that do not oblige one to bow and scrape, as he puts it, are still a nuisance: they take time.

A *fortiori*, Michel and Fernande are not the type of people who, armed with letters of introduction, are burning to visit the collections of Prince Colonna or Baron de Rothschild, which are for the most part closed to the public and which it is therefore a mark of distinction to have seen. Those of the museums suffice for them and indeed more than satisfy their hunger. They visit the galleries hoping to find here and there some lovely object that instantly charms or moves them, but any masterpiece that does not immediately appeal to them, however many stars it may boast in the guidebook, is not given a second glance. This free-spirited approach, though it fails to make them enlightened amateurs, at least saves them from having to express obligatory admiration and partake of fashionable enthusiasms. To Michel's eyes, most of the paintings at the annual exhibition seem ridiculous, which in fact they are. History has more of a hold on their attention, and the catastrophes of the past give them, in contrast, the feeling that they are vegetating in an age of stifling security. In Prague, Fernande, who is well versed in German history, evokes for Michel the principal actors in the Defenestration of 1618 (that of Jan Masaryk, in 1948, is yet to come), when haiduks or reiters, at the orders of the Protestant faction, threw from the windows of Hradčany Castle two of the king's Catholic councillors, who plunged seventy feet into the moat. A guide who is passing by with a group of tourists, and who understands French, informs Madame that she is looking at the wrong side of the building. They will have to pack up their emotions and move them to another site, so to speak. They are seized with uncontrollable laughter. They felt then that when it comes to grand historical memories, as with all things, faith makes all the difference.

I know what attaches me to these two strays, as one might call them, amid the throngs of Time Past. In this world where everyone thinks of putting himself forward, such ambition did not occur to them. The range of their learning, which I can see has many gaps, isolates them. It soon becomes apparent to Michel that the grand duchess has read virtually nothing. This man who instinctively forms a bond with every animal he meets detests hunting and is too fond of horses to enjoy racing. He can smell the fakery and pretentiousness in the Grand Prix, as he can in everything else. The fine foods and wines of fashionable restaurants hold no appeal for Fernande, who is content to dine on an orange and a glass of water. Monsieur de C., whose capacity for food is Homeric, likes only the simplest dishes: the delight of delights, for him, is to go to Larue's and order a plate of perfectly cooked eggs or some delicious boiled beef. The cabarets for vagrants, the basement clubs whose stairways may be missing a step and where new arrivals are greeted with a rowdy chorus ("Here they come, the swine!") entertain them for a mere half hour. They sample the bitter genius of Bruant and the touching argot of Rictus but sense all the artifice in these low hangouts for the worldly set. Only one vice links them to this fast society: the passion for gambling. But Fernande has for the moment exorcised it. Michel will take it up again only after her death.

From time to time, distant rumblings seem to herald a storm that never comes or that erupts so far away that the danger is imperceptible. Beginning in 1899, the Boer War raises French Anglophobia to a fever pitch, and Michel, when he is asked whether he supports Kruger or the English, answers that he is for the Kaffirs. In 1900 the couple, like everyone else, devour the newspaper accounts of the Boxers' atrocities, but above all Michel remembers how the ambassadors' wives, holding up their long skirts, ran as fast as they could to be the first on the scene at the looting of the Summer Palace. The assassination of Umberto I of Italy is nothing more than a dreadful item from the daily news. Flames of rebellion blaze up here and there in the Balkans or in Macedonia—mere brushfires. Sometimes a reference to the "affair," an allusion to the conflict between Church and State, once again revives Michel's interest in these matters. Out of a love for justice, he supports Dreyfus; out of a love for liberty, he is on the side of the persecuted Congregations. Moreover, he does not claim, in the first instance, to measure the enormous mass of deceptions and outrages that have accumulated in France over the years or, in the second, to ally himself with the Church, whose errors and oversights he deplores. His indignation is always short-lived, like his personal anger. Europe, through which he is wandering accompanied by a lady in boa and veil, is still a lovely park where the privileged can stroll about as they please and where identification papers are most useful when one is calling for letters at the General Delivery window. He tells himself that someday there will be war and that times will be hard for a while and that afterward the lamps will be lighted once again. If the Great Darkness comes, the middle class, which he detests, will have got what it deserves, but this upheaval will doubtless take place only after he himself is gone. England is solid, like the Bank of England. There will always be a France. The German Empire, nearly new, gives the impression of a gaudily painted metal toy that no one ever imagined would fall to pieces so soon. The Austrian Empire is majestic by reason of its very decrepitude: Michel is not unaware that the kind old emperor ("The poor man! How he has suffered!") was formerly known as the King of the Hanged, but in those remote histories of Hungary and Lombardy, how can one distinguish the just from the unjust? The Russian Empire, which he caught glimpses of on his travels with Berthe, resembles a sort of monarchy of the Great Mogul or the Grand Dairi, a kind of subarctic Orient. A vast Christianity frozen in rites older than those of the West, a sea of muzhiks, a continent full of nearly virgin land, the mummified saints in the crypts of the Kiev cathedral, and, high above the rest, the golden crosses atop the church domes, the sparkling tiaras, and the shimmering enamels of Fabergé. Against all this, what good are the efforts of an old man of God like Tolstoy and a few handfuls of anarchists? Michel would be quite surprised to learn that these three great imperial structures will not last even as long as the well-made garments that he orders from his tailor and prides himself on wearing for twenty years.

During those three years, Michel took hundreds of photographs. Many of them, almost stereoscopic, are in the form of long papyrus-like bands that roll up from each end when I try to lay them out flat. Scenes of life among the common people: farmers prodding their donkeys, peasant women balancing pitchers of water on their heads, rings of little girls in Italian piazzas, Bavarian farandoles. Monuments that he saw at such-and-such a time on such-and-such a date and whose images, thus captioned, would remind him (or so he thought) of the minor happy incidents of a day gone by. He was mistaken, apparently never having taken the time to cast another glance at those soon faded snapshots. Their sepia coloring imbues them with a disquieting melancholy: they look as if they had been taken under that infrared light which supposedly makes ghosts more easily perceptible to the eye. Venice seems to be suffering in advance from the disease it is dying of today: its palaces and churches look crumbly, as though they are being eaten away. Its canals, less crowded then than they are nowadays, are bathed in an unhealthy twilight, which Barrès compared at about that time to the baleful glow of an opal. The shadow of a storm is spreading over Lake Como. The palaces of Dresden and Würzburg, captured slightly askew by this amateur photographer, seem already distorted by the bombardments to come. The objectivity of this passerby without preconceived ideas reveals after the fact, like an X-ray, the wounds of a world that did not realize it was so threatened.

Now and again a presence enlivens the luxurious settings. Here is Trier, a sleek and glossy puppy, who was purchased in and named for Trèves and whose crooked paws have trotted about the Roman ruins of his native city. He is attached by a long leash to one of the bronze flagpoles located in front of Saint Mark's and jealously guards his master's overcoat, cane, and binoculars—a complete still life of the turn-of-the-century traveler. And of course here is Fernande. Fernande leaning toward the fountain at Marienbad, holding in one hand a bouquet of flowers and a parasol, in the other a glass of water, which she sips with a charming expression. Fernande slim and straight in her traveling suit—her skirt a bit shorter than usual, giving a glimpse of her high boots—on the snow-covered grounds of some nameless Alpine resort. Fernande in city clothes, the inevitable parasol in hand, advancing with little steps across a rocky land-

Fernande at Marienbad, 1900

Monsieur de C. on horseback at Mont-Noir, 1902

scape, while her stepson, perched like a cat atop a dolomitic formation, looks for all the world like a young troll. Fernande in a white blouse and light-colored skirt, crowned with one of those enormous beribboned hats she was so fond of, strolling with book in hand through some dark Germanic forest and, to judge from appearances, reading a few lines out loud. One of these images seems to testify to a happiness that Michel must have known at least intermittently during those years, the memory of which evidently faded afterward like the photographs themselves. The snapshot shows a room in an inn on Corsica. Vile flowered wallpaper, a dressing table that looks a bit rickety. A young woman sitting before the mirror inserts a last hairpin in the ornate coils of her chignon. Her upraised arms have let the loose sleeves of her white peignoir slip down to her shoulders. Her face is a reflection to be guessed at rather than perceived. On a little stand next to her are the portable stove and foot warmer used by travelers. I imagine Michel would not have taken the time to capture this scene if it had not summed up for him a morning of tender intimacy. He must have had quite a few such mornings in the course of those three years.

And yet, imperceptible rents are appearing in their simple life, as in a piece of silk that is worn in spots. It seems that Fernande, like many women in those days, harbored within her a Hedda Gabler, contorted and wounded. The shadow of the music-loving baron sometimes appears on the horizon. On days when there are sharp disagreements, Michel goes out for a long walk and comes back having regained his calm: he is not the type to prolong a quarrel. I have already spoken of his annoyance over lost rings and quickly disheveled toilettes. Fernande, who is nearsighted and declares she is delighted to be so ("Everything looks more beautiful, from afar, when you can't see the details"), nevertheless uses at the theater and elsewhere a lorgnette—

that arrogant device which transforms an infirmity into a sort of haughty reserve and of which she owns a whole collection in gold, silver, and (I am ashamed to say) tortoiseshell and ivory. The dry click of their spring causes Michel the same spasm of irritation as the click of an insolent fan.

Fernande's indolence limits the husband to unexciting strolls. Her riding lessons have failed to cure her of her fear of horses. For the little yacht that succeeds the ones Michel had with Berthe, the *Peri* and the *Banshee*, she has chosen the name of another legendary woman, the *Valkyrie* (unless the former owner, Countess Tassencourt, likewise a Wagnerian, had already given it this name, which would then have been one of the reasons for the purchase). But she has nothing of the Brünnhilde in her. They return from Corsica via the reliable mail coach. The *Valkyrie*, with its captain and crew of two, follows in its wake up and down the Italian coast, the three sailors lingering in each port where they have family, friends, or girls that strike their fancy. Michel merely laughs at their telegrams of regret: "TEMPO CATTIVISSIMO. NAVIGARE IMPOSSIBILE." But Fernande deplores the useless expense. Sometimes—at Genoa, at Livorno—their little boat catches up with them, and Monsieur de C. cannot resist the pleasure of spending a night on board, rocked gently by the waves. But he feels remorseful. It is not in his nature to leave a woman alone in her room in an Italian hotel, with a volume of Loti as her sole consolation. He rejoins her early in the morning and lingers to buy her flowers in some square named for the Risorgimento.

The cracks widen at Bayreuth. Fernande immerses herself in German legends and poetry. Monsieur de C. follows Wagner up to and including *Lohengrin* and *Tannhäuser*: he has been heard humming the "Song to the Evening Star." Beyond this point, the Music of the Future seems to him nothing but incessant noise. The stocky Tristans and the fat Isoldes, Wotan with his beard and belly, and the Rhinemaidens resembling stout, red-faced village girls fill him with mocking disdain; and he is scarcely less amused by the foods displayed at the buffet or pulled from spectators' pockets at intermission, the uniforms and helmets that are as theatrical as the barbaric finery on the stage, the stiff dresses of Berlin or the exaggeratedly languorous ones of Vienna. He eyes the worldly people who have come from Paris to applaud the New Music; Madame Verdurin is there with her coterie ("We'll form a clique! We'll form a clique!"); the shrill voices of the Parisian women can be heard over the rumbling tones of the Germans. Leaving Fernande to enjoy the third act of *Die Meistersinger* by herself, he returns to the hotel and takes Trier out for his evening walk. The glowing gas lamps observe this strolling pair, who are friendly and cynical in the true sense of the words, these two individuals frankly bound to each other, each with his own more or less limited sphere of action, his inherited tastes and personal experiences, his caprices, his urges to growl and sometimes to bite: a man and his dog.

The letters from her sisters brought Fernande round to a more accurate view of the pleasures of her own life. Jeanne's were limited to a weather report, with occasional news of a marriage, an illness, or a death in their immediate circle; Jeanne never imparted any details about her own existence, which she assumed would be of interest to no one. Several times, Michel had invited her to make a trip to Lourdes with him and Fernande: it seemed to him that her unusual ailment could benefit from the shock of immersion in the pool and from the charged atmosphere of a pilgrimage. Moreover, he did not deny the possibility of divine intervention—he did not deny anything.

But each time, Jeanne had answered coldly that miracles were not for her.

Zoé's letters are infused with a gentle piety. Describing the confirmation of Fernand, her oldest son, she mentions with emotion the touching address given by the priest, the almost celestial effect of the bouquets, the tapers, and the canticles sung by the little girls from the catechism class, and finally the excellent meal served by the Good Sisters in a nearby convent. Zoé does not add that she was unable to ask Monseigneur to dine at the godless man's château, still less in the restaurant of Cécile's nieces. What would she have said had she known that she would die two years later and that her Fernand would be carried off at the age of fifteen by a malignant fever? I imagine she would have accepted God's will without a word of protest. Shortly before her death, she bequeathed to her husband the share of wealth at her disposal, wishing despite everything to give him this proof of her confidence. In a farewell message perhaps inspired by Mathilde's, or perhaps intended to mislead everyone, this saint who was infused through and through with the teachings of her mother, her Fräulein, and the Dames Anglaises, and with the counsel of the parish priest, humbly demanded pardon from Hubert and her three children for the trouble she may have caused them and asked them to remain loyal to the spirit of the family. Hubert would demonstrate this spirit by eventually marrying Cécile.

In January 1902 at Pas de Calais, Michel and Fernande attend the funeral of another saint, Michel's sister Marie, killed accidentally during a stroll in the woods by a gamekeeper, whose shot ricocheted and struck her through the heart. I shall speak again elsewhere of Marie's life and death. Here let me say merely that, firmer in body and soul than Zoé, less wounded in her self-respect as a woman, she accomplished her ascension toward

God by instinct, by a sort of impulse of her entire being, supported by the mental discipline of the austere Christian France of earlier times. Michel no doubt suffered much more at this funeral service than he had at a certain anniversary Mass nearly three years earlier. Marie, fifteen years his junior, was probably the only person, with the exception of his father, whom he had both venerated and tenderly loved. But winter in the north of France is unbearable for Michel and Fernande: the vision of blue skies and waves soon leads them back to Menton or Bordighera.

The life he led with his second wife was expensive, as he had suspected it would be. Madame Noémi, who had permanent legal control over the inheritance, refused to consider any supplementary largesse, and Michel hesitated to resort to money-lenders, as he had during his years with Berthe. The solution, a classic one, was to spend the summer in the country. The dowager, closeted in her apartments and perpetually occupied in hatching or thwarting intrigues among the servants, scarcely ever bothered them. Michel did not fail to take Fernande to F. and introduce her to Berthe's brothers and sisters, with whom he had been friends for twenty years. An equine photograph shows him in boots and a high hat, side by side with those Messieurs de L. in bowlers, posing for a moment, on the way back from a local race or exhibition, by the front door of one of the neighborhood's rustic restaurants: my thoughts are drawn less to the horsemen than to the beautiful, docile horses, whose names are unknown to me. Photographed about the same time against the background of Mont-Noir's stables, Fernande in a riding habit keeps her seat as best she can on the pretty mare that Achille the groom controls with the aid of a long halter, smiling all the while so as to put Madame at ease.

But these outings and lessons will soon come to an end.

Even on foot, and beneath the gentle September sun, a tour of the estate with its meadows and stands of fir trees is too tiring for Fernande. Like a traveler on the deck of a transatlantic liner, she reclines on a chaise longue at the edge of the terrace, from which one sees, or thinks one sees, beyond the pale green expanse of the rolling plain, the distant gray line of the sea. Majestic clouds drift in the open sky, like those once sketched in this same region by painters of seventeenth-century battles. Fernande spreads a lap robe over her knees, languidly opens a book, and gives a caress to Trier, who is curled up by her feet. My face begins to take shape on the screen of time.

Author's Note

Translator's Notes

Author's Note

As indicated along the way, I have written this book with the aid of documents and oral traditions passed on to me. I have also made use of certain well-known genealogical compilations and, in the sections concerning Flémalle-Grande, of newspaper articles or publications by local historians. Here and there I have found contradictions, albeit trivial ones, among these various sources. In such cases I have not always tried to track down proofs that would be difficult and often impossible to locate; it matters little to me, and still less to the reader, that some obscure uncle of one of my great-grandfathers may have been named Jean-Louis or Jean-Baptiste, or that such-and-such an estate may have changed hands on the date I have given or ten years earlier. We are dealing here with history of a very minor sort.

The passages concerning the two Pirmez brothers, Octave and Fernand (known as Rémo), draw extensively on the writings of Octave Pirmez himself, and particularly on his book *Rémo*, which is devoted in its entirety to his brother's life and death. *Rémo* contains numerous excerpts from the letters and diaries of the younger brother, which are all the more precious because the papers that he left behind and that Octave said he was preparing for publication have never appeared. I have also taken into account some unpublished letters from Octave's correspondence in the collection of the Bibliothèque Nationale of Brussels, though they add but little to what was already known about their author; and especially a letter from Octave to Félicien Rops, published in *Le Mercure de France* on July 1, 1905, that reveals a good deal about the writer's literary behavior, explaining in part his mental reservations and his often disconcerting periphrases.

The long list of articles devoted to Octave Pirmez and his work, a list that was very kindly sent to me by M. Roger Brucher, director of the Bibliothèque Royale, who published it in his monumental *Bibliographie des Ecrivains Français de Belgique*, may give readers a mistaken impression by virtue of its very richness: it seems to indicate that this author, who is virtually unknown in France, has been carefully and rigorously studied in his native country. In fact, this is not the case. Apart from the surprising and touching portrait sketched from life by his contemporary James Vandrunen, engineer, geologist, and man of letters who became vice-chancellor of the University of Brussels, the articles on Octave Pirmez and the references to his life and work are nearly all misleading. Most are swimming in that atmosphere of almost mawkish esteem that is so often accorded great amateurs who leave behind them a respectable, reliable body of work and whose poetic or romantic personality has left its mark. Moreover, it is apparent from the tone of his books, and especially from the confidences revealed in his letters, that it was precisely this haze of somewhat flaccid hagiology that Octave Pirmez himself liked to have around him. I think he becomes more interesting as a person when viewed in a different way.

The work by the local scholar Paul Champagne, *Nouvel essai sur Octave Pirmez*, which appeared in 1952 and which can be found in the catalogue of the Académie Belge de Langue et de Littérature Françaises—as well as some other pieces by the same author on the same subject, likewise written in hagiographic style—preserve the somewhat conventional image that the poet and his family strove to give of him and his milieu around 1883. No more than seven or eight lines in these works are devoted to Fernand-Rémo, the younger brother viewed as liberal and rebellious according to the ideas of the family group, and only one line alludes to his death from a gunshot in Liège in 1872, even though this event and indeed his entire tragic career had obviously been profoundly disturbing to Octave. Paul Champagne's book, rich in minor but often significant biographical details, was valuable to me for the many extracts from letters and unpublished diaries that it contains. I found in it, for example, new information about the Drion sisters, my great-grandmothers and great-aunts; and the letter from Arthur de Cartier de Marchienne, my grandfather, to his first cousin Octave, from which I in turn quote several lines, is taken from the same source. I did, however, turn up a certain number of more or less considerable errors in Paul Champagne's text: my great-great-grandfather Joseph de Cartier de Marchienne was not a baron; my grandmother Mathilde did not have fourteen children; the year of Rémo's birth was not 1848 but 1843—a simple misprint, no doubt, but one that conjures away five years of the life of this man who died before he was thirty and one that also tends, curiously, to diminish still further the role he played in his brother's life. I am only too aware that such errors are almost inevitable in the fluid and inconsistent substance that composes the history of families, as well as the history of individuals still too close to us and yet already too far away, and I am afraid my own work likewise offers a fair sampling of these. It is no less true that a comprehensive biography of Octave Pirmez and his brother has never been written, and probably never will be written, since changes in ideas, sensibilities, and conditions of life make it difficult today to appreciate these two men for what they are truly worth and since too many indispensable documents have doubtless been irretrievably dispersed.

I should like to mention here the names of some people who helped me by providing letters, photographs, genealogical facts, and illuminating anecdotes or by procuring books for me that have become virtually impossible to find. In particular, without the friendly goodwill of Jean Eeckhout, Esquire, of Ghent, certain pages of this book could certainly not have been written. I likewise thank Mme de Reyghère of Bruges, M. Pierre Hanquet of Liège, and M. Joseph Philippe, director of the museums of Liège, as well as M. Robert Rothschild, Belgian ambassador to London, and M. Jean Chauvel, former French ambassador to the United Nations, who helped me add numerous details to the portrait of their former colleague Emile de Cartier de Marchienne and to that of his nephew Jean, killed in the Resistance in 1944. I should also like to express warm thanks to Mme Jeanne Carayon, who was always willing to give me information about certain historical incidents or certain individuals located in the background of my narrative—for example, the December Second exile Désiré Bancel, friend of the two Pirmez brothers. To M. Louis Greenberg, a specialist in the history of the Commune, I owe my knowledge of certain texts concerning another of Rémo's friends, Gustave Flourens, "the red knight, exceedingly brave and slightly mad," mentioned in Hugo's notebooks, who was executed by royalist soldiers in April 1871.

Finally I should like to thank M. Marc Casati, who identified for me the "good Monsieur Feuillée" mentioned by Fernande.

Among the people connected either closely or distantly to my maternal family who agreed to meet with me, I should like first of all to thank Mme Rita Manderbach, widow of "Cousin Jean" and, if I am not mistaken, the only survivor other than myself of Arthur and Mathilde's grandchildren and their spouses; Baron Drion du Chapois and Countess Norbert de Broqueville, née Drion; Baroness Hermann Pirmez; Baron de Cartier d'Yves; Baron de Pitteurs; M. A. Mélot of Namur; Countess Claude de Briey; and especially my second cousin M. Raymond Delvaux, who, after providing me with numerous details, frequently new to me, about the history of his grandparents and great-grandparents, said that he hoped I would evoke the psychological climate of those lives and added:

"Even if historical truth were not respected, no one could reproach you for it. Besides, it is not an easy task to render this truth, for in that vicious circle of contradictory emotions, with their multiple interactions, it is impossible to say which is cause and which is effect."

Remarks like these cannot but reassure all biographers, historians, and novelists who are searching for a truth that is multiple, unstable, evasive, sometimes saddening, and at first glance scandalous but that one cannot approach without often feeling for human beings in all their frailty a certain measure of kinship and, always, a sense of pity.

Translator's Notes

Madame Yourcenar took a keen interest in the translation of her works, particularly into English (a language she knew very well), and made a number of changes and corrections in the manuscript of this book. Unfortunately she died after reviewing only eight chapters, and the translation had to be completed without the benefit of her insights and guidance. She had an impressive knowledge of specialized terms and shades of meaning, as well as a gift for hitting upon peculiarly apt and satisfying renderings; it was she, for example, who chose the title *Dear Departed*, with all its resonant irony.

In the notes that follow, I have explained her emendations and also some possibly obscure passages in the text, knowing full well that it would take a great deal more space to do justice to the wealth of her literary, historical, and cultural allusions. I have tried to steer a reasonable middle course between burdening the book with intrusive, unwieldy documentation and leaving the reader with no clarification at all. The genealogical chart is offered in a similar spirit, as an optional aid to readers in sorting out the large cast of characters; it does not appear in the French text.

The basis for this translation is the edition of *Souvenirs Pieux* published by Gallimard/Folio in 1974. There exists another edition, published by Editions Alphée in Monaco in 1973 and now out of print, which differs in a number of respects from the later, revised version. The photographs are a selection from those that appear in the Alphée edition; the Gallimard/Folio volume contains no illustrations.

For his invaluable assistance in the preparation of this translation, I am deeply grateful to Walter Kaiser, whose discerning eye and sensitive ear helped purge the text of numerous errors and awkwardnesses. My gratitude also goes to George Savidis, who taught me much about the art and craft of translation and who motivated me to begin this project. In addition I owe thanks to Jane Bobko, Roslyn Schloss, and Lynn Warshow for their expert editing; to Jean Lunt for her assistance in obtaining the illustrations; and, as always, to David Sykes for his unfailing support and encouragement.

———

page

4 *"Mildly curious":* In a comment written on an early draft of this translation, Mme Yourcenar indicated that the phrase "avec curiosité" should not be rendered by too forceful an expression here: "It is *very important* that the reader *not* get the impression that the author is greatly or personally interested about her origins, since the whole quest is more sociological and historical than personal."

7 *"Bois de la Cambre":* Author's emendation. The 1974 Gallimard/Folio edition (p. 16) reads simply "Bois."

9 *"Mademoiselle de T.":* Author's correction. The Gallimard/Folio edition (p. 18) reads "Mademoiselle G." Also corrected on pp. 262 and 314.

25 *"Nord":* A *département* in northern France, bordering the North Sea and Belgium. Its capital is Lille.

34 *"Headed to the railway station, and thence sped home to Mont-Noir":* Author's addition. The Gallimard/Folio edition (p. 46) reads "remonta dans la voiture qui l'attendait et repartit pour le Mont-Noir" ("climbed back into the waiting carriage and left again for Mont-Noir"). The author commented on an early draft: "Would it be clearer to say 'to the station, and from there home to Mont-Noir'? I am trying to avoid the notion that Bruxelles is *near* Mont-Noir—at that time, four or five hours by train."

44 *"Before my tenth year":* Author's correction. The Gallimard/Folio edition (p. 57) reads "vers ma dixième année" ("around my tenth year").

56 *"Seven silver lozenges"*: Author's correction. The Gallimard/Folio edition (p. 69) reads "dix losanges d'argent" ("ten silver lozenges").

56 *"Carnet de bal"*: Mme Yourcenar preferred this to the English term "dance card."

56 *"La Semeuse"*: Female figure of a sower, seen most commonly on French coins. It was the emblem of the Third Republic (1870–1940).

62 *"The letter Q having some rather crude associations in French"*: Author's addition; the phrase does not appear in the original. In French, Q rhymes with *cul* (the *l* is not pronounced), which is an impolite word meaning "rump" or "ass."

63 *"Commynes"*: Philippe de Commynes (also spelled Comines and Commines; lived c. 1447–c. 1511), French historian, courtier, and diplomat. His *Mémoires sur les règnes de Louis XI et de Charles VIII* (*Memoirs of the Reigns of Louis XI and Charles VIII*) is an important historical and literary work celebrated for its penetrating analyses of individuals and institutions.

63 *"Théroigne de Méricourt"*: Ardent, outspoken radical and one of the most colorful figures in Paris during the Revolution, known for her fiery speeches and picturesque garb (including pistols, saber, and plumed hat). She was often referred to as "la belle Liégeoise." She participated in the taking of the Bastille on July 14, 1789, and distinguished herself in battles with royalist troops. After 1793 her mental health deteriorated; she died insane in 1817 at the age of fifty-five.

66 *"Oradour"*: Oradour-sur-Glane, village in south-central France, near Limoges. On June 10, 1944, the village and its 642 inhabitants were destroyed by German troops, who imprisoned the men in barns and the women and children in the church, and then set fire to the whole village. The name Oradour has become a synonym for "atrocity."

68 *"Grignoux"* and *"Chiroux"*: Terms designating the political factions in the principality of Liège during the seventeenth century. The Grignoux (whose name, in the regional patois, meant "grumblers" or "malcontents") were those who favored the interests of the people. The Chiroux, or "swallows," whose name derived from their style of dress (black coats and breeches, and white stockings), were the partisans of the court.

85 *"The shock of the suddenly revealed past"*: The phrase is from Sacheverell Sitwell's *Monks, Nuns, and Monasteries* (New York: Holt, Rinehart and Winston, 1965). Sitwell is describing the chantry chapel at Tewkesbury, Gloucestershire: "On the north side of the choir is the Despenser tomb with the kneeling, mailed figure of its long-dead occupant, Sir Edward le Despenser [d. 1375], kneeling with his face towards the altar. It is as effective and shattering in that silence as a trumpet blown from a tower in the dark of night . . . It is not a lifesize figure, being in fact no more than half-lifesize. But if we walk round the choir so as to get the best view of him, which is from over the roof of the chantry chapel opposite, the effect, almost the sound of it, is as strange and haunting as that first time one hears the muezzin calling from a minaret, and we come out of Tewkesbury Abbey and back into the present enriched by an experience

in its little way as marvellous and memorable as any shock of the suddenly revealed past in whatever other land" (pp. 5–6).

148 *"Napoleon the Small"*: "Napoléon le Petit" was a scornful name that Victor Hugo frequently applied to Napoleon III, especially after Hugo went into exile. The term makes an explicit and unfavorable comparison between Napoleon III and his famous uncle, Napoleon I ("Napoléon le Grand"), and is the title of a satirical tract that Hugo wrote in Brussels in 1852.

158 *"Palikars"*: Soldiers of the Greek militia who fought against Turkey in Greece's war for independence (1821–28).

160 *"La Païva"*: Celebrated Parisian courtesan (1819–84), whose real name was Thérèse-Pauline-Blanche Lachmann. She made a fortune from her lovers, who were among the richest and most powerful men of the day. Her sumptuous mansion on the Champs-Elysées still stands. Hortense Schneider (1838–1920) was both a grand courtesan and an operetta star, known for her performances in Offenbach's works. Mademoiselle Thérésa was a singer of popular songs who was admired by many (and disparaged by others) for the singular force and harshness of her vocal effects.

161 *"Liberal Empire"*: From 1860 to 1870 Napoleon III gradually liberalized his policies in order to win public support. He expanded civil liberties and the powers of the legislative assembly, causing members of the opposition to hope that the reforms would be lasting and far-reaching. The Liberal Empire came to an end with France's defeat in the Franco-Prussian War.

162 *"December Second exiles"*: Many republicans fled or were driven from France after Napoleon III overthrew the Second Republic on December 2, 1851, and declared himself emperor on December 2 of the following year. The most famous of these so-called December Second exiles was Victor Hugo.

162 *"Terrible Year"*: The phrase refers to 1870, a year of disasters for France. The nation was soundly defeated in the Franco-Prussian War. Napoleon III himself was captured at the battle of Sedan on September 1, his armies lost the will to fight, and the Parisians suffered great hardships during a four-month siege of their city.

194 *"Télémaque"*: *Les Aventures de Télémaque* was written in 1699 by the churchman Fénelon for his pupil, Louis XIV's grandson. Presented as a continuation of the *Odyssey*, it tells of the further adventures of Odysseus' son, Telemachus, and is designed to show the young prince, by indirection, the rewards of righteous behavior and good government. For approximately two centuries it was required reading for all French students, but its measured, classically inspired moralizing is not to modern tastes.

198 *"Catharist"*: The Cathari (from the Greek word meaning "pure") were members of a widespread religious movement of the Middle Ages. They believed in a dualistic universe and in absolute surrender of the flesh to the spirit.

200 *"Monsieur Homais"*: The apothecary in Gustave Flaubert's *Madame Bovary*. The epitome

of the self-satisfied country busybody, he prides himself on being anticlerical and Voltairean and tirelessly defends his views to the local curé, Monsieur Bournisien.

202 *"Kolokotronis"*: Theodore Kolokotronis (1770–1843), Greek patriot and general. During the 1820s he was a leader in the Greek war of independence against Ottoman rule, and has been the inspiration for numerous folk songs.

210 *"Faublas"*: Hero of *Les Amours du Chevalier de Faublas* (1790), a novel by Jean-Baptiste Louvet de Couvray that recounts the amorous exploits of an amiable young rake. The work is typical of many frivolous, licentious novels of its time.

224 *"Quarantines"*: A quarantine is a Lenten period (forty days) and is one of the units of time in which indulgences are normally given, according to Roman Catholic doctrine. An indulgence is a remission before God of the temporal punishment due for one's sins, and can be earned on behalf of souls in Purgatory through prayers and good works.

226 *"De Coster"*: Charles-Théodore-Henri De Coster (1827–79), Belgian medievalist, born in Munich. His best-known work, *La Légende d'Ulenspiegel* (*The Legend of Till Eulenspiegel*), recounts the fabulous exploits and practical jokes of a North German peasant clown of the fourteenth century.

259 *"Almanach de Gotha"*: A widely used annual reference work giving data on the royal families and nobility of Europe. First published in Gotha, Germany, in 1763.

285 *"Thaïs"*: Novel by Anatole France, published in 1890, which depicts early Christianity in an ironic light. *Madame Chrysanthemum* (in French, *Madame Chrysanthème*) is a novel by Pierre Loti, published in 1888 and set in Japan. Paul Bourget's *Cruel Enigma* (French title: *Cruelle Enigme*), published in 1885, is a novel of psychological analysis that explores the emotions and passions of a group of aristocrats.

285 *"Duc de Brancas"*: Louis-Léon-Félicité de Brancas (1733–1824), soldier, scientist, playwright, political writer, and revolutionary, famous for his boldness and amorality. His life was marked by controversies and scandals, including an adulterous liaison with the actress and courtesan Sophie Arnould, who bore him three children.

285 *"Maria Walewska"*: Countess Maria Walewska (1789–1817), Polish noblewoman. She became the mistress of Napoleon I in 1807 and bore him a son, Alexandre Walewski, in 1810.

307 *"The Lohengrin suspected of madness"*: Ludwig II, King of Bavaria, became increasingly irrational during the course of his reign (1864–86); in one of his many fantasies, he identified himself with Lohengrin, the Knight of the Swan. His ministers eventually had him confined in his château on Lake Starnberg. On June 13, 1886, he went for a lakeside stroll with Dr. Bernhard von Gudden, a distinguished expert on mental illnesses. A few hours later, their bodies were found in the lake. It seems likely that Ludwig intended to commit suicide and that von Gudden died attempting to save him, but their deaths have never been satisfactorily explained.

309 *"Helleu"*: Paul-César Helleu (1859–1927), French etcher and painter best known for his drypoint studies and portraits of fashionable women.

312 *"Caudine Forks"*: Two narrow passes in the southern Apennines near Caudium, Italy, where in 321 B.C. the Roman army was routed by the Samnites. Latin: *Furcae Caudinae.* "To pass through the Caudine Forks" means to undergo a painful or humiliating experience.

317 *"Nothing human should be alien to us"*: An allusion to Terence's famous declaration "Homo sum; humani nil a me alienum puto" ("I am a man; I consider nothing human to be alien to me").

320 *"Andalusian women of Barcelona"*: Barcelona is not in Andalusia; but the reference is to a poem by Alfred de Musset entitled "L'Andalouse," which sings the beauties of an Andalusian woman living in Barcelona.

321 *"Barnabooth"*: Character created by the novelist Valéry Larbaud (1881–1957). In 1913 Larbaud published *A. O. Barnabooth: Ses oeuvres complètes, c'est-à-dire un conte, ses poésies et son journal intime* (*A. O. Barnabooth: His Complete Works—i.e, a Tale, His Poems, and His Personal Diary*). Archibaldo Olson Barnabooth is a wealthy, jaded young South American who wanders through Europe in search of distraction and spiritual fulfillment.

322 *"Haiduks"*: The name of a special body of Hungarian foot soldiers who in 1605 were given lands and noble rank. "Reiters" were German cavalry soldiers, especially those employed in the wars of the sixteenth and seventeenth centuries.

323 *"Bruant"*: Aristide Bruant (1851–1925), songwriter and cabaret singer, made his first appearances at the Chat-Noir in Paris and then established his own cabaret, the Mirliton. His publications include collections of his songs (e.g., *Dans la rue* and *Chansons et monologues*), as well as a dictionary of argot (1901). Jehan Rictus (pseudonym of Gabriel Randon; lived 1867–1938) wrote slangy, frequently touching poems and ballads of Parisian low life which were published in such collections as *Soliloques du pauvre* (1897) and *Les Cantilènes du malheur* (1902).